The History of
American Foreign Policy

The History of American Foreign Policy

Volume I To 1917

Jerald A. Combs
San Francisco State University

ALFRED A. KNOPF   NEW YORK

For Art and Meg Combs

First Edition

9 8 7 6 5 4 3 2 1

Copyright © 1986 by Newbery Award Records, Inc.

Cover design by Nancy Sugihara

Library of Congress Cataloging in Publication Data

Combs, Jerald A.
  The history of American foreign policy.

  Bibliography: p.
  Includes index.
  1. United States—Foreign relations. I. Title.
E183.7.C656 1986   327.73'009   85-12644
ISBN 0-394-34146-5
ISBN 0-394-35689-6 (v.1 pbk.)
ISBN 0-394-35690-X (v.2 pbk.)

Manufactured in the United States of America

PREFACE

Anyone who has experienced the bitter debates over United States policy toward Iran, El Salvador, or Vietnam understands that American foreign policy inevitably generates controversy. Yet most people expect a history of American foreign policy to be a simple narrative of the "truth" about the past. They seem unaware that events of the distant past created just as much controversy as those of the present day. They also seem to assume that historians will be unaffected by past controversies, let alone by present ones.

Unfortunately, historical study cannot provide a final truth about the past. Historians can approach the truth by close study of the documents surrounding critical events in America's diplomatic history, but their accounts are still affected by their own experiences, judgments, and predilections. These differences have given rise to several opposing views of the history of American foreign policy.

Some historians see American diplomacy as having been a fairly successful blend of democratic idealism and realistic concern for American national interests. They generally assume that American values of liberty, democracy, and free enterprise are worthy goals which, if encouraged throughout the world by American diplomacy, will benefit all the people of the earth as well as the United States. They portray most of America's wars as justified resistance to foreign aggression. For instance, they see the American Revolution and the War of 1812 as necessary battles against British tyranny. They look upon westward expansion as the spread of liberty and civilization against reactionary colonial regimes and tragic but doomed Indians. They emphasize the aggressiveness of the Mexicans leading to the Mexican War and the tyranny of Spain in Cuba and the Philippines prior to the Spanish American War of 1898. They regard the two world wars as gallant crusades to save Europe from the tyranny of Kaiser Wilhelm's Germany and then of Hitler's Nazis. Finally, they tend to see the events of the Cold War, including Korea and Vietnam, as part of a noble if occasionally inept resistance to the expansion of Soviet and Communist plans for world domination.

This view, which I will call the nationalist interpretation of American foreign policy, represents the outlook of many secondary school texts, politicians, newspapers, and television commentaries. It also continues to have strong support in the academic world. It can lead to blatant superpatriotic flag waving, as in the speeches of some politicians, but it also can be the sophisticated conviction of scholars who have examined the realistic alternatives available to American statesmen at various times and concluded that in most circumstances America's leaders chose properly.

For the most part, those who hold the nationalist view are politically conservative. Among politicians, Ronald Reagan in his more ideological and less pragmatic moods would be a good example. An extraordinarily informed scholarly account of American foreign policy from this point of view is the classic text, *A Diplomatic History of the United States* (4th ed., 1955) by the dean of American diplomatic historians, Samuel Flagg Bemis. Some liberals, however, also hold to the nationalist view. Liberal journalists, for instance, often write exposés of American blundering or cruelty in a particular instance such as the Vietnam war, but contrast that with the rest of America's supposedly decent and successful history. Good examples of such journalistic liberal nationalism are David Halberstam's account of the Vietnam war, *The Best and the Brightest* (1972), and Seymour Hersh's biography of Henry Kissinger, *The Price of Power* (1983).

A second and more critical interpretation of the history of American foreign policy is the so-called realist view. This has probably been the dominant interpretation among diplomatic historians since World War II. Realists insist that American foreign policy generally has been too naive, idealistic, and moralistic. They believe that Americans, regarding their own nation as more peaceful and moral than others because of America's democratic form of government, have oscillated foolishly between a policy of isolation designed to insulate themselves from evil foreigners and their meaningless wars, and a policy of crusading internationalism designed to eliminate foreign evils by making nations over in America's image. For instance, realists argue that America's devotion to total victory over Nazi Germany and unconditional surrender destroyed Central Europe and left a vacuum of power that naturally tempted the Soviets to expand. Instead of meeting that expansion with a realistic negotiating stance, the United States first hoped to deter it by peaceful intentions and goodwill, then overreacted to the failure of this naive approach by embarking on an excessive military buildup and an anti-Communist crusade. Realists believe the United States must follow a steadier policy based on national interests rather than grandiose democratic ideals, and seek peace through a balance of power rather than some utopian vision of a world without conflict.

Although many American diplomatic historians share this realist outlook, they often divide over its application to particular events. Hard realists emphasize the need for the United States to protect its national interests and the world balance of power by dealing with adversaries from a position of unassailable strength. America must be willing to take significant risks, including major military action, to prevent the expansion of its adversaries even in morally ambiguous situations or in areas others might see as unimportant to America's most vital interests. Thus, they favor a very activist American foreign policy. Henry Kissinger is a good example of a contemporary politician and historian who operates from this perspective. For a good history of American foreign policy written from this point of view, see Thomas A. Bailey's popular *A Diplomatic History of the American People*, now in its tenth edition (1980).

There are a number of soft realists, however, who argue that a proper analysis of America's national interest, the balance of power, and the limited ability of military action to accomplish worthwhile policy goals should have led the United States to greater restraint in its relations abroad. Soft or restrained realists generally think that greater patience and more expert diplomacy might have saved the United States from some of its wars and crusades and avoided its present overextension. The most prominent advocates of this view among diplomats and publicists have been George Kennan, Walter Lippmann, and Hans Morgenthau. In general, it is the view to which I subscribe and from which I have written this account.

While realists have chastised American foreign policy for excessive idealism and moralism, another group of critics known as revisionists argue that American diplomacy instead has been realistic and self-interested to the point of rapaciousness. Revisionists regard the primary theme of American diplomatic history not as an oscillation between isolationism and interventionism, but as continuous aggressive expansion. They see American imperialism beginning with the westward movement, extending through America's attempts to protect its markets and capitalist economy in the first and second world wars, and culminating in recent efforts to preserve American economic interests in Vietnam, the Middle East, and Central America.

The most radical of these revisionists believe that American imperialist foreign policy will not change unless the United States becomes a socialist nation. They agree with Lenin's theory that imperialism is the product of capitalism's intrinsic need to expand its markets and sources of raw materials. Capitalist nations must continually expand their economies by acquiring either formal or informal colonies, because only in this way can the elite that monopolizes the internal wealth of the nation find new resources to buy off the masses, whose exclusion from the benefits of their labor would otherwise lead to a revolutionary redistribution of the nation's goods. Radicals believe that this redistribution of goods would enhance the purchasing power of the vast majority of the people, augment economic demand, and thus increase production and jobs. America's prosperity would no longer depend on overseas expansion and aggression, and the major motive behind imperialism and war would be gone. Failing this, the United States and the other capitalist nations would continue to expand, inevitably clash in their competition for markets and resources, and bring war and destruction on the earth. You will not find many American politicians who hold this point of view; they have difficulty being elected in the present American political climate. But you will find a strong statement of this perspective in Gabriel Kolko, *The Roots of*

American Foreign Policy (1969), and Sidney Lens, *The Forging of the American Empire* (1971). An excellent scholarly survey written with similar assumptions but with a much more restrained tone is Lloyd C. Gardner, Walter F. LaFeber, and Thomas J. McCormick, *Creation of the American Empire* (1976).

Moderate revisionists also criticize America's rapacious expansionism and imperialism, but they tend to stress the economic factor in foreign policy somewhat less than the radicals. They see American diplomacy as the product of bureaucratic as well as economic elites, of ideological and psychological factors like racism and fear of communism as well as capitalist expansion, and of well-intentioned error as well as malevolence. They also find some leaders and episodes in American history with which they sympathize, especially Franklin Roosevelt's attempts to accommodate the Soviet Union during World War II. An excellent survey of American diplomacy from this moderate revisionist point of view is Thomas G. Paterson, J. Garry Clifford, and Kenneth J. Hagan, *American Foreign Policy: A History* (2d ed., 1983).

In the following work, I, like the authors of all the other texts mentioned above, have tried to write a balanced account of the history of American foreign policy. But like them, I cannot help but be affected by my own experiences and point of view. I have tried to compensate for this by ensuring that even when the narrative expresses strong opinions about an episode, it presents other interpretations as well. The reader will also find detailed discussions of conflicting interpretations in the historiographical essays that follow each chapter. These essays trace the development of the major schools of historical thought outlined in this introduction, schools I think affect not only histories of past American diplomacy, but the making of present policy as well.

ACKNOWLEDGMENTS

I have incurred many debts in writing this book. I had a chance to compose several of the Cold War chapters in a National Endowment for the Humanities Seminar with Robert A. Divine at the University of Texas in the summer of 1982. Professor Divine and the members of the seminar have been extremely helpful. One member, Professor Wayne Knight of C. Sergeant Reynolds College, read the entire manuscript and made many useful suggestions. He also did much of the work researching and obtaining the illustrations. Professor Richard H. Immerman of the University of Hawaii gave an excellent critique of the chapters on later American diplomacy. Others who generously donated their time and knowledge to the project include Professors John Tricamo of San Francisco State University, Herbert Margulies of the University of Hawaii, Lou Gomolak of the University of Texas, and Kathy Scott of the Iowa State Historical Society. Readers for the press at various stages of the manuscript include Professors Walter LaFeber, Kinley J. Brauer, Mark Lytle, Robert C. Hildebrand, and Franklin W. Abbot. My wife, Sara P. Combs, helped edit the manuscript and locate the maps. With all the help I have received, any errors of fact or interpretation that remain are my own fault.

All Chinese names are Romanized according to the more familiar Wade-Giles system because this was the system in use for most of the period covered in this book and the system used in all the reference materials.

CONTENTS

MAPS

The History of
American Foreign Policy

CHAPTER 1

The American Revolution and the Origins of American Diplomacy

EARLY AMERICAN FOREIGN POLICY: NEUTRALITY AND EXPANSION

One of America's leading diplomatic historians, Ernest May, has characterized early American foreign policy as "pacifist and isolationist." There is much truth in this label. Americans did try to avoid entanglement in the wars and alliances of the great powers of Europe, just as George Washington had advised them to do in his famous Farewell Address. President Martin Van Buren said in the 1840s that Americans still regarded nonintervention and neutrality "with a degree of reverence and submission but little, if anything, short of that entertained for the Constitution itself." With its neutralist stance and its tiny army and navy, the United States seemed a peaceful haven to many Europeans who immigrated to escape the continuous wars and burdensome military obligations of their homelands.

Yet the image of early America as "pacifist and isolationist" is misleading. Americans did not want total isolation from Europe: They avoided political entanglements as best they could, and some even sought cultural isolation to prevent contamination by Europe's supposedly corrupt antirepublican society. But Americans did not want commercial isolation. Trade with Europe was vital to the American economy, and if Americans designed their neutrality to avoid entanglements in Europe's wars, they also designed it to increase their foreign trade. Under international law, neutral nations could trade unmolested with nations at war, and the United States intended to benefit from this protection. Americans also hoped to reinforce the protection of international law by making their trade so valuable that no nation would risk interfering with it. So, early American policy toward Europe is far better characterized as neutralist rather than isolationist.

Nor was early American diplomacy truly pacifist. Even though Americans wanted neutrality to keep them out of European wars, they were ready to fight for their neutral rights, as they proved in 1812. In addition, despite the reverence Martin Van Buren insisted Americans held for noninterven-

1

tion, the United States joined the major powers of Europe in claiming and exercising the right to intervene in other nations to protect the lives and property of its citizens abroad. The United States considered this to be "nonpolitical" intervention and therefore a legitimate function of diplomacy. America conducted over one hundred such interventions prior to 1900, ranging from forced debt collection to the bombardment of towns that had imprisoned American sailors.

It was not only the belligerent pursuit of neutral rights and "nonpolitical" interventions that belied the image of early American foreign policy as pacifist and isolationist; on the North American continent and in the Caribbean, the United States was aggressively expansionist. It conquered the Indians, purchased Louisiana from France, extorted Florida from Spain, and took the Far West from Mexico. There were even profound expansionist aspects to episodes that were essentially defensive efforts to secure independence and neutrality, such as the American Revolution and the War of 1812.

The twin themes that dominated American foreign policy prior to the twentieth century were neutrality and expansion, rather than pacifism and isolationism. Of the two themes, neutrality was at first the more important. Until after the War of 1812, the nation's diplomacy was essentially defensive rather than offensive. The desire to expand American trade and territory always hovered in the background, but it remained secondary to the desire of the United States simply to survive and preserve what it already had. After the War of 1812, however, Americans felt secure from destruction at the hands of hostile European powers for the first time in their history and could turn their attention with confidence to westward expansion. Neutrality toward Europe remained a cornerstone of American diplomacy for the rest of the nineteenth century and occasionally, as during the Civil War, it reemerged as the dominant concern. But for the most part territorial expansion became the primary theme.

THE ORIGINS OF EARLY AMERICAN FOREIGN POLICY

"These United Colonies are, and of a right ought to be free and independent States," and as such should seek "foreign alliances." So proclaimed Richard Henry Lee of Virginia to the Continental Congress in June 1776. After vigorous debate, the Congress agreed. This famous resolution embodied the contradictory impulses that would compete for dominance in America's foreign policy during much of the new nation's early existence—the desire for independence from Europe and the need for foreign connections. Nonentanglement was the eventual victor. Washington's Farewell Address, warning against foreign influences and permanent alliances, became almost an eleventh commandment for Americans of the nineteenth century. But it was neither an easy nor a permanent victory.

The American Revolution probably did more than anything to turn Americans against European entanglements. Behind the primary grievance of the colonists against England, taxation without representation, was the conviction of many Americans that the connection with Great Britain had impeded expansion of their trade and territory. The British mercantile system had monopolized American commerce and limited the growth of manufactures. Parliament had frustrated the territorial ambitions of the Americans. Acting on the assumption that they would gain access to vast tracts of land, the colonists had cooperated with the British to eliminate French control of Canada and Louisiana during the French and Indian War. Yet with the Proclamation of 1763, the British had temporarily halted settlements beyond the Appalachians. Then the Quebec Act had given administration over much of the Ohio Valley to Canada rather than to claimants in the original thirteen colonies. In their disappointment, many Americans recalled still another instance of British betrayal. In the 1740s, during the War of the Austrian Succession, New Englanders had captured the strategic French fortress of Louisbourg, guardian of the mouth of the St. Lawrence River. In the final peace treaty, however, the British had returned it to the French in exchange for concessions in Asia of no value to the colonists. Such incidents convinced many Americans that their ties to Europe through Great Britain had involved them in wars so little related to American interests that the United States would be well advised to avoid such bonds in the future.

American attitudes toward Britain's European rivals reinforced this disposition to shun alliances. Most potential allies had long been enemies of the colonists. Spain had made the initial claim to the Western Hemisphere and viewed the British as trespassers. A long period of desultory warfare on America's southern frontier resulted, stimulating hatred between the Spanish and the settlers. The French in Canada and Louisiana also had been bitter antagonists of the Americans, and these colonists murdered one another enthusiastically during the century of warfare between their mother countries. Americans regarded France and Spain as corrupt and effete Catholic regimes whose superstitious subjects were willing victims of perpetual inquisition and enslavement. The American image of the French was summed up in a line from a popular song of the time—"When Gallick hosts, ungrateful men, our race meant to extermine. . . ." To most Americans, an alliance with such powers was no improvement on their old colonial relationship with Great Britain.

America's geographical situation reinforced the colonists' inclination to keep the Europeans at arm's length. All the great powers were three thousand miles across the Atlantic. The United States was surrounded by the colonies of these nations, but such thinly populated neighbors posed no threat without the long-distance backing of the mother countries. As America's population grew, military invasion from any source would become even more difficult. Benjamin Franklin calculated that the nation's population was doubling every twenty-three years. John Adams figured that this growth guaranteed the addition of twenty thousand fighting men each year. He thought the physical size of America might protect against invasion as well. Only a "multitude of posts" and an army a hundred thousand strong, Adams argued, could hope to conquer and garrison even a few of the states. Intellectual tradition also supported separation of the two hemispheres. More than two centuries before the revolution, the pope had drawn a line of demarcation down the Atlantic to separate the colonial spheres of Portugal to the east and Spain to the west. The British and French disregarded the papal proclamation to plant their own colonies, but the line still had some influence. European leaders came to disregard many conflicts "beyond the line" as somehow outside the realm of civilization and not necessarily cause for war between the mother countries.

British Whig reform tradition, the same philosophy that so influenced American resistance to taxation without representation, confirmed the revolutionaries' inclination for nonentanglement. The British Whigs had long sought to avoid excessive entanglements with European powers. They urged concentration on overseas trade and empire rather than on continental politics. Such trade would promote a strong navy that could defend the moat of the British Isles, the English Channel, and thus prevent an invasion of the homeland. This would make a large standing army, the traditional enemy of internal liberty, unnecessary.

The Americans, already disposed to agree with the Whig outlook on domestic affairs, readily adopted much of Whig foreign policy as well. Like the British Whigs, Americans would avoid foreign entanglements. They would rely on an even larger moat than the English Channel, the Atlantic Ocean, to protect the homeland. They too would avoid the large standing army that might threaten internal liberty. Even for the frontier, no large army would be necessary, because Americans were certain that the country's rapid population growth, the local militias, and a few regular troops at strategic frontier forts would be adequate for the purpose of westward expansion.

The British Whig emphasis on a navy, however, was more debatable in America. Many Americans thought a navy essential to defend their ships and coastline, and they echoed the British Whigs in pointing out that a navy did not threaten internal liberty in the same manner as an army. Ships could not be used so easily to disrupt legislatures or coerce farmers. Opponents, however, warned that naval building and maintenance would require heavy taxation which would strengthen a potentially despotic central government. They argued that the Atlantic moat supplemented by coastal defenses would suffice to protect America against a major invasion from the sea, and that America's neutral policy toward Europe combined with Europe's need for American commerce would deter interference with American shipping.

The belief that Europe desperately needed American trade undergirded much of America's early attitudes toward foreign affairs. It allowed Americans to rationalize their desire for nonentanglement and peace with their equal desire for the profits of overseas commerce. Like the eminent French *philosophes* who wrote at the time of the American Revolution, many Americans hoped that free and extensive commerce would render balance of power politics and warfare obsolete. If each nation's prosperity depended upon a network of international trade, no country would risk attacking another. Militarism, "a dangerous prejudice, a carry-over from barbarism, a remnant of former chaos," would be replaced by free commerce that pacified and unified the peoples of the world. So Americans urged that colonialism be ended and other artificial barriers to world trade abandoned. Free governments responsive to the will of their people should be established. These governments would be more peaceful than monarchies, many Americans believed, since only monarchs stood to gain by war while their people supplied the deaths and taxes.

Free trade and anticolonialism gratified America's interests as well as its ideological proclivities. America could afford to support free trade because it needed access to foreign markets. In the absence of large-scale domestic manufactures, it had little need to protect its home markets against foreign competition. America could oppose colonialism because it had no colonies of its own and was surrounded by the colonies of European powers, which severely restricted foreign commerce. Foreigners were expected to trade with colonies only through the mother countries. This worked little hardship on European nations, since they were neighbors. But these mother countries were thousands of miles away from the United States.

In its desire for freer trade, America naturally championed such doctrines as neutral rights and freedom of the seas. The United States saw these doctrines as both morally correct and helpful to American interests. Since the United States expected to be a neutral and to have a navy inferior to those of the major powers, it was to America's interest to promote an international law that protected the trade and shipping of neutrals against the desire of powerful warring nations to interfere with them.

While all Americans hoped that extensive commerce might help the United States protect its neutrality, a good many recognized that this neat package of ideals and interests might not always hold together. Thomas Jefferson, for instance, warned that America's determination to share in the world's commerce and shipping meant "Frequent wars without a doubt," as America's ships, property, and seamen might be insulted or captured. Occasionally Jefferson saw this danger as a reason to abandon commerce and navigation entirely, but most of the time he was confident that America's trade itself could be a powerful enough weapon to deter war. Jefferson and other Americans had had considerable experience in wielding trade as a weapon. Before the revolution, their boycotts of British goods helped to force repeal of the Stamp Act of 1765 and the Townshend Duties of 1767. Most Americans were quite prepared to follow the same policy again if it became necessary. They would use commerce to manipulate the balance of power system if the Europeans refused to accept free trade as a substitute for outmoded military competition.

THE FRANCO-AMERICAN ALLIANCE: CHALLENGE TO NONENTANGLEMENT

In the revolutionary tract *Common Sense*, which circulated in America almost as widely as the Bible and crystallized opinion in favor of independence, Thomas Paine spelled out America's developing attitude toward foreign policy. He denounced the British connection because it tended "directly to involve this continent in European wars and quarrels. . . . As Europe is our market for trade, we ought to form no partial connection with any part of it. It is the true interest of America to steer clear of European connections." Commerce, "if well attended to, will secure us the peace and friendship of all Europe; because it is the interest of all Europe to have America a free port."

Despite this inclination to avoid European connections, Americans desperately needed foreign help to win the revolution against Great Britain. The Continental Congress therefore tried to secure French aid without violating Paine's philosophy of nonentanglement. This contradiction appeared graphically in the model treaty Congress adopted to serve as a guide for all its ministers abroad. John Adams, its primary author, was so determined to avoid military or political ties with France that he was prepared to refuse French troops and naval support. The United States was to make only a "marine treaty."

America would exchange its commerce for supplies and economic aid. When the inevitable war between Britain and France resulted, the United States would promise only to refrain from support of England. The standard provisions of European alliances should be avoided: America must retain its ability to make peace separately, and should not guarantee protection of any French territory. Adams and his allies successfully resisted congressional proposals to offer France just such concessions. They warned particularly that France should be kept out of North America. Since the French wanted to break Britain's monopoly of American trade, Adams seemed confident that this alone would be sufficient incentive to make France finance the revolution.

Congress sent the model treaty to Europe with a group of talented but amateur diplomats. Because Great Britain had conducted all foreign policy for the empire, Congress had to turn to American merchants for its diplomatic corps. The secret congressional committee of correspondence, formed to secure foreign aid and intelligence, was composed largely of merchants and chaired successively by partners in one of the most influential trading houses of Philadelphia, Thomas Willing and Robert Morris. These merchants knew where and how to obtain weapons, supplies, and loans from overseas, and they took a healthy commission for their services. The first diplomat the committee sent to Paris was Silas Deane, also closely associated with Willing, Morris, and Company. Fearing British detection, Deane was melodramatically covert: He composed dispatches in invisible ink. He chose the none-too-original code name "Jones." He pledged to speak nothing but French when unsure of his company, leading French Foreign Minister Vergennes to quip that Deane had to be "the most silent man in France" because he was unable to put six French words together.

When Congress realized the need for more than material assistance, it sent Benjamin Franklin to join Deane in Paris. Franklin's name had preceded him; his scientific experiments and homespun philosophy had made him the most famous of Americans. By lobbying in Parliament as a colonial agent for Pennsylvania and Massachusetts, he had gained diplomatic experience. His list of influential contacts abroad was as lengthy as his reputation was impressive. Franklin was lionized in Paris; he frequented salons and boudoirs, charming the French ladies. He played the role of innocent rustic to his French audience, which anticipated little else from an American. To them he was a representative colonial as well as a colonial representative in the plain frontier clothing he affected. He even let them assume that as a Philadelphian, he was necessarily a Quaker, the symbol of New World simplicity.

America's greatest bargaining tool, however, was France's hatred of Britain, not its love of Franklin. France still smarted at the British victory in the French and Indian War which, in 1763, had stripped France of its North American possessions. Americans and their republican ideals did not mesmerize Foreign Minister Vergennes and the French court as they did Franklin's salon clique. Vergennes, a dedicated and conservative servant of an imperial monarchy, distrusted colonial rebels. Nevertheless, he was ready to support the American Revolution because he saw in it the opportunity to restore French supremacy in the European balance of power. Humbling Britain would not only satisfy Vergennes' desire for revenge, but also perhaps make the British more willing to cooperate with France in restraining the increasingly aggressive eastern empires, Prussia, Austria, and Russia. Those three nations had partitioned Poland in 1772 and were planning new moves against the Ottoman Empire. Vergennes saw this aggressiveness as a threat to continental stability and resented Britain's contemptuous dismissal of France's concern.

Vergennes also saw a chance for more direct gains. He might secure new West Indian islands and regain French rights in the Newfoundland fisheries. His main goal, however, would be the independence of America. He believed that the loss of the American colonies would be a devastating blow to Britain's commercial and financial strength and would undermine much of Britain's naval power. To further his larger goals, Vergennes would even renounce the chance to exploit the revolution to regain Canada. He hoped that Britain's presence in Canada would force the United States to continue to rely on French protection.

Vergennes won royal consent for covert aid to the Americans in 1776, before Franklin's arrival. Playwright-inventor Pierre Augustin Caron de Beaumarchais, author of "The Barber of Seville" and "The Marriage of Figaro," helped initiate Vergennes' project. Beaumarchais had been converted to the American cause by the Virginian Arthur Lee, whom he had met, ironically, in London. Beaumarchais and Vergennes established a bogus Spanish corporation, Roderique Hortalez et Compagnie, through which the French and Spanish governments could covertly buy arms and ship them to the American rebels. Ninety percent of the gunpowder Americans used in the first third of the war came from Europe, primarily through Hortalez. Faced with a massive British invasion force, however, Congress recognized the need for more than money and gunpowder; the United States had to have an open alliance with France. The French navy could divert British attention from America to the protection of the rest of the British Empire. But could France be lured into this arrangement without the permanent political "strings" against which the model treaty warned?

This delicate task, which fell to Franklin, called for more than friendly persuasion. Baron Turgot, finance minister to the French court, feared the costs of the war. They might lead to national bankruptcy or to taxes so exorbitant they would trigger a French revolution. Fortunately for the United States, King Louis XVI rejected this prophetic vision and Turgot resigned. Early American military setbacks also worried the French. Vergennes went so far as to halt the secret sponsorship of Hortalez and Co. for a time. Still, he was eager to help America win its independence, and he fostered a rapid building program to prepare the French navy for war. He was ready to intervene after the Americans captured a mighty chunk of the British army in the Battle of Saratoga in 1778. In case further incentive were needed, Franklin and Deane reminded the French that Britain's defeat at Saratoga might stir George III to offer new and attractive terms for peace and imperial reconciliation. A reunited British empire might then take the French West Indies. Vergennes agreed to an official alliance, but he held out for promises of no separate peace and territorial guarantees. Under the pressure of the war, the American diplomats decided to ignore their instructions and accept Vergennes' offer. Almost simultaneously, Congress prepared new orders to permit just such a pact, orders that arrived in the nick of time.

These orders coupled the concessions to the world of power politics with some audacious requests. France and the United States should take joint action against Canada, Nova Scotia, Newfoundland, and the West Indies. The United States intended to annex all but the Caribbean islands. Should the Spanish climb aboard this bandwagon, they were welcome to Florida and Portugal. Congress might bluster with such grandiose statements, but it had now accepted the kind of alliance it had disdained earlier. Neither side could sign a peace treaty without the consent of the other. America would guarantee protection of French possessions in perpetuity—but only in the Western Hemisphere, and only in a defensive war. In exchange, France would guarantee American independence and whatever borders America succeeded in wresting from the British. The accompanying treaty of commerce did reflect many of the liberal premises of *Common Sense* and the model treaty. But clearly nonentanglement had fallen by the wayside. Even John Adams praised the alliance, and Thomas Paine accepted money from the French secret service to act as a propagandist for the pact.

STRAINS ON THE ALLIANCE

The Franco-American alliance tilted the scales of war in favor of the United States. The British were put on the defensive when a joint French-Spanish force threatened invasion of southern England. After this, the British cabinet kept ships and supplies close to home rather than use them in America. The French also kept Britain occupied by harassing British colonies in the East and West Indies. Finally, in 1781, the French made a major contribution to the crowning American victory of the war. A French fleet drove off the English ships sent to rescue General Cornwallis from the Yorktown peninsula while a French army joined Washington's forces to surround Cornwallis's troops and obtain their surrender. The alliance proved indispensable, yet the allies discovered conflicting interests. The most important of these involved a new combatant in the war against England: Spain.

In April of 1779, without informing the Americans, France had lured Spain into the war by promising no peace with Britain until the French had helped Spain retrieve Gibralter from the British. This made the United States the prisoner of Spanish policy. America could make no peace without French consent; France could make no peace without Spanish consent; and Spain would refuse consent until it got Gibraltar. Spain also refused to ally itself directly with the American rebels against monarchy and imperialism, despite the fact that the two countries were fighting a common enemy. Spain feared especially for its North American colonies bordering the avaricious revolutionaries. It wanted desperately to keep the Americans away from the Mississippi River, the only means by which farmers west of the Appalachians could profitably export their crops.

Without the right to navigate the Mississippi, American settlements beyond the mountains could never be more than tiny groups of subsistence farmers which would offer no threat to the equally weak and thinly populated Spanish possessions on their borders. In hopes of pinning the Americans to the strip of land between the Atlantic and the Appalachians, Spain reconquered Florida from the British and sent expeditions up the Mississippi to lay claims as far as the Ohio Valley.

In pursuing this policy, Spain fumbled its best chance to contain the Americans. In 1780, at a particularly ominous point in the war, Congress instructed John Jay, whom it sent to Spain to gain recognition and an alliance, to part with the Mississippi if such a sacrifice was necessary to get a Spanish treaty. Reluctantly, Jay made the offer. The Spanish rejected it, confident they could hold the Mississippi with or without American consent. One reason the Spanish were so cocksure was the leverage they had over France.

France had little interest in the conflict between Spain and the United States over territory in North America, but it needed Spanish consent to conclude the war. The French were becoming desperate for peace because they had borrowed heavily to finance the war effort, and their economic situation was deteriorating rapidly as the war dragged on. They had good reason to believe that their military position might fade along with their economy. Since it seemed increasingly unlikely that they could take Gibraltar to satisfy the Spanish conditions for peace, Vergennes thought he might induce the Spanish to forfeit that hope if France successfully supported Spain's claims in the Mississippi and Ohio valleys.

America had little claim on those territories. They had not been administered by any of the thirteen colonies before the revolution and the American military expeditions to the West, notably those of George Rogers Clark, had been hit-and-run affairs resulting in no permanent occupation. French observers in the United States mistakenly wrote back to Vergennes that the Americans had no great interest in the trans-Appalachian West anyway. Vergennes consequently believed that France's guarantee of American independence and territory did not include an obligation to support America's extravagant western claims, and he tended to discourage those claims in favor of Spain's.

Some Americans were alarmed and angered by this divergence from American interests. One of these was Arthur Lee, whom Congress had sent from his post as Massachusetts' colonial agent in London to join Franklin and Deane in Paris. Lee distrusted not only the French, but his fellow commissioners as well. He wrote virulent letters to Congress calling Franklin and Deane French sycophants. He specifically accused Deane of profiting from speculations that sacrificed American interests to the French. Congress recalled Deane, and the vitriolic public debate which followed drove Deane to join the Loyalists and split Congress into bitter pro- and anti-French factions.

In Deane's place, Congress appointed John Adams, an ally of Arthur Lee and the anti-French faction. Adams was a man of deep integrity, but he was prickly, vain, and self-righteous. He already mistrusted Franklin for straying so far from Adams's own model treaty, and his outlook was not improved by closer scrutiny of the situation in Paris. Franklin, basking in French admiration, was swirling from one soirée to another. He left Adams to attend to all the drudgery and paperwork. Adams decided it was his duty to offset Franklin's indolent and compliant style. Since France was so obviously in the war for its own interests, Adams saw no reason to couch his requests for further aid in flattering terms. Vergennes bristled under Adams's continual hectoring and ultimately refused to do business with any American representative but Franklin. Vergennes was appalled, therefore, when he learned that Congress had appointed Adams as the commissioner to make peace with England. In early 1781, he instructed the French minister in America to seek Adams's dismissal.

The French had many friends in Congress, including at least one who was on their payroll. But Adams had his own allies. Instead of replacing him, Congress surrounded Adams with a new commission designed to be favorable to France. Franklin, Thomas Jefferson, and John Jay, all considered part of the pro-French faction of Congress, would share the responsibility for peacemaking with Adams and his one possible supporter, Henry Laurens of South Carolina. To further hamstring Adams, Congress instructed the commission to do nothing without the "knowledge and concurrence" of the French and "ultimately to govern" itself by French "advice and opinion." Congress then sent the mortified Adams to Holland to seek a loan.

So Franklin was alone when British commissioner Richard Oswald arrived in Paris to open peace negotiations after Britain's bitter defeat at Yorktown. Franklin dutifully informed the French of the British overture, but in his private conversations with Oswald, he disobeyed the instructions tying him to French advice. In addition to demanding absolute independence and the Mississippi River border, he recommended that Britain cede Canada to the United States. He implied that the elimination of this British threat to North America would render America's "perpetual" alliance with France obsolete. Naturally Franklin neglected to inform Vergennes of this suggestion. Shortly afterward, Franklin was joined by John Jay, who was even less concerned about French sensibilities. Jay had been known as a strong supporter of the French connection when Congress had sent him to seek Spanish recognition and alliance in 1779, but he thought he had received inadequate help from the French during his unhappy stay in Madrid. He arrived in Paris in an angry and suspicious mood, to discover that Oswald's commission empowered the British envoy to treat with the American "colonies" rather than with the independent United States. He objected strongly to this wording. Dubiously, he joined Franklin to ask Vergennes' "advice and opinion" about the matter.

Vergennes dismissed the discrepancy as trivial; only the final treaty need recognize America's independence. Vergennes also expressed support for Spanish and English claims to some of the territory east of the Mississippi which the United States sought so ardently. Franklin, true to his subtle style, seemed inclined to accept Vergennes' advice, at least on the issue of Oswald's commission, and to continue following congressional orders. But Jay would have none of it. When they returned to the American residence, Jay told Franklin they should ignore Vergennes' opinions, demand a new commission for Oswald, and negotiate independently. "Would you deliberately break Congress's instructions?" asked Franklin, as though he had not already done so himself. "I would break them like this," Jay responded, smashing his clay pipe in pieces on the brick fireplace.

Thus, at Jay's insistence, the Americans delayed negotiations with Britain until Oswald's commission could be revised. Then Jay found himself driven to further defiance. He discovered that Vergennes' secretary, Joseph Rayneval, had disappeared after ostentatiously taking leave for a short holiday in the countryside. Rayneval had been Vergennes' spokesman in support of Spanish claims in the trans-Appalachian West. Coincidentally, the British had just turned over to Jay and Franklin an intercepted dispatch from another French diplomat, one stationed in America, who urged that the United States be excluded from the Newfoundland fisheries. Jay correctly surmised that Rayneval was on a secret mission to discuss peace in London and that America's interests in the West and the fisheries might suffer. Jay ignored congressional instructions and, without telling Franklin or the French, sent his own messenger to warn the British against Rayneval. He later explained to Congress that he would have preferred to act with Franklin's consent, but that Franklin had disagreed with Jay's assessment of the situation and had felt constrained by his confidence in Vergennes and his instructions from Congress.

When John Adams joined the delegation fresh from his mission in the Netherlands, he backed Jay to the hilt.[1] He had long assumed what Jay had

[1] He was the only other commissioner to arrive in time to take a significant part in the negotiations. Jefferson had declined his nomination. The British captured Laurens en route to Europe

Figure 1   The American commissioners who negotiated the peace treaty with Great Britain ending the Revolutionary War—from left to right, John Jay, John Adams, Benjamin Franklin, Henry Laurens, and the secretary to the commission, William Temple Franklin. Unfinished painting by Benjamin West. Courtesy The Henry Francis du Pont Winterthur Museum.

recently decided—that the French were actively opposing American interests to keep their ally permanently under their influence. With Jay and Adams in agreement on a unilateral approach independent of France, Franklin acquiesced; henceforth the Americans excluded the French from all their deliberations and negotiations. This was a risky diplomatic strategy. The British could use the rift between the allies that Jay's messenger had revealed to play one off against the other. (Actually the British would have known of the rift anyway, if not from Rayneval himself, then from the British spy who served as Franklin's secretary throughout the negotiations.) Fortunately for the United States, the British decided to play the Americans against the French rather than vice versa. They offered the most liberal of peace terms to the United States in hopes of weaning America away from its French alliance, regaining the lion's share of American commerce, and buying off any further American contribution to the war.

While Jay's diplomacy thus seems to have had some good results, the delay caused by his insistence on a reworded commission for Oswald may have cost the United States something. During that interim, news arrived that the final French-Spanish assault on Gibraltar had failed, and the British stiffened their terms. And in all probability, the risks taken by Jay and Adams

---

and imprisoned him in the Tower of London. They released him only in time to participate in a few last-minute diplomatic details.

were unnecessary. They exaggerated France's hostility to American interests. France was caught in a Hobson's choice between the conflicting claims of its allies. Rayneval indeed implied lack of support for America's claims to the West and the fisheries during his secret mission to London, as Jay and Adams suspected. But the French did not pursue these issues seriously or maliciously. Franklin's more subtle approach to independent negotiations might well have sufficed. Certainly Jay need not have invited the British into the Mississippi area as a counterweight to Spain. He did so later in the negotiations, offering Britain joint navigation of the Mississippi River and promoting a secret article in the peace treaty that would place the Florida border at 31 degrees if Spain held the province, but farther north if the British regained it.

Fortunately for Jay and Adams, however, Jay's rash generosity cost the Americans little. The British were never able to make use of their rights to navigate the Mississippi because, as later mapping expeditions proved, the river did not cross the border into Canada. Therefore the British needed permission to cross American territory in order to reach the river, permission Britain never got.

THE TREATY OF 1783

Whatever the merits of the Americans' diplomacy, the result was a treaty so favorable to the United States that Vergennes remarked the British had bought peace, not made it. To the west, the United States reached to the Mississippi River. To the north, although America lost its first proposed border enclosing present-day Ontario, the modified line through the Great Lakes gave the United States access to that vital waterway. John Adams's advocacy won the "liberty," if not the "right," for Americans to catch and dry fish off Newfoundland. In turn the United States would put no legal impediment in the way of British collection of private debts from American citizens. The promise of a Congressional recommendation to the states that Loyalists be compensated for their war losses helped Britain save some face, but both sides knew that the states would ignore the recommendation.

While the United States won its independence and a territorial bonanza in the Peace of 1783, none of the other participants in the war fared very well. Great Britain lost the heart of its empire. The French monarchy, weakened by its war expenditures, set the stage for its own demise. The Spanish helped create for themselves an exuberant neighbor whose expanding population regarded Spain as a temporary custodian of territories destined sooner or later to be part of the United States. Americans liked to think of themselves as innocents abroad, the victims of the subtle and cynical machinations of the Old World. But occasional use of that smokescreen by Jay, Adams, and Franklin could not obscure the machinations behind their own diplomatic coup.

Vergennes was naturally chagrined by the American diplomats' conduct toward France. He had to acknowledge that technically they had not broken

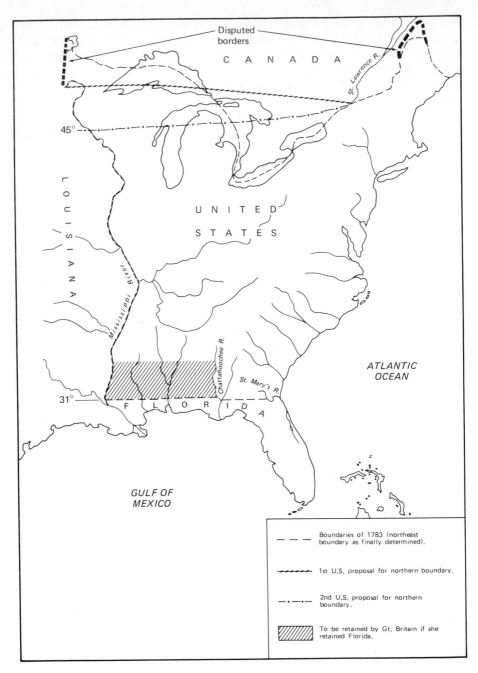

Map 1 Boundary Negotiations of the American Revolution

their pledge against a separate peace, since they had not signed a final peace treaty, but a preliminary agreement to go into effect only when an official pact was signed by all combatants. Nevertheless, America had weakened the position of its allies. Britain could increase its demands against France and Spain knowing that America's belligerence on the battlefield declined in proportion to its diplomatic victory. But Vergennes could find a silver lining even in this. He could use the defection of the United States to press Spain into making peace without Gibraltar or territory in America's hinterland. When Vergennes castigated the Americans for excluding him from their negotiations, he permitted Franklin to dissuade him from any serious retaliation. Franklin blandly warned against allowing the British to flatter themselves that they had split the allies. Vergennes accepted this and even granted Franklin's request for a new loan.

Despite the negotiators' success, their conduct did not receive unanimous approval in the American Congress. A substantial portion of the pro-French faction, led by James Madison, proposed to censure the American delegation for defying its instructions and keeping the negotiations secret from the French. The taste of diplomatic triumph and Vergennes' mildness soon dampened this carping, but the issue did not die. Members of the pro-French faction—James Madison, Thomas Jefferson, and Robert R. Livingston—would soon form the Jeffersonian Republican party. During the war between Great Britain and the new revolutionary French regime in the 1790s, these Republicans would recall the diplomacy of Benjamin Franklin as justification for continued adherence to the French alliance. The opposing Federalists also would appeal to the history of the negotiations, but to remind their constituents that their Federalist compatriots, John Jay and John Adams, had rescued the Mississippi and the fisheries from the French and their compliant dupe, Franklin. Thus America's revolutionary diplomacy lived on, first as the football of politicians, later as a bone of contention among historians.

CONTROVERSIAL ISSUES AND FURTHER READING

Nationalist historians cite the diplomacy of the revolution as a prime example of successful American foreign policy. They especially praise John Jay and John Adams for taking an independent line to defend American interests against the cynical maneuverings of the French. Hard realists too appreciate the vigor and tenacity with which Jay and Adams bargained for America's desires and regard Franklin's diplomacy as too weak and compliant. Samuel Flagg Bemis, author of the classic study *The Diplomacy of the American Revolution* (2nd ed., 1957), actually thinks Jay and Adams should have taken a still harder line. [Richard B. Morris's *The Peacemakers: The Great Powers and American Independence* (1965), the most extensive account of this issue, sees Jay's position as just hard enough. Cecil Currey, in his controversial *Code Number 72: Ben Franklin, Patriot or Spy* (1972), asserts that Franklin was not just wrong but treasonous in his dealings with France and Britain.]

Restrained realists tend to favor Franklin's equally independent but more subtle defense of American interests. They condemn Jay and Adams for being excessively abrasive and taking unnecessary risks. They also regard French maneuvering as to be expected in the pursuit of national self-interest and far less malevolent than Adams and Jay had feared. [Gerald Stourzh's *Benjamin Franklin and American Foreign Policy* (1954) is the best modern defense of the Philadelphian. Stourzh calls John Adams's conduct "pretentious diplomacy of the big stick." James H. Hutson, in *John Adams and the Diplomacy of the American Revolution* (1980), says that Adams's constant mistrust of Franklin and the French was literally paranoid. The best study of the alliance itself is William C. Stinchcombe's *The American Revolution and the French Alliance* (1969). Stinchcombe discovered the list of paid American agents in the French archives and emphasized the conflicts of interest within the alliance. Jonathan R. Dull, *The French Navy and American Independence: A Study of Arms and Diplomacy, 1774–1787* (1975), argues convincingly that Vergennes' policies toward America were largely the product of military necessity and pressures from the other great powers of Europe, rather than any hostility toward the United States. The 1978 bicentennial of the signing of the French alliance inspired two collections of essays reflecting the latest thinking on the Franco-American alliance, Ronald Hoffman and Peter J. Albert, eds., *Diplomacy and Revolution: The Franco-American Alliance of 1778* (1981), and Lawrence S. Kaplan, ed., *The American Revolution and "A Candid World"* (1977). An older yet still valuable history of the alliance is E. S. Corwin's *French Policy and the American Alliance of 1778* (1916).]

The argument between nationalist and realist historians over the relative merits of Jay, Adams, and Franklin is built on a long line of quarrelsome accounts dating back to the revolution itself. In those early days, the basic issue was which of the negotiators best lived up to the sacred injunction of Washington's Farewell Address against permanent foreign alliances. Most early American historians were New Englanders who echoed and endorsed the public accusations John Adams made against Franklin and the French throughout his long life. [See, for example, Theodore Lyman, *The Diplomacy of the United States* (1826–1828).] Then, in the 1830s, Franklin's historical reputation received a powerful defense from Jared Sparks, the first professor of American history and the first American to gain access to the French archives. As a New Englander, he could hardly be accused of pro-Republican bias, and his favorable interpretation of French conduct and Franklin's diplomacy was therefore dominant for half a century. [See, for example, Jared Sparks, *The Writings of George Washington*, Vol. I (1834).] His success was somewhat surprising, because by Sparks's time, anything that implied approval of foreign alliances was suspect as heresy.

In the 1870s, George Bancroft, the greatest American historian of his day, further improved Franklin's position, bringing it more in line with Washington's admonitions against permanent foreign alliances. Bancroft discovered that Franklin himself had been the first to defy Congress's instructions to seek French advice when he secretly suggested British cession of Canada. This revelation offset an additional finding Bancroft made that might have discredited Sparks and Franklin. Sparks had blatantly distorted the French records only he had been privileged to see in order to portray the French as more beneficent than they had been. [George Bancroft, *History of the United States*, Vol. VI (1876).]

The State Department assigned Francis Wharton to issue a correct version of the diplomatic correspondence of the revolution to replace that of Sparks, but he too found support for Franklin's approach to the negotiations. He thought the record of British responses showed that Franklin might well have won Canada from the British if not for John Jay's delays in search of a properly worded commission. [Francis Wharton, *Revolutionary Diplomatic Correspondence of the United States* (1889).] Then, the Jay family struck back. John Jay's grandson and nephew separately wrote books using the newly opened French archives to demonstrate that the opposition of Vergennes and his cohorts to America's claims in the West and the fisheries might have justified Jay's suspicions and the separate negotiations. [John Jay, "The Peace Negotiations of 1782 and 1783," in Justin Winsor, *Narrative and Critical History of America,* Vol. VII (1889). George Pellew, *John Jay* (1890).]

While these opposing interpretations continue to influence histories of revolutionary diplomacy, the fading of Federalist-Republican partisanship, filial piety for the Founding Fathers, and the pride of the Jay and Adams families has muted the debate, and the gulf between assertions has narrowed. All historians now agree that Franklin was not adamantly opposed to separate negotiations, as he was the first to undertake them. No one looking closely at the British records now believes that Great Britain ever intended to surrender Canada, so negotiating delays probably had only a minor impact on the liberality of peace terms. Most of the best modern surveys of revolutionary foreign policy agree that defiance of congressional instructions was in order. They therefore tilt slightly in favor of Jay and Adams.

While nationalists and realists have built upon the old historical disputes over which American negotiators best lived up to the precepts of the Farewell Address, revisionists, with their concern for American expansionism and imperialism, have also been able to build on a foundation of older classic histories. Frederick Jackson Turner, the historian who did the most to call attention to the influence of the frontier on American history, was the first to view revolutionary diplomacy through an expansionist lens. [Frederick Jackson Turner, "The Policy of France toward the Mississippi Valley," *American Historical Review,* 10 (1905).] He inspired a longer and still worthwhile exploration, *The West in the Diplomacy of the American Revolution* (1913), by P. C. Phillips. Of course, both Turner and Phillips regarded westward expansion with favor, while the later revisionists take a considerably more jaundiced view of it. Revisionists portray the territorial demands of the Americans during the revolutionary negotiations as greedy and aggressive and find no reason why France should have been expected to support them. The best case against American revolutionary diplomacy as imperialistic is made by Richard W. Van Alstyne's *Empire and Independence: The International History of the American Revolution* (1965). Van Alstyne himself is not a revisionist, but since no radical historian has yet published a comprehensive study of the diplomacy of the revolution, revisionists cite Van Alstyne to support their imperialist image of America. [The classic work examining the foundations of American foreign policy is Max Savelle's *The Origins of American Diplomacy: The International History of Anglo-America, 1492–1763* (1967). It should by augmented by Felix Gilbert's *To the Farewell Address: Ideas of Early American Foreign Policy* (1961), and the conflicting view taken by James Hutson in his book cited above.]

CHAPTER 2

The Diplomacy of a New Nation: 1783–1800

FOREIGN POLICY UNDER THE ARTICLES OF CONFEDERATION

As the newly independent United States began to formulate its policies, Americans did not find the international atmosphere nearly as accommodating as they had expected it to be. The British and their Parliament had become increasingly disgruntled over the defeat they had suffered. They were less and less satisfied with the liberal terms by which they had secured peace from their rebellious colonists. Lord Shelburne, whose cabinet had made the peace, had hoped that generous terms, followed by a mutually advantageous trade treaty, would regain much of the economic and strategic advantage Britain had formerly enjoyed from possession of the American colonies. Not only had he been ready to offer a liberal trade arrangement between England and the United States, but he had been willing to permit continuation of America's important prewar trade with Canada and the British West Indies. This flew in the face of Britain's mercantilist policy, which closed colonies to the ships of outsiders. Many Britons feared that the West Indies trade would provide too much incentive for American commerce, shipbuilding, and naval power. They overturned the Shelburne government and abandoned his conciliatory approach: The new cabinet closed all British colonies to American ships and refused to sign a trade treaty. It counted upon the infant nation's weakness and its need for profitable trade with the British home islands, which were still open to the Americans on quite liberal terms, to prevent American retaliation.

The British also abandoned conciliation on the American frontier, angered by the discovery that the strategic forts controlling the passageways between the Great Lakes were on America's side of the Canadian border. These forts were traditional fur-trading posts for Indian tribes who trapped beaver for England's thriving hat industry. British fort commanders warned that the Indians were seething because the British government had negotiated no protection for them or their lands in the peace treaty with the United States. This left the Indians technically still at war. The United States could be expected to take advantage of this state of war to extort concessions of Indian lands in the Ohio Valley. Should the forts be given to the United States, the Indians would be dependent on the new nation and might well vent their fury on the scattered frontier population of Canada. So the British declined to turn over the posts. They justified their refusal by pointing to America's own violation of the peace treaty. The United States had neither compensated the Loyalists nor enforced collection of the private debts owed to the British. Adding insult to injury, Britain refused to send a minister to the United States in exchange for the dispatch of John Adams as the first American minister to Great Britain. Adams reported that the British expected preference over France before they would treat with the United States. In his anger he came close to agreeing with Jefferson, America's new minister to France, that the British were "rich, proud, hectoring, swearing, squibbing, carnivorous animals."

As might be expected, the Spanish were no more accommodating than their traditional enemies, the British. The Spanish had already made their decision to confront rather than conciliate the Americans when they had rejected America's offer to exchange the Mississippi River for an open alliance. There were means other than conciliation by which to limit America's westward expansion. First, Spain claimed a Florida border extending far north of the 31st parallel that the United States accepted as the proper line. Even if America prevailed in this border dispute, possession of West Florida and Louisiana guaranteed Spanish control of the river from 31° south to the Gulf of Mexico. By international law, the nation owning both banks of a river could close its portion of the waterway to foreign navigation. Spain did this by proclamation in 1784, effectively blocking the only practical route by which most farmers west of the Appalachians could send their goods to the markets of the East Coast, the West Indies, or Europe.

Spain counted on the blockade of the Mississippi to prevent westward expansion; but it also had an alternative plan. If Americans continued to migrate across the Appalachians, the Spanish hoped to lure them into secession with promises of access to the Mississippi once they had become Spanish subjects. They even paid some prominent western Americans like General James Wilkinson to help inspire secessionist sentiments. Meanwhile, like the British, the Spanish supplied neighboring Indian tribes and urged them to resist United States encroachments on their lands. And again like the British, they refused to sign a trade treaty with the United States. The Spanish trade was not nearly so important as the British, which supplied nearly 90 percent of America's imports and accounted for 75 percent of America's trade overall. But Spain was the only nation to which America exported more than it imported, making the Spanish trade the major source of hard currency. A firm trade treaty with Spain was obviously desirable.

Even the French were less forthcoming than many Americans had expected. France had no territorial conflicts with the United States, but its continuing need for Spanish aid to balance British power put France's ultimate loyalties in doubt. Franco-American trade, which Americans had expected to burgeon, instead grew rather slowly. The French did not manufacture the range of goods the British did, and contacts between French and American merchants were not as familiar and trusting as those with the British. The French merchants refused to emulate the British by extending credit or permitting American merchants to obtain goods on consignment and sell them before paying their bills. Consequently, the volume of American trade with France could never approach that with Great Britain. The French, unlike the British, did permit American ships to trade on a limited basis with their West Indies colonies. Yet ironically this trade did not much exceed that with the British West Indies, because the British islands were often thrown open to American ships by emergency decrees of the local governors in defiance of the wishes of the home government.

Many Americans could not understand why the Europeans were not more forthcoming. After all, Americans sought little more than mutually beneficial trade and security within their proper borders. Freer trade was not merely a matter of self-interest, but of justice and peace, according to the American outlook. The mercantile system was especially unjust to the United States because America was the only independent nation among the colonies of the Western Hemisphere. Colonialism barred America from trading with its neighbors and confined it to the markets of the mother countries three thousand miles away. For the European powers, on the other hand, it was their neighbors' markets that were open, and only the distant colonial ports that were closed. Surely, Americans believed, fairness and the interests of peace required the opening of colonial ports in the Western Hemisphere to the United States. This would provide profits for all and an interdependence that would encourage peace between nations. European obtuseness had to be more than mere self-interest; it had to indicate a malicious hostility to the United States and its republican system.

Americans regarded European intransigence on territorial issues as equally unjustified and spiteful. They blamed every Indian raid in the Northwest on the British, whom they accused of using the Indians to keep Americans away from the Great Lakes posts. They assumed quite correctly that the British were holding the posts for economic and strategic purposes, not just in reprisal for America's noncompliance with the peace treaty. With equal accuracy, they regarded Spanish border policy as hostile. Yet the Spanish had considerable legality and reason on their side. The administrative border of Florida had actually been moved north of 31° when the British had occupied it before the revolution. In asserting their border claims, closing the Mississippi, supporting Indian resistance, and bribing Americans to stir up secession, the Spanish were defending themselves against an attitude they knew to be common in the United States—that the Spanish colonies were empty; dominated by a corrupt, tyrannical, superstitious government; and therefore a legitimate future target for American expansion. Jefferson, for one, worried only that the Spanish might be too feeble to hold their border territories "till our population can be sufficiently advanced to gain it from them peice by peice [sic]."

As the leading political figures in the United States came to realize that the value of America's commerce would not bring the European powers hurrying to grant liberal trade treaties or to accept American domination over the Mississippi and Great Lakes systems, they began to reconsider their foreign policies. Humiliated by the lack of British and French respect, Adams and Jefferson wrote home urging more unified and vigorous action. If European powers were unwilling to adopt reciprocal trade concessions, then America must adopt reciprocal trade exclusions. John Jay, George Washington, James Madison, and Alexander Hamilton agreed.

Under the Articles of Confederation, however, the national government had no control over foreign trade. This put commercial retaliation out of the question. The Articles also prohibited most other means of diplomatic leverage. They denied Congress the power to tax or to raise an army. Congress had to request money and troops from the states, which it did with little success. Consequently, it could not build a navy adequate to protect America's shipping or guard its coasts. It could not build an army to regain the Great Lakes posts or control the Indians. It could not even enforce its own treaty obligations. State courts often defied congressional orders to enforce the collection of British debts, and state legislatures ignored congressional suggestions that they compensate the Loyalists.

Hamilton and Madison, as members of Congress, tried to win some of these powers for the national government. They proposed an amendment to the Articles of Confederation giving Congress the right to levy a tariff on imports. This would enable the federal government to retaliate commercially against hostile powers by assessing higher tariffs against them than against friendly nations. It would also provide revenue with which to build a navy and pay a militia. But a unanimous vote was required to amend the Articles of Confederation, and both New York and Rhode Island vetoed the tariff the two times it came before the Congress—New York the first time; Rhode Island the second.

If the United States did not have the power to achieve its goals, there seemed to be only one other recourse—assistance from foreign nations. No American leader considered this desirable. Even such a friend of the French as Thomas Jefferson had been made wary by the diplomatic experience of the revolution and its aftermath. When John Jay, secretary for foreign affairs, told Jefferson to seek French help against the British occupation of the Northwest posts, Jefferson declined. He preferred not to remind France that the United States had reciprocal obligations under the alliance to protect French territory. Jay had some other alternatives: The United States could ally with the British against Spain to force open the Mississippi. Or it could ally with the Spanish to remove the British from the Northwest posts. But each had its price. The British would demand the posts and American withdrawal from the West Indies trade in exchange for their help, while alliance with the Spanish would cost America the Mississippi. Despairing of any chance that the states would consent to strengthen the national government, Jay decided to bid for Spanish help. Once again, the Mississippi would be the main bargaining chip.

In 1786 Jay negotiated a preliminary agreement with Diego de Gardoqui. Spain would grant the United States a liberal trade treaty and guarantee America's borders against the British in exchange for a compromise on Florida's border, America's sacrifice of Mississippi navigation rights for twenty-five to thirty years, and a guarantee of Spanish possessions in the Western Hemisphere. Jay then went to Congress to seek approval of the agreement before negotiating the final treaty. But he told Congress only of the provisions concerning navigation of the Mississippi and trade with Spain, omitting any mention of the mutual territorial guarantees that committed Spain to help America retrieve the Northwest posts and the United States to respect and protect Spanish colonial possessions. If he had revealed these provisions, no approval would have been forthcoming.

Even so, Jay stirred up a storm that threatened the new union. Southerners accused him and his supporters of sacrificing the Mississippi to northern interests in foreign commerce. James Monroe distrusted Jay as a potential traitor from that day on. Jay encountered so much opposition to those portions of the agreement he revealed to Congress that he dropped the entire negotiation. Even so, southern delegates to the Constitutional Convention of 1787 and subsequent state ratifying conventions would cite the Jay-Gardoqui Agreement as a warning against too much power being given to a federal government that might become the instrument of the more populous North.

THE CONSTITUTION AND AMERICAN FOREIGN POLICY

But Jay's fears had been premature. The Philadelphia Convention of 1787 created a new Constitution, granting the federal government the three crucial powers it had been denied under the Articles of Confederation—the power to tax, to raise an army, and to control commerce.

Of all the constitutional provisions affecting diplomacy, contemporaries probably attributed the most importance to the commerce clauses. Americans expected commercial retaliation to be the primary weapon of their foreign policy. The South supported such action but feared that the North, with its larger voting bloc, might make southern rather than northern products the sacrificial goats. So a southern-dominated committee proposed to prohibit taxes on exports and any interference with the slave trade. It also sought to require a two-thirds vote of both houses to pass any navigation act. Northerners whittled back these demands. They secured the right of Congress to control the slave trade after 1808 and to pass navigation laws by a simple majority of the two houses. But they accepted the prohibition on export taxes. Thus the United States could wield its commercial power by taxing imports or embargoing exports, but even today it is constitutionally prohibited from taxing exports.

The members of the convention also were determined to prevent the states from flouting federal treaties, as they had under the Articles of Confederation. The first comprehensive proposal offered in the Constitutional Convention, the Virginia Plan, sought to do this by giving Congress the right to veto all state laws. This, however, was too much of an invasion of states rights for most of the convention members. Instead, the Constitution and treaties were made the supreme law of the land. In addition, the Supreme Court was given original jurisdiction over cases involving other nations, foreclosing any state control over foreign policy through the legal system.

Having increased federal power over international relations, the convention had to decide with which branch of the government that power ought to lie. The members had no difficulty deciding that the power to make war should be lodged with the legislature. It was a staple fare of British reformers and their American disciples that the people who supplied the taxes and the soldiers were far less likely to agitate for war than monarchs seeking glory and treasure. The convention made an interesting modification, however, when it permitted Congress to "declare" rather than "make" war. This would allow the president as commander-in-chief to "repel sudden attacks." In later times, of course, it enabled the president to commit the nation to full-scale wars without an official congressional declaration.[1]

The president received much of the rest of his power over foreign policy almost accidentally. The Virginia Plan granted the right to make treaties and appoint ambassadors to the Senate. Then the Great Compromise eliminated the provision that membership of both House and Senate would reflect the number of inhabitants in each state. The Senate would be composed of two senators per state, regardless of population, meaning that states with less than one-third of the population could conceivably outvote the remainder of the nation. The large states rebelled against empowering such a Senate to control foreign policy. They gave the president the right to make treaties and appoint ambassadors, leaving the Senate only the power to advise and consent by a two-thirds vote. On occasion the Senate has used this role to great effect, but its power has declined over the years.

When George Washington appeared personally in the Senate to ask for advice on a treaty, the senators asked him to leave so they could debate in private. Washington never went back. Ever since, the Senate has done more consenting than advising. More important, presidents found ways to circumvent the senatorial power over treaties. They have used joint congressional resolutions or executive agreements that require no congressional consent at all to make what are in effect treaty commitments. They have also lessened Senate power over appointments, lodging much authority over foreign policy in officials of the White House staff, such as the National Security Advisor, who unlike the secretary of state do not require senatorial confirmation.

---

[1] After such an action had led to the Vietnam debacle, Congress passed a joint resolution in November of 1973 requiring the president to secure congressional approval or withdraw American troops within sixty days if he intervened without a declaration of war.

In fact, the Constitution did not provide specifically for a cabinet or for a secretary of state, just unnamed executive departments. The first Congress created the Department of State and gave it jurisdiction over foreign policy. But diplomacy was thought a small enough task that the department could also be responsible for the mint and various domestic affairs. Thomas Jefferson, the first secretary of state, presided over a department consisting of only six employees and a handful of ministers and consuls abroad. Another of Congress's most significant decisions affecting the State Department was to reject the contention that it should require a two-thirds Senate vote to dismiss cabinet ministers as well as to appoint them. Instead, the president could fire his cabinet secretaries at will. This made the Department of State a creature of the executive, not an independent entity or a servant of the Senate. Still, the role of the cabinet remained a bit hazy. One member of Washington's administration meant to make the most of that situation. That man was Alexander Hamilton.

THE DIPLOMACY OF THE FEDERALIST ERA

John Adams, who came to hate Alexander Hamilton, called him "the bastard brat of a Scotch peddlar." Hamilton indeed had been born out of wedlock to a West Indian woman who had left her husband for a wandering Scottish laird. She bore the Scotsman two children, whereupon he unceremoniously left her. Alexander was left the breadwinner in his impoverished family, serving as an eleven-year-old clerk in a merchant firm on the island of St. Croix. This inglorious heritage produced in Hamilton a gnawing ambition. He thirsted for heroism, and what he wanted for himself, he naturally wanted for his adopted nation as well. He came to the United States under the sponsorship of a group of West Indian planters who sent him to study medicine on the condition that he would return to practice in the islands. Once in America, he became one of the revolutionaries, an officer in the artillery, and then General Washington's aide-de-camp. The childless Washington virtually adopted Hamilton as a surrogate son. Hamilton's patron permitted him to lead the charge on a critical fortified redoubt at the Battle of Yorktown and cover himself with military glory. Hamilton also profited from his connections at Washington's headquarters, marrying the daughter of the powerful Schuyler clan of New York. Upon leaving the army, Hamilton studied law and became a member of the Confederate Congress, where he teamed with James Madison to lead the movement toward a more powerful federal government.

When Washington appointed him the first secretary of the treasury, Hamilton saw himself as prime minister, and modeled his office on that of the British prime minister, who was usually the chief economic officer in his own cabinet. Hamilton thus took it upon himself to direct much of America's foreign as well as economic affairs, a task made easier by Jefferson's late arrival from France to take his position in the first cabinet as secretary of state.

Figure 2 George Washington (left) and his secretary of the treasury, Alexander Hamilton, were the key figures in making American foreign policy following adoption of the Constitution. Portraits courtesy of the National Archives.

Even after Jefferson assumed control of foreign policy, Hamilton used his private British contacts to direct diplomacy behind Jefferson's back. This might not have made much difference had Hamilton not been moving away from some of the ideas he had seemingly shared with Jefferson and Madison. All three had agitated for federal power to control trade, arguing that this would permit the United States to retaliate against British intransigence. Hamilton and Madison had even made this a central point in their famous collaborative effort in support of the Constitution, the *Federalist Papers.* But when Madison proposed such retaliation from his position as leader of the House of Representatives, Hamilton worked successfully behind the scenes to defeat it. It proved to be the first divergence among the organizers of what would become the Federalist and Republican parties.

Hamilton's goal for America was truly heroic: He wanted to build the nation's military power so that it could assume the leadership of the Western Hemisphere. Too long Europe had plumed itself as the master of the world, Hamilton wrote. The mission of the United States, therefore, was "to vindicate the honor of the human race, and to teach that assuming brother moderation." But Hamilton leavened his romanticism with a substantial dose of realism. The federal government needed money to build its power, and it was clear that a tariff on imports would have to be the primary source of federal funds. The alternative of an internal tax would be highly unpopular to a people fresh from a successful revolution triggered by Britain's attempt to impose an internal stamp tax.

The money to be derived from the tariff was crucial to Hamilton's vision. In his famous Report to Congress on the Public Credit, he proposed to use the tariff revenue to begin paying off the national and state debts. With America's credit restored, foreign governments would once again be willing to loan the nation money in case of war or emergency. The government's newly funded bonds also would circulate at full face value, giving America a much-needed money supply. Hamilton welcomed the fact that funding the bonds at face value would enrich commercial speculators, many of whom had bought the bonds at depreciated prices from needy farmers and soldiers. Farmers and soldiers would invest their profits in land and slaves; speculators were far more likely to invest in commerce and manufactures, which Hamilton regarded as the sinews of modern power. His Report also proposed a national bank, where the government could deposit excess revenue and in turn see to it that bank loans went exclusively to commercial and manufacturing projects. Finally, in a separate Report on Manufactures that Congress ultimately defeated, Hamilton advocated direct subsidies to critical manufactures. Thus, Hamilton would encourage a modern balanced economy and provide the wherewithal for a strong military and a powerful, heroic nation.

Since Great Britain supplied 90 percent of the imports on which the tariff would be levied, Hamilton argued against commercial retaliation for fear of starting a tariff war. (Subsidies rather than high protective duties would encourage American manufacturers to compete with the British.) France, Spain, and the Netherlands could not replace the immense volume of British trade because they could not furnish credit. Worse yet, a tariff war could lead to a shooting war, and Great Britain was the one European power with enough naval strength to support an invasion of the United States from its adjacent province of Canada. It would be better to appease Britain, perhaps even ally with it to force the Spanish to open the Mississippi. Then, in fifty years or so, a more mature United States could turn to the task of teaching Great Britain "moderation."

James Madison also supported a strong national government, but he did not aspire to heroism for himself or his nation. Where Hamilton strutted, Madison stooped. Where Hamilton was a dandy, Madison wore sober black. Where Hamilton was a soldier, Madison was a scholar. Madison spoke so softly his colleagues in the House of Representatives had to crowd around his desk to hear his speeches. He insisted to the House that commercial retaliation was a viable weapon. The British West Indies would starve without American foodstuffs. Manufacturers and workers in Britain's home islands would suffer terrribly if deprived of their American market. Americans would suffer far less from an interruption of the British trade because theirs was a self-sufficient agricultural economy. American citizens were virtuous, independent republican farmers who could feed, clothe, and house themselves without foreign help and who were willing to sacrifice for liberty and national dignity. The British, on the other hand, had been corrupted and made effeminate by manufacturing and trading in luxuries. They were dependent on the United States for necessities, where America got from the British only dispensable "gew-gaws."

Madison disdained Hamilton's warnings that commercial retaliation and the potential loss of tariff revenue might destroy the funding system, the national bank, and Hamilton's entire financial system. Madison would not mourn the collapse of Hamilton's financial program because he regarded it as overblown, corrupt, and inclining toward the same dependence on luxuries, speculation, and vice that plagued the British economy. Madison did not oppose trade and shipping, but he wanted only enough to carry off America's agricultural surplus and return with imported necessities. Trade in luxury goods was debilitating. To expand American shipping to the point that it would dominate the carrying trade of other nations was to invite conflict and war.

Madison did not oppose manufacturing either, but he wanted only limited home manufacturing of necessities for domestic consumption. Like many people of the eighteenth century, he asssociated large-scale manufacturing for export with extremes of luxury and aristocracy on the one hand and poverty-stricken masses and vice on the other. These ideas derived from the first large manufacturing establishments of that century, which tended to be workhouses, where minor criminals and the poor were forced to earn their keep, or royal establishments like the Gobelin factory, which produced magnificent tapestries for the French court. Madison and his friend Jefferson feared that Hamilton's attempt to subsidize manufactures would lead to the same extremes of poverty and wealth, the same division between a foppish upper class and a vicious, dependent urban laboring class as they believed already existed in England. Madison and Jefferson also did not believe that commercial retaliation would risk much harm to America. They thought Great Britain would cave in quickly, and in the meantime the few imports America truly needed could be supplied by France and Holland. British credit led only to an unhealthy dependence on British trade and an excessive volume of luxury goods.

By 1793, Madison had organized a faction of Congress in permanent op- position to Hamilton's program. This faction feared that Hamilton was forming a "corrupt squadron" in Congress made up of speculators whose fi- nancial position was in the hands of the secretary of the treasury and whose votes could be manipulated much as prime ministers like Robert Walpole had manipulated the British Parliament. Madison's allies were angry that Hamilton favored trade, shipping, and manufacturing over agriculture, and thus northeastern interests over those of the agricultural South and West. Yet so long as the issues remained complicated economic ones, they failed to strike much spark among the people at large, who preferred to trust that President Washington was doing the right thing.

Then events abroad made the issue of commercial retaliation against Great Britain dramatic and vital enough to galvanize even ordinary people into action and expand congressional factions into grassroots parties. First, the French Revolution, which all Americans had cheered in its early stages, took a sharp turn toward radicalism and violence in 1793 with the execution of the king and large numbers of the nobility. Hamilton's Federalists, some of whom had been part of the anti-French faction during the American Revo- lution, were generally conservatives who disliked radical and anticlerical tendencies. This attitude further reinforced their inclination to avoid offend- ing Britain. The Republicans, on the other hand, led by members of the for- mer pro-French faction of the Continental Congress, emphasized the kinship between the French and American revolutions, accused the Federalists of fa- voring Great Britain from monarchical and aristocratic sentiments, and con- tinued to urge retaliation against the British.

Shortly after the execution of Louis XVI, France declared war on England and began still another world conflagration. American policies toward Britain and France now involved not just financial consequences or democratic sym- pathies, but national survival. The United States was "perpetually" bound by its treaties of alliance with France, which required America to defend French possessions in the Western Hemisphere should France request it. The alli- ance also gave France special privileges in American ports that were to be de- nied to France's enemies. Adherence to this alliance could quite easily lead to war with England; renouncing it would bring at least some danger of war with France. The vast majority of Americans still sympathized with France and its revolution; but they also wanted political isolation from Europe, the commercial benefits of foreign trade, and above all, peace. Washington, Hamilton, Madison, Jefferson, and their colleagues would have to put to- gether a policy consistent with this rather paradoxical consensus.

Virtually the only thing they could agree upon was that the United States should remain neutral. None of the major leaders wanted to join the European fight, however strong their sympathies for England or France. The form American neutrality should take, however, became a source of bitter controversy between Federalists and Republicans. Hamilton advised President Washington to practice absolute impartiality. He wanted to renounce the French alliance and make an immediate public declaration of neutrality. This would allay the natural suspicions of Great Britain that the United States meant to go to war on the side of its French ally. Perhaps then America could avoid a break with its most important source of supplies and revenue. Jefferson, on the other hand, said America should not declare neutrality, but bargain with it. Great Britain should be threatened rather than bribed. Keep the French alliance, and when the British, who could not afford another enemy, came to beg for American neutrality, demand that they abandon the Northwest posts, open the West Indies to American ships, and respect neutral rights. If, in accordance with the alliance, the French did request American intervention to protect their Western Hemisphere possessions, there would be time enough to remind them that the United States did not have the army or navy to do so.

Washington compromised. He issued a Proclamation of Neutrality, as Hamilton wished.[2] But he refused to renounce the French alliance. Instead, he recognized the legitimacy of the new revolutionary government in France and received the new French minister, Citizen Edmund Genêt. He assumed that the Proclamation of Neutrality made it apparent to both the French and the British that the United States would not honor the alliance to the point of endangering America's peace. Jefferson and Madison remained opposed to this tepid form of neutrality, but Washington was so revered by his constituents that Jefferson and Madison could not risk a frontal attack on his policies. Their opposition had to take the form of minor quibbles about Washington's failure to consult Congress before declaring neutrality.

Jefferson and Madison had to abandon even this caviling when the tactless Genêt embarrassed them and the other friends of France. Lacking the prudence of the Republican leaders, Genêt openly defied Washington's narrow interpretation of America's obligation to its French ally. He recuited American citizens to fight against the British and used American ports to fit out captured British merchant ships as raiders. He even threatened to instigate an American uprising against Washington if the president hampered his efforts. An outraged Washington demanded Genêt's recall. The discredited French envoy wisely chose to retire quickly to New York, where he married the daughter of Governor George Clinton and thus avoided the guillotine that might well have awaited him had he returned to France.

By dampening some of America's pro-French fervor, the Genêt incident strengthened Washington's hopes for neutrality. Genêt had already boosted those hopes when he had revealed that France had no intention of asking the

---

[2] Ironically, in deference to Jefferson's opposition, the word "neutrality" was omitted from the text of the proclamation.

United States to join the war in defense of the French West Indies. The United States was far more valuable to France as a neutral. French ships and trade were largely swept from the sea by the superior British navy. The Americans, however, had the universally recognized right as neutrals to trade with warring nations. They could rescue France from economic collapse by carrying on the vital trade with the French colonies. Naturally, the British tried to interrupt this effort. They repeatedly devised legal technicalities to narrow the range of neutral rights. They knew they could rely on their navy rather than international law to protect their own commerce. The disputes occasioned by their defiance of America's concept of neutral rights destroyed all hope that the United States might enjoy an easy and profitable neutrality and soon brought the two nations to the brink of war.

France and the United States, as nations with small navies, had taken the precaution of writing a broad spectrum of neutral rights into their treaties of alliance and commerce during the revolution. They had agreed that "free ships meant free goods." Under this doctrine, a neutral ship could carry almost everything, including enemy property, to a nation at war. The British adhered to an older doctrine which gave them the right to confiscate enemy property wherever it was found. The United States protested in vain, since Britain had the bigger guns. But American shippers found a clever way around their dilemma; they bought the French property. This meant Americans were carrying neutral goods aboard neutral ships, which was legal by any definition.

The British cried "fraud" because Americans often paid far less than the goods were worth, after arranging in advance to sell them for less on arrival in France. The Americans in this way would collect only the equivalent of their shipping costs. The British then found another way to interrupt American trade. International law permitted Britain to confiscate as contraband any war materiel headed for an enemy port even if the ship and cargo were owned by neutrals. The British simply expanded their definition of contraband to classify food as war materiel because it was necessary to the enemy. To assuage American anger, they offered to pay for any food they confiscated, but the issue continued to rankle.

The British still thought too much trade was getting through to the French. So they appealed to a supposed Rule of 1756 to stop neutral ships carrying goods from the French West Indies to France. The Rule of 1756, a British creation, declared that trade closed to foreigners in time of peace could not be opened in time of war. Since direct trade between France and the French West Indies had been monopolized by France under its mercantilist system, opening it to Americans after hostilities broke out was an act of war, one the British claimed the right to counteract. Soon the Americans steered around this as well. Since trade between the United States and the French islands had been open in peacetime, as had trade between the United States and France, American ships simply detoured to America on their way between the West Indies and France. Thus they were no longer following a route that had been closed before the war.

At this point the frustrated British abandoned all niceties. They were worried by a sudden flood of supplies being sent off by French islanders trying to salvage the goods from a terrible slave uprising. In late 1793 the British declared an illegal blockade of the French West Indies. Without informing the Americans of their new policy, they swooped down upon nearly three hundred unsuspecting American ships and forced them into British ports for trial before British admiralty courts. At the same time that news of this outrage reached the American government, newspapers were printing a speech by the British governor of Canada to the Northwest Indians. He said war was imminent between England and the United States and pledged British support in expelling American settlers from the Ohio Valley.

Again Federalists and Republicans quarreled over the proper response to these threats. Hamilton and his group urged Washington to send a friendly negotiator to Britain to iron out the differences between the two nations. Jefferson, Madison, and the Republicans argued that America should first cut off trade with the British so the envoy could bargain from strength. Federalists insisted that this would antagonize the British without accomplishing much, since the United States needed trade with Great Britain more than the British, and the British knew it. Federalists argued instead for military preparations. They especially wanted to hurry construction of six frigates already being built for use against the Barbary pirates.

Washington sided with the Federalists. He appointed John Jay, second only to Hamilton in prestige among the Federalists, to be the special envoy. Jay immediately warned Congress against any hostile commercial measures prior to the negotiations. The House of Representatives, at the urging of Madison, insisted on a nonintercourse act against Britain. Only the tie-breaking vote of John Adams defeated it in the Senate. Congress then passed a temporary embargo to prevent American ships from leaving port and so removed such targets from the seas in case of war. Since the embargo affected trade with all nations, not just England, Jay was able to approach his negotiations in the conciliatory posture he thought suitable. He would try to persuade the British that America was truly neutral and not intent on helping the French. America's measures of military preparedness would serve as subtle reminders that failure to reach agreement would mean almost certain war. He was convinced that overt threats could add nothing to this leverage and might sabotage agreement by convincing the British that America was inveterately hostile to them.

Historians ever since have wondered whether a more assertive approach might have won a better agreement than Jay was able to negotiate. The British may have thought him easy to manipulate. One British official who knew him advised the British negotiator that Jay "argues closely but is long-winded and self-opinionated. He can bear any opposition to what he advances provided that regard is shown to his abilities. He may be attached by good treatment, but will be unforgiving if he thinks himself neglected . . . almost every man has a weak and assailable quarter and Mr. Jay's weak side is *Mr. Jay."* Jay apparently never attempted to use threats. Had he tried that approach, he would have found that Alexander Hamilton had already undermined the credibility of his major threat. The secretary of the treasury indiscreetly and secretly informed the British minister to the United States that America would not join other neutrals in Europe who were contemplating a league to resist with force British searches and seizures on the high seas.

Certainly Jay's results were less than sensational. True, the British returned the Northwest posts. They also opened the West Indies to small American ships, although they hedged the concession with so many limitations that the Senate rejected the proposition. The British also agreed to compensate Americans for illegal captures of ships during the blockade of the West Indies. The amount of damages would be set by a neutral commission. Another such commission would settle the disputes that had arisen over the location of the Canadian-American border. Of course, the greatest benefit of the Jay Treaty was that it would maintain the peace between Great Britain and the United States.

But Jay paid a high price. There was no agreement on neutral rights, so British ships would continue to disrupt Franco-American trade. Americans would be bound to pay off their prewar debts to the extent decided by a neutral commission. Above all, Jay had agreed to sacrifice the one weapon Republicans believed might have coerced a better agreement from the British—the treaty prohibited any change in the regulation of Anglo-American trade for ten years.

Historians with access to the British archives have generally agreed, however, that Jay obtained about as much as the British had been willing to give. The English could hardly undermine their war against France by bowing to the American view of neutral rights. Some figures high in the British cabinet were adamantly opposed even to those concessions Jay did win. The Republicans, nevertheless, were livid. They thought the Jay Treaty was a sellout, a purposeful attempt of pro-British Federalists to aid England by permitting interruption of the neutral trade vital to the French war effort. If the United States had used its economic weapons instead of bargaining them away for a pittance, Britain might have conceded America's neutral rights. The Federalists could only respond that unsatisfactory as the treaty was, it was better than the alternative of war. The debate ultimately stirred such emotions among the general population that it turned the two congressional factions into grassroots parties with mass followings and semi-permanent organizations.

At first the public debate was rather tentative because it was based on unsubstantiated rumors of the terms Jay had accepted in London, terms kept secret during the Senate deliberations. This changed once the Senate consented to the treaty by a vote of twenty to ten, precisely the two-thirds vote necessary. Some Republicans immediately broke the seal of silence, and newspapers published the treaty terms around the country. The treaty aroused a chorus of criticism. Congressional Republicans urged their local followers to take advantage of the situation by organizing mass meetings and signing petitions to Washington to ignore the Senate's advice and refuse ratification. Hamilton attempted to address a hostile meeting in New York and was stoned by the crowd, causing one Federalist to remark that it was the first sensible thing the Republicans had done; by dashing out Hamilton's brains, they might reduce him to an equality with themselves. Jay lamented that he could have found his way from Charleston to Boston at midnight by the light of his burning effigies.

Washington was deeply offended by the pressures the Republicans and their petitions brought on him. But he had been disappointed at the treaty himself. At the urging of Edmund Randolph, a moderate Republican who had replaced Jefferson as secretary of state, he decided to delay ratification because the British had resumed captures of American foodstuffs. Fortuitously for the Federalists, they found a way to change his mind. A British ship had recently captured some dispatches en route to France from the French minister to the United States. These dispatches seemed to implicate Secretary Randolph in a convoluted bribery scheme. The British turned them over to his Federalist enemies and they showed them to Washington. This convinced the president to fire Randolph and immediately ratify the treaty.

On the face of it, Washington's ratification should have completed the constitutional process of treaty-making. But Republicans controlled the House of Representatives and saw one last chance to defeat the Jay Treaty. Since all money bills had to originate in the House, Madison and the other Republican leaders organized an attempt to refuse the appropriations necessary to implement the treaty. Again they launched a campaign of mass meetings and petitions, hoping to influence the votes of wavering House members. This time, however, the Federalists abandoned their aristocratic disdain for such methods and matched the Republicans meeting for meeting and petition for petition. The Federalists warned that rejection of the treaty would mean a devastating war with England. Slowly they turned the tide of public opinion in their favor and used their increasing popular support to frighten some fence-sitters. The Republican majority in the House melted. One intimidated Congressman decided he had to leave the House to mail a trunk. When the Committee of the Whole took the critical vote, the result was a tie. The tie-breaking vote rested in the hands of the chairman of the committee, a Pennsylvania Republican named Frederick Muhlenberg. A passionate Federalist had warned Muhlenberg earlier that a vote against the treaty would doom the prospective match between Muhlenberg's son and the Federalist's daughter. Whether that threat had any influence or not, Muhlenberg voted for the treaty.

The treaty fight was over, but the party battle endured. The Republicans used the party organization they had developed in the struggle to promote Thomas Jefferson against Federalist Vice-President John Adams as successor to the retiring President Washington. The Federalists considered such organized opposition to be dangerous and disloyal, particularly because the French were openly supporting Jefferson in hopes of overturning the treaty with Great Britain. Washington agreed and assisted by Hamilton, composed a Farewell Address to caution his countrymen against the dangers of parties and foreign intrigue. He did not advocate violation of the French alliance, but warned against any extension of it. The United States should have as little political connection with Europe as possible. It should build its own unity and strength, steer clear of permanent alliances, and accept temporary alliances only for extraordinary emergencies. Although many Republicans were not yet convinced of the wisdom of Washington's advice, the address quickly entered the realm of American gospel. Americans printed it in children's schoolbooks, engraved it on watches, and wove it into tapestries. The Farewell Address was a ringing blow in the struggle between neutrality and foreign alliances.

Despite Washington's endorsement, John Adams found himself in a neck-and-neck race for the presidency. Gone were the days when a president could be elected unanimously. The Republicans used the emotional reactions to the French Revolution and the Jay Treaty to mobilize a large and organized vote for their candidates. But Adams could point to some Federalist accomplishments in foreign policy that were not so controversial as the Jay Treaty. Thomas Pinckney, Washington's minister to Spain, forced concessions from the Spanish by playing on their fear that the negotiation of the Jay Treaty might produce an Anglo-American alliance aimed at their North American possessions. The Spanish were susceptible to such fears because they had just withdrawn from their alliance with Great Britain to make a separate peace with France. In 1795, Pinckney concluded the Treaty of San Lorenzo with Spain, a treaty known familiarly in America as the Pinckney Treaty. It finally opened the Mississippi to American navigation and settled the boundary of Florida at 31° in line with the claims of the United States. The Pinckney Treaty was so popular that the Federalists threatened to stall its ratification as a means to force congressional acceptance of the Jay Treaty.

In addition to the Pinckney Treaty, Adams and the Federalists could brag about the victory of General "Mad Anthony" Wayne over the Northwest Indians at Fallen Timbers in 1794. This resulted in the Treaty of Greenville of 1795, which opened much of the Ohio Valley to American settlement. These two boons to American expansion, the Pinckney and Greenville treaties, along with the swing of public opinion in favor of the Jay Treaty, permitted Adams to defeat Jefferson by the slim margin of three electoral votes.

JOHN ADAMS AND THE QUASI-WAR OF 1798

With this narrow mandate, Adams faced a formidable problem. While the Jay Treaty preserved peace with Great Britain, it also came close to provoking war with France. The French economy depended on America's neutral trade. Great Britain would now interrupt a large portion of that trade with impunity because the United States had not forced British recognition of the broad spectrum of neutral rights embodied in the Franco-American treaties. In retaliation, the French announced a new version of the Golden Rule—they would do to the Americans whatever the Americans permitted the British to do. Under this rubric, they detained or captured over three hundred American ships suspected of carrying British goods.

Adams decided to treat the French just as his predecessor had handled the British. He urged naval appropriations and authority to increase the army, avoided commercial retaliation, and sent emissaries to France to negotiate. To avoid Republican charges that the diplomatic mission would be a partisan one anxious to sabotage the negotiations in order to justify war against France, Adams asked first Jefferson and then Madison to be one of the envoys. Both rejected the appointment, so Adams sent another Republican, his old Massachusetts friend Elbridge Gerry. Gerry would join two Federalists, John Marshall and Charles Cotesworth Pinckney, to demonstrate that the mission would negotiate in good faith.

Unfortunately, the French were not ready to accept the mission in a similar spirit. The new French foreign minister, the Marquis de Talleyrand, did not want war. But he thought France would benefit if prolonged negotiations allowed partisan quarrels to weaken the United States while French ships continued their plundering. He sent three underlings to inform the American delegates that they would have to explain away the Jay Treaty's supposed betrayal of the French alliance, approve an American government loan to France, and pay a bribe before they would be permitted to open official negotiations. When finally convinced that Talleyrand was serious, the two Federalists indignantly reported their reception to Adams and left the country. Gerry, however, remained in France at Talleyrand's urging to forestall a complete breakdown of relations and possible war. His was a praiseworthy effort, but one that encouraged the Republicans in Congress to suspect that the Federalists themselves had provoked the crisis. The Republicans demanded that Adams turn over the delegation's correspondence to prove otherwise. Adams confounded them by doing so, substituting for the names of the three French underlings who had requested the bribes the letters X, Y, and Z. The XYZ Affair destroyed almost all pro-French sentiment in America, discredited the Republicans, and rallied the nation around Adams, who now called for military preparations.

Yet the president did not request an immediate declaration of war. Instead, he ordered American naval vessels to retaliate against French attackers. A two-year quasi-war followed, in which there were numerous small-scale naval engagements resulting in the capture of eighty-five French ships. Meanwhile, Congress enacted additional taxes, authorized construction of ships for the newly created naval department, and voted to raise a 50,000-man army whose command Adams gave to the one man who could unite Federalists and Republicans in a war against France, George Washington. Without Adams's encouragement, Congress also passed the Alien and Sedition Acts, giving the government extraordinary powers to silence Republican dissent that might undermine the war effort and just incidentally overturn the Federalists in the next elections.

To the surprise of many, Adams never did carry through with the war. Although he was second to none in his dislike of France, he disliked Great

Britain as well. His inclination against war was further dampened when Washington insisted that Hamilton be promoted over the heads of all other officers to be inspector-general and second in command of the army. Not only was Hamilton too pro-British for Adams's taste, but Hamilton had tried to manipulate the electoral vote to elevate the Federalist vice-presidential candidate over Adams into the presidency. Then, following the appointment of Hamilton that Washington had coerced from Adams, Hamilton whirled through the capital urging Congress to appropriate less money for the navy than Adams had requested and to give it instead to the army. Hamilton dreamed of leading this army on an expedition against the Spanish border colonies and beyond, supported by the British navy and by Latin American rebels under the leadership of Francisco de Miranda.

Understandably, Adams was relieved when he heard from reliable sources in Europe, including his own son John Quincy Adams, that Talleyrand wanted peace and was ready to accept with dignity a new American negotiator. Adams immediately appointed one in defiance of his own cabinet, many of whose members were holdovers from Washington's administration and more beholden to Hamilton than to their own president. They and other "high Federalists" insisted that since France had so rudely rejected the previous emissaries, Adams should require that France send a delegation to the United States. Some of them made this demand in the hope that it would bring war with France. Hamilton's own motives are not so clear. Nevertheless, Adams's appointment of an envoy to France split his party. The peace with France also gave Americans a chance to reconsider and resent the taxes and the Alien and Sedition Acts passed in expectation of war. The way was paved for Jefferson and the Republicans to defeat Adams in the election of 1800.

Adams took his defeat hard. He left the capital immediately on the expiration of his term of office without even participating in Jefferson's inaugural. He believed he had sacrificed his political career and reputation in pursuit of the right and said he desired nothing more on his gravestone than the inscription "Here lies John Adams, who took upon himself the responsibility of the peace with France in the year 1800." Recent historians have cast some doubt on Adams's claim to transcendent moral courage. They cite evidence that public opinion was already moving toward peace when Adams made his decision, and that his defeat would have been even more likely had he taken America to war. That debate probably never will be settled. But it is indisputable that the XYZ Affair and the quasi-war ended the Republicans' emotional attachment to France. The Federalists never tired of claiming that the Republicans were the treacherous tools of French policy, but actually Republicans too were ready to accept the advice of Washington's Farewell Address.

Jefferson announced in his Inaugural Address that America sought "peace, commerce, and honest friendship with all nations, entangling alliances with none." Even the French alliance would no longer challenge this unanimous sentiment for nonentanglement. That alliance had been terminated by the Treaty of Mortefontaine, the pact that ended the quasi-war. The United States would not sign another treaty of alliance until World War II.

EXPANSIONISM IN EARLY AMERICAN DIPLOMACY

The primary theme of American diplomacy in this era was defensive, a striving for survival, independence, and respect in the relations of the United States with the formidable powers of Europe. Accompanying this was a secondary theme, the hunger for expansion. Occasionally this secondary theme surfaced in a dramatic fashion. During the Confederation period, for instance, Congress had established a format for governing new territories, the Northwest Ordinances. The ordinances imposed congressional rule on inhabitants of the territories and deprived them of full self-determination, but promised to bring them into the Union as equal states once they had achieved sufficient population and agreed to a republican form of government. This arrangement, remarkably liberal in an age when the only known means of governing new territories was an empire dominating colonies, gave Americans confidence that they could acquire new lands without breeding the same problems England had faced with its American colonies.

At least this would be the case so long as the alien inhabitants of these new lands, be they Indians or the colonists of a foreign power, were few enough that their natural resentment against the American conquerers could be overwhelmed by American settlers moving into the territory. The Northwest Territories themselves were a major arena for this expansionist process. Settlers swarmed into the Ohio Valley and intruded on Indian lands. The army inevitably followed to suppress Indian resistance and negotiate a treaty solidifying United States government control. The Department of War rather than the Department of State conducted all such diplomacy with the Indians under the assumption, dominant throughout Europe, that Indians were not totally sovereign over their lands. Indians were what the Supreme Court later called "domestic dependent nations," entitled to negotiate treaties only with the truly sovereign state whose claims were recognized as valid by the European powers.

Thus, the United States had the so-called right of preemption over the Northwest Territories, and legally the Indians of the area could negotiate only with the American government. Great Britain had maintained agents with those tribes, supplied them, traded with them, encouraged their resistance, and even sought to negotiate an Indian border state with the Americans. This project would have reserved for the Indians a broad swath of land south of the Canadian border extending from the Great Lakes to the Atlantic. The Indian border state would be guaranteed jointly by Britain and the United States. The United States resisted this British demand because the border state would have been formed entirely from land claimed by the United States, without any Canadian territory being sacrificed, and because it would permanently bar American access to the Great Lakes and the St.

Lawrence. Wayne's victory at Fallen Timbers and the near clash of his army with the British at Detroit put an end to this British project for the time being, much to the distress of the Indians, who had hoped to keep their lands.

American expansionism also showed up as a minor theme in the Constitution. One of the primary arguments of the opponents of the Constitution was that a republican form of government was appropriate only in a small area. In a small area, a homogeneous population could come to an easy consensus and make rule by elective legislatures possible. A larger area, opponents insisted, required a stronger, more arbitrary rule by a monarch to hold its disparate peoples together. James Madison countered this in his famous Federalist Paper No. 10, arguing that a republic could actually survive better in a large area than a small one. The multiple interests and factions in a large area could prevent the tyranny of a permanent majority so likely to arise in a small, homogeneous area. Some historians have seen this argument as a significant blueprint for imperialism. But Madison was not so much arguing to accommodate expansion as he was trying to convince the American people that the United States could rule that territory it already had in a republican yet efficient manner. Expansion may have been in the back of the minds of Madison and many other Americans, but survival, independence, and neutrality were in the forefront.

CONTROVERSIAL ISSUES AND FURTHER READING

The conflict between Federalists and Republicans over American foreign policy still stirs considerable passion among historians, although few go so far as to join the partisans of the 1790s and some early American historians to accuse opponents of having been the willing dupes of a foreign power. [For the rather rare examples of this, see the mid-nineteenth-century multivolume histories of the United States by pro-Republican James Schouler and pro-Federalists Richard Hildreth and Hermann Von Holst.] Increasingly, historians see these accusations as near-paranoia produced by the relative newness of the concept of a loyal opposition and the suspiciousness encouraged by libertarian thought of the time. [See John Howe, "Republican Thought and the Political Violence of the 1790's," *American Quarterly*, 19 (Summer 1967); and James H. Hutson, *John Adams and the Diplomacy of the American Revolution* (1980).] Still, many studies of this period remain rather strongly partisan in outlook.

Samuel Flagg Bemis established the standard for research in this period. His *Jay's Treaty* (1923) and *Pinckney's Treaty* (1926) thoroughly exploited foreign as well as American archives. A strong nationalist, Bemis praised the Republicans for their desire to stand up against England, but doubted the efficacy of their means, commercial retaliation. He also disapproved of their reliance on France, although he made clear that Jefferson and Madison were far from French sycophants. He disapproved even more heartily of the Hamiltonian maneuverings on behalf of Great Britain, and praised instead the prudent but sturdy independence of men like Washington and Adams, who best enabled the United States to wring American benefits from European distress.

Rather than debating whether Jeffersonian Republicans were too pro-French or Hamiltonian Federalists too pro-British, more recent historians have argued over which were the more realistic in their foreign policy. Paul A. Varg's survey, *The Foreign Policies of the Founding Fathers* (1963), portrays the Federalists as realists and the Republicans as hapless idealists. Varg is heartily seconded by Charles R. Ritcheson, *Aftermath of Revolution* (1969), based on thorough research in the British documents, and Gilbert Lycan, *Alexander Hamilton and American Foreign Policy* (1970). My own book, Jerald A. Combs, *The Jay Treaty* (1970), attempts some corrective to this interpretation by arguing that there were some realistic aspects to the Jeffersonian approach and that while Hamilton may have been a realist in some of his diplomacy, he was rash and romantic in much that he did.

Significant works by Alexander De Conde and Albert Hall Bowman take a much more Republican view of things. They praise the Jeffersonians for their idealism and claim that the Republicans managed to combine that idealism with realism, while the Hamiltonian Federalists were simply cynical and devious reactionaries. [Alexander De Conde, *Entangling Alliance* (1958) and its sequel, *The Quasi-War* (1966), and Albert Hall Bowman, *The Struggle for Neutrality* (1974). An important challenge to Bowman is William Stinchcombe, *The XYZ Affair* (1980). All these books make excellent use of the French archives.]

There have been only a few extensive radical treatments of early American diplomacy asserting that expansion rather than neutrality was the primary theme of these years. William Appleman Williams gave the expansionist interpretation of Madison's stand on the Constitution in his *Contours of American History* (1961). Jack Ericson Eblen used American territorial government to demonstrate the undemocratic, imperial tendencies of the United States in *The First and Second United States Empires* (1968). Burton I. Kaufman rather unsuccessfully sought expansionist overtones in "Washington's Farewell Address: A Statement of Empire," in Kaufman, ed., *Washington's Farewell Address: The View from the 20th Century* (1969). [For a history of this period emphasizing expansion but from a more traditional view, see Richard Van Alstyne, *The Rising American Empire* (1960), or Arthur Burr Darling, *Our Rising Empire* (1940).]

Drew R. McCoy, *The Elusive Republic* (1980), gives a fascinating analysis of the ideological and economic premises behind the clash of the Hamiltonian and Jeffersonian systems. Arthur P. Whitaker's *The Spanish-American Frontier* (1927) is still excellent on the events leading to the Pinckney Treaty. Frederick W. Marks's *Independence on Trial* (1973) is the most recent work on the role of foreign affairs in the Confederation period and the making of the Constitution. Stephen Kurtz makes the argument that John Adams was not defying but responding to popular opinion when he made peace with France in his book, *The Presidency of John Adams* (1957).

CHAPTER 3

Republican Diplomacy: The Louisiana Purchase and the War of 1812

LOUISIANA AND FLORIDA

Jefferson's dedication to "peace, commerce, and honest friendship with all nations, entangling alliances with none" was quickly put to the test. Shortly after he took office, he received disturbing information that Napoleon had forced Spain to sign a secret treaty retroceding Louisiana to France. Spanish control of New Orleans and the mouth of the Mississippi might be tolerable because Spain posed little threat to the United States. It also had committed itself in the Pinckney Treaty of 1795 to allow American navigation of the river. France in control of the Father of Waters would be an entirely different proposition. Not only was France a formidable power and Napoleon a ruthless expansionist, but there was no guarantee that France would feel itself bound by the Pinckney Treaty. Indeed, there was ominous evidence to the contrary. Spain suddenly announced that it was suspending the right of Americans to deposit goods from their Mississippi flatboats at New Orleans for transfer to ocean-going vessels. This violation of the Pinckney Treaty would render the right to navigate the river useless. Naturally, Jefferson assumed that Napoleon had instigated the Spanish decision, although historians have found nothing to indicate this in the French or Spanish archives.

The outcry from the West and Jefferson's Federalist opponents was immediate. Jefferson instructed the American minister in Paris, Robert R. Livingston, to try to purchase New Orleans from France and to acquire Florida as well if possible. This would assure American control of the Mississippi's mouth. To add to Napoleon's incentive to sell New Orleans, Jefferson indicated that upon French occupation of the city, the United States "would marry itself to the British fleet." This may not have been pure bluff; Jefferson did order America's minister in Great Britain to open negotiations for an alliance without further instructions if France took New Orleans and closed the Mississippi. Clearly Jefferson was no ideologue. He had moved rapidly from embracing the French alliance to a statement of nonentanglement comparable to Washington's, and now he was considering an alliance with Great Britain.

Few historians believe that Jefferson's threats much affected Napoleon's plans for Louisiana, but events in the West Indies did. Napoleon had earmarked Louisiana to be the source of foodstuffs and lumber for France's immensely profitable sugar islands, just as the United States had served that purpose for Britain's Caribbean islands before the revolution. But the slave rebellion of Toussaint L'Ouverture on the main French island of Santo Domingue undermined the potential rewards of Napoleon's dream. Yellow fever and rebel attacks decimated the armies he sent to put down the revolution, so Napoleon capriciously decided to get rid of his newly acquired white elephant, Louisiana. He would not return it to Spain, though his treaty of retrocession with that country required that he do so if ever France parted with it. Instead, he decided to sell it to the United States.

At first Livingston hesitated. He had instructions to buy New Orleans and Florida for $10 million, not to spend $25 million for Louisiana. But with the support of James Monroe, the newly arrived special envoy, Livingston offered Napoleon $15 million, and Louisiana became American territory. Livingston was only chagrined that he had to share credit for his coup with Monroe. America received his unauthorized action ecstatically, and Jefferson's popularity soared. Even Federalist leaders like Alexander Hamilton, John Adams, and John Marshall endorsed the purchase, although a good many other prominent Federalists denounced it.

Federalist opponents doubted that a Republican government could effectively govern so vast an area, and they feared that the civilized East would lose its political supremacy to the barbaric West. Jefferson brushed this op-

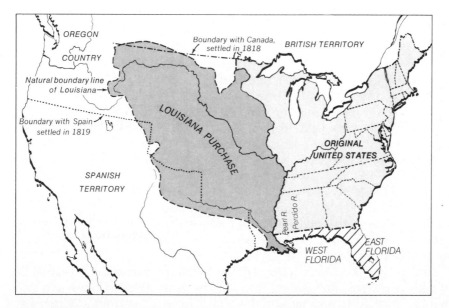

Map 2   Louisiana Purchase, 1803

position aside, along with whatever uneasiness he may have felt about the federal government acquiring territory without a constitutional amendment permitting it to do so. When Spain complained that the purchase violated France's promise not to alienate the territory to any third party, Jefferson told the Spanish to take their complaints to Napoleon. The United States, he reminded them, had never been privy to the agreement between France and Spain. He welcomed the opportunity Louisiana offered to guarantee the availability of land in the United States for years to come, thus ensuring the supremacy of agricultural interests in the political councils of the nation. He even began to contemplate the use of the purchase as leverage for further expansion.

This opportunity arose because Louisiana's borders were extremely vague. France had sold the province to America with the borders "it now has in the hands of Spain, and that it had when France possessed it." Ever since Spain had acquired Louisiana in 1763, West Florida had been administered as a separate entity. But Livingston and Monroe discovered that France had ruled the Florida territory up to the Perdido River as part of Louisiana prior to 1763. They advised Jefferson that he might use their discovery as a precedent to claim West Florida as part of the Louisiana Purchase. This required the Americans to argue that, in historian Henry Adams's pungent phrase, "Spain had retroceded West Florida to France without knowing it, that France had sold it to the United States without suspecting it, that the United States had bought it without paying for it, and that neither France nor Spain, although the original contracting parties, were competent to decide the meaning of their own contract."

The Americans seemed to make this claim without embarrassment. Talleyrand, the French foreign minister who sold them Louisiana, even encouraged them in their convoluted case. When asked the boundaries of Louisiana he professed ignorance, and archly told the American negotiators: "You have made a noble bargain for yourselves, and I suppose you will make the most of it." Jefferson did. He constantly pressed Spain to relinquish West Florida, and sought East Florida as well. At his direction, Congress established a customs district that encompassed most of West Florida. He pressed Napoleon to intervene with Spain on America's behalf and got a secret appropriation from Congress of $2 million with which to bribe the French leader. He even toyed briefly with the possibility of a British alliance to confront Spain and France should all else fail. Finally, in 1810, James Madison brought this unseemly effort to a climax. He took advantage of the invitation of a small group of American rebels in West Florida to occupy some of the area not actually garrisoned by Spanish troops. Congress excused the action on the grounds that Britain, then warring with France and Spain, might interfere in the Floridas.

Jefferson could be more straightforward with the Barbary pirates than he had been with Spain and France. Although he generally sought ways to gain American objectives without actual warfare, he was far from a doctrinaire pacifist. He had argued for using naval force against the pirates since the

Figure 3 Thomas Jefferson (left) and his secretary of state (later president) James Madison were the key figures in making American foreign policy after the Jeffersonian Republican party defeated the Federalists in 1800. Portraits courtesy of the National Archives.

1790s, taking issue with John Adams and most of the European nations, who believed that paying ransoms was easier and cheaper in the long run. Upon becoming president, Jefferson did fulfill his campaign promise to reduce naval expenditures to a minimum, even to the extent of replacing existing larger warships with ineffective coastal gunboats. But he sent the navy into the Mediterranean against the North African corsairs. After some sensational exploits, including Stephen Decatur's burning of the captured American ship *Philadelphia* in Tripoli harbor and an overland desert expedition led by William Eaton, the Barbary states accepted a temporary truce. The piratical career of those states was not finally ended, however, until after the War of 1812, when the joint efforts of the American navy and an Anglo-Dutch fleet extorted a permanent peace.

JEFFERSON AND GREAT BRITAIN: THE EMBARGO

Jefferson's difficulties with Great Britain were not so simply resolved. Relations had been pleasant enough during Jefferson's first administration for him to flirt occasionally with an Anglo-American alliance. But this happy state of affairs did not survive the resumption of the Napoleonic Wars in Europe in 1803. Once again England began interrupting America's neutral trade to France. At first these annoyances did not create a serious crisis. The Jay Treaty was still in force, and flawed as it had seemed to the Republicans, at least its terms had defined a *modus vivendi* between the two nations. Anglo-American commerce remained voluminous. The British still confiscated food as contraband, but they paid for it, so Jefferson and Madison contented themselves with nothing more than written protests. The British also allowed the United States to circumvent the Rule of 1756 and carry considerable trade between the French West Indies and France. In 1802, a British admiralty court had set a precedent in the case of the American ship *Polly* permitting French West Indies goods to be taken to France as long as they had been unloaded in America and a duty paid. The British allowed this trade despite the fact that the United States rebated almost the entire duty to the shippers when they left with their goods for France.

In 1805, British treatment of Americans stiffened. Another admiralty court decision, this time involving the ship *Essex,* set a new precedent for America's reexport trade. The court decided that any rebates given American shippers were proof that the circuitous shuttling between France, the United States, and the West Indies was a continuous voyage subject to interruption under the Rule of 1756. The *Essex* decision also transferred from the capturing vessel to the neutral ship the burden of proving that its voyage was not a continuous one. Properly interpreted, this decision only made the reexport trade more difficult; it did not stop it. But British ships enforced the decision with an overabundance of enthusiasm. Sixty-one American ships, sailing blithely in the belief that their conformance to the *Polly* case immunized them from capture, were unceremoniously hauled off to admiralty courts. American anger ran deep.

That anger intensified as 1805 also brought a substantial increase in British impressment of American seamen. The British had long used kidnapping to staff their navy, and they took British subjects as well as Americans. America had protested against the practice since colonial days, and John Jay had tried unsuccessfully to include an article against interference with American crews in his Treaty of 1794. The British, however, considered impressment essential because conditions aboard their own ships were too terrible to attract volunteers. Most earlier British impressment had been confined to crews that were ashore in Great Britain. Such seizures merely inconvenienced American shipping, however traumatic they may have been for those impressed. But when Britain began impressing men from ships already on the high seas, entire crews, cargoes, and ships suffered from being perilously undermanned. The offense to American honor and sovereignty was also more blatant. It was one thing to haul an American sailor away from a London pub; it was quite another to take him from a ship flying an American flag.

The issue was very difficult to resolve. The British never claimed the right to take American seamen, only British subjects. But the two nations disagreed on the nature of American citizenship. Britain refused to recognize America's right to make Englishmen into naturalized United States citizens. Consequently, it would not accept citizenship papers as proof of the nationality of American sailors. The United States did not want to limit its protection against impressment to sailors with citizenship papers anyway. Foreigners manned nearly 50 percent of America's merchant marine, and many of these were British deserters. To permit Great Britain to impress from aboard an American vessel any sailor who did not have citizenship papers would cripple American shipping. Thus, neither side had much incentive to compromise. The British saw impressment as a vital deterrent to desertion and a cornerstone of their naval power; the Americans saw it as a mortal insult and a threat to their prosperity.

The crisis toward which impressment and ship seizures were inevitably leading finally erupted in 1806. In a well-intentioned but maladroit action, the British cabinet of Charles James Fox sought to reduce the effects of the *Essex* decision on American trade. The cabinet announced that American ships could bring goods from the French West Indies to Europe as long as they did not try to enter French ports which the British now designated as blockaded. To pacify the hawks at home, Fox proclaimed that the blockade would extend almost the full length of Europe facing the English Channel. Quietly he let the Americans know that it would be enforced only in the narrow but strategic area bounded by the Seine and Ostend rivers. Nevertheless, the Americans were outraged by the illegal blockade. Their emotions intensified with news of the accidental killing of an American sailor by a British cannonball that had been intended as a warning shot across his ship's bow. The Republicans now faced a dilemma very similar to the one their Federalist predecessors resolved with the Jay Treaty.

Naturally they turned to the same alternative they had offered at the time of the Jay Treaty: commercial retaliation. The Republican-controlled Congress enacted the Non-Importation Act of 1806. The intention was to prohibit the importation of British goods, but the act exempted those goods the United States needed most, including cottons, cheap woolens, and iron products. Since these were also the goods Britain most wanted to sell to the United States, the Non-Importation Act would not exert much leverage. To add to this inherent weakness, the act was not to be enforced for several months. With this gesture of commercial retaliation, Jefferson was ready to bargain. He sent William Pinkney of Maryland to join James Monroe in London with instructions to negotiate a replacement for the Jay Treaty, the commercial articles of which were expiring.

Jefferson and Secretary of State Madison gave their negotiators some audacious instructions. Britain was to abandon all impressment from American ships on the high seas. The British were to treat American trade with France and the French West Indies as it had been under the *Polly* precedent. Without these concessions, there would be no agreement. Less urgently, the American negotiators were to request British adherence to "free ships, free goods" and a more limited contraband list. Jefferson even wanted the British to accept the Gulf Stream as America's boundary rather than the traditional three-mile limit. This would remove the British fleet farther from the American coast and make interruption of American trade far more difficult.

Of course Monroe and Pinkney had no hopes whatever of achieving such terms. Instead, they negotiated a severely compromised agreement, as had Jay ten years before. Britain would treat the reexport trade from the French West Indies more liberally. If West Indian goods were physically unloaded in America and a 2 percent duty paid, the goods could be reshipped to France without being condemned by the Rule of 1756. Great Britain would not make a treaty stipulation against impressment, but agreed to an official note in which it promised to use exceptional care to avoid impressment of Americans. Most of the other commercial stipulations paralleled those in the Jay Treaty, including the commitment to avoid commercial retaliation for ten years.

But half a loaf would not satisfy Jefferson and Madison, as it had their Federalist predecessors. They refused the Monroe-Pinkney Treaty of 1806 because it failed to halt impressment. They were also disturbed by a reservation the British had appended to the treaty which left Britain free to retaliate against Napoleon's new Berlin Decree, which proclaimed a blockade of the British Isles.[1] Jefferson ordered Monroe and Pinkney to renew negotiations, hoping that time and commercial pressure, such as the Non-Importation Act of 1806, would move Great Britain in America's favor.

The American envoys had no chance to negotiate a better agreement. They suspected as much, and the British records confirm their opinion. They

---

[1] Since Napoleon had few ships to enforce such a blockade, he would have to wait until ships that had violated the blockade and traded with England had arrived in a French-controlled port, whereupon he would confiscate them. It is interesting that Napoleon delayed enforcement of the Berlin Decree until Jefferson and Madison had rejected the Monroe-Pinkney Treaty and thereby reduced the chances of an Anglo-American settlement.

continued their bargaining, however, until the whole negotiation was interrupted by a dramatic incident that produced a fervent demand for war in the United States. In 1807, the British ship *Leopard* attacked an American naval vessel, the *Chesapeake*. The *Leopard* had demanded that the *Chesapeake* turn over four seamen suspected of being British deserters. This was the first attempted impressment from an American naval as opposed to a merchant ship. When the surprised and unprepared *Chesapeake* refused, the *Leopard* poured a series of broadsides into her hull, inflicted twenty-one casualties, and finally took the four seamen.

The British were prepared to apologize for the *Chesapeake* affair and to avoid impressment from naval vessels in the future. But Jefferson decided to use the incident to coerce Britain into abandoning all impresssment. When Britain refused to give Jefferson what it had denied to Monroe and Pinkney, the president called upon Congress to impose an embargo prohibiting all American ships and products from leaving the country. He also put the Non-Importation Act into effect. An embargo was a traditional prelude to war, a means by which a nation could retrieve and protect its shipping before the beginning of hostilities. But the Republicans, with their long devotion to commercial retaliation, also saw the embargo as a weapon in itself. It cut off trade with France as well as with Great Britain, but since both were capturing America's ships, that did not seem inappropriate. And clearly the embargo would hurt the British the most. The rival decrees of the two belligerents had already halted most trade to France, so trade with the British would be most affected. In combination with the Non-Importation Act, which was directed solely at Great Britain, perhaps the embargo would bring Britain around without the need for actual war.

Jefferson never did make clear whether he intended the embargo as a prelude to war or a substitute for it. At times he spoke as though he intended war. But he let time pass, and as the war fever dwindled in the countryside, it became doubtful that Congress would give him a declaration of war even if he wished it. Plagued by migraine headaches and indecision, he retreated to his study. James Madison, always more enthusiastic and consistent in his support of commercial retaliation, became by default the embargo's public defender. Albert Gallatin, the secretary of the treasury, became its chief administrator. Jefferson watched with disillusioned passivity as the embargo proved impotent and domestic opposition to the administration mounted.

The embargo simply did not have the desired or expected effect on the British. Great Britain's warehouses were already full of American products, and British merchants welcomed the chance to sell off their excess stock at better prices. These same products also were becoming available in South America, where Spanish colonists used their mother country's preoccupation with the Napoleonic Wars to declare their independence and open their ports to the English. In addition, so many loopholes had been left in the hastily drafted embargo that six hundred American ships left port legally in 1808, the first year of the embargo's operation. Many more departed illegally. Smuggling flourished, especially in New England, the center of opposition to

Jefferson and to the Republican idea of commercial retaliation. Jefferson, Madison, and Gallatin tried to plug the leaks, even sacrificing their devotion to civil rights by allowing widespread and arbitrary searches and seizures. Still they could not stop the hemorrhaging of the embargo despite the kind help of Napoleon, who ordered all American ships in French-controlled ports to be confiscated on the pretext that they must be embargo violators or British ships in disguise.

By 1809, most members of Congress, even Republicans, had concluded that the embargo had failed. They took advantage of Jefferson's lame-duck period, when he had completely dropped the reins of government, to replace the embargo with a far weaker measure. The Non-Intercourse Act of 1809 allowed American ships and products to leave port if not destined for territory controlled by Great Britain or France. Of course, once the ships left American waters, the United States had no effective way to ensure that they avoided these countries. Enough ships ostensibly left for the Azores to supply these islands many times over. The embarrassed Madison and Gallatin preferred war to admitting the embargo's failure, and their transparent attempts to represent the Non-Intercourse Act as the beginning of forceful measures only accentuated the American humiliation. Their warnings that they would reopen trade with the belligerents only if they respected American neutral rights rang hollow.

Yet ironically it did seem for a moment that the Republican maneuver had succeeded. The British minister to the United States, David Erskine, made an executive agreement with President Madison to stop interrupting American commerce under the Orders in Council if the United States would reopen trade with Great Britain. Not knowing that Erskine had drastically exceeded his instructions, the euphoric Republicans assumed that their advocacy of commercial retaliation had been vindicated. But the British cabinet rejected the Erskine Agreement in insulting terms and replaced Erskine with a minister obnoxious enough to ensure that the United States could not mistake the British position again.

After this new humiliation, the demoralized Republicans turned from the blackmail of the Non-Intercourse Act to the bribery of Macon's Bill No. 2. Under this act, Congress reopened trade with everyone but promised to close it to the enemy of any nation that would recognize America's neutral rights. The clever and cynical Napoleon saw the opening. He had his foreign minister, the Duc de Cadore, inform the United States that France would stop seizing American ships, "it being understood" that the United States would then force Britain to abandon its interference in American trade. Macon's Bill No. 2 had promised only to cut off trade with Britain; it could not guarantee that Britain would abandon its Orders in Council. Napoleon and Cadore had left themselves an escape hatch through which they could excuse their continuing confiscations of American ships.

As obvious as Napoleon's ruse was, Madison accepted the Cadore letter at face value. Perhaps he was duped. Or perhaps he was desperate to concentrate America's efforts on one belligerent at a time. However weak the pretext, he would close British trade while leaving that with Britain's enemy open. He hoped this would bring the British around, allowing him to turn on the French and use the British as a lever against them.

If this was his thinking, it was a wild gamble, and ultimately a disastrous one. The Cadore letter was too weak a pretense with which to pressure the British, and too flimsy an excuse to convince the American public to unite in support of confrontation with Great Britain. Yet having made the challenge, the Republicans could not back down again. Another retreat would be ruinous to the Republican party and to the nation's reputation in the world. When the Republican-controlled Congress cut off trade with Britain in response to the Cadore letter and Britain still refused to retract the Orders in Council, Madison and the Republicans could see no alternative but to declare war.

MADISON AND GREAT BRITAIN: THE WAR

In his request for war, Madison listed Great Britain's obvious offenses of impressment and interference with neutral trade to justify his course of action. Contemporary opponents of the war and later historians, however, noted some disturbing anomalies in the idea that these maritime grievances were the basic causes of the war. With few French ships challenging British control of the seas after the Battle of Trafalgar in 1805, the rate of impressment had dwindled. The United States had few instances of impressment to protest in the years immediately preceding the war. And although Britain had continued to harass American trade under the Orders in Council, the French had seized just as many American ships as the British. Ironically, Madison learned shortly after the war began that the British had already repealed their Orders in Council in the wake of a serious economic depression and the assassination of the prime minister. Yet Madison and the Republicans continued the war, supposedly to end impressment as well.

If maritime grievances were the genuine motivation for the war, why did the declaration come after the offenses had diminished so greatly? Why did the opposition to war center in the New England area, where maritime grievances were most felt, while young western war hawks like Henry Clay, John C. Calhoun, and Felix Grundy led the congressional movement for war? Why did America declare war against England rather than France, when the one had captured as many American ships as the other? Opponents of the war accused Madison and the Republican leaders of being in league with Napoleon. They also thought the Republicans had chosen to fight England rather than France because it gave them an excuse to conquer Canada and to take Florida from Britain's sometime ally, Spain. Thus opponents charged that the war was not a defense of maritime rights against British arrogance and rapacity, but an aggressive grab for territory.

There were indeed some important expansionist factors operating in the decision for war in 1812. Americans had long coveted Canada and Florida.

Frontier settlers also felt menaced by Indians they firmly believed to be supplied and supported by the British and the Spanish. The Battle of Tippecanoe dramatized the Indian problem in 1811. Two Shawnee brothers, Tecumseh and the Prophet, had been trying to organize the Ohio Valley and Southwest Indians into a confederacy. They sought solidarity to resist the corruptions of Anglo civilization and the loss of Indian lands through treaties that avaricious American settlers made with pliable village chiefs. The British did supply and encourage resistance among these Indians, but they also discouraged premature hostilities that might provoke war between Britain and the United States. Tecumseh and the Prophet established a town at the confluence of the Tippecanoe and Wabash Rivers. Governor William Henry Harrison of Indiana feared the town would be a rallying point for a British-supported Indian war against the frontier and stormed it while Tecumseh was absent on a recruiting trip to the south. Harrison then exaggerated his account of the events to claim a great victory over British-supported Indians. Consequently, Madison could mention Indian depredations and British complicity in his request for war. Later he also instructed his peace negotiators to try to acquire Canada in the settlement.

Yet it seems clear to most modern students of the War of 1812 that these expansionist factors were secondary to the maritime grievances of impressment and ship seizures. The United States had recently acquired Louisiana and still had much good unsettled land in the Northwest, so land hunger was not exceedingly strong in 1812. In addition, sectional jealousies tempered some expansionist passions. Southerners especially feared that acquisition of Canada would fuel northern political interests, and some northerners had similar reservations about Florida. Judging by the private and public comments of contemporaries, Canada was more a bargaining chip than an object of annexation. Republican leaders seemed more inclined to trade Canada for British concessions on impressment and neutral rights than to keep it. Westerners also shared the East's interest in Great Britain's maritime offenses. They may not have had many ships or seamen, but they blamed the severe depression that beset the nation's farming areas in 1811 on British interference with America's agricultural exports. Thus maritime grievances contributed substantially to the near-unanimity of western congressmen and senators in favor of war in 1812.

Nevertheless, the unsettled West could contribute comparatively few votes for war; most votes had to come from the more populous East. The maritime areas of New England did tend to oppose war, partly because merchants there were prospering in spite of European depredations on their shipping, and partly because their districts would be the most exposed to British naval bombardment or invasion. Yet representatives of other areas interested in overseas commerce, such as Philadelphia, Baltimore, and Charleston, voted for war. Thus sectional interests do not fully explain the congressional lineup. Party loyalty seems to have been more significant.

All the Federalists in the House of Representatives voted against the declaration of war with Great Britain. All but twenty-two of the Republicans voted for it, most of those dissenters hailing from states vulnerable to British attack. Such a partisan lineup makes sense. The Republicans feared that their party could not survive another humiliating retreat. Since they regarded the Federalists as antidemocratic as well as treasonably pro-British, they believed that a Federalist victory in the coming elections would doom America's experiment in republicanism. Despite their historical reputation as the party of the war hawks, most Republicans were not eager for war; they merely saw it as the best of unhappy alternatives. There was little of the buoyant belligerence one would have expected if the war had been a crusade for Canada.

Not only did the Republicans enter the war without enthusiasm, they entered without military preparations. They authorized army recruitment and naval building, but appropriated almost no money to carry them out. They detested Napoleon too much to make advances toward formal cooperation or alliance with France, yet they counted on French success in the continental war to preoccupy the British and ultimately force concession to America's neutral rights. Their calculations went awry. Within a year, Napoleon suffered a disastrous defeat in his Russian invasion. America then stood alone and unarmed against the most powerful nation left in the world.

The Federalists rushed to make political capital of the Republican plight. Before and during the war, they answered Republican denunciations of Britain with reminders that Napoleon too seized American ships and disregarded American rights. They mocked Madison's naive faith in the Cadore letter. They actually supported war preparations in the months before the declaration, but for the sole purpose of embarrassing the Republicans. Federalists hoped to pick up the political pieces when, as they confidently but mistakenly expected, the Republicans backed away from actually going to war with Great Britain. After the Republicans won the vote for war, the Federalists proposed a simultaneous fight with France and lost by only two Senate votes. Their obstructionist tactics continued throughout the war, culminating in the Hartford Convention of 1814. There the Federalists called for peace at any price, demanded constitutional restrictions on all future commercial retaliation, and hinted at the possibility of secession if the Republicans persisted in their misbegotten war.

As the American war effort stumbled from fiasco to fiasco, Federalist strength grew steadily, especially in New England. But the British saved the Republicans when they decided not to pursue the war with the United States even though Napleon had been beaten. There were many Britons who wanted to fight until they had extracted a peace that would teach the American upstarts a lesson in humility. One newspaper close to the government laid out the terms that should be required of the United States: Canada should have a new boundary giving it a monopoly of the Great Lakes–St. Lawrence system. Americans should be excluded from the fisheries and barred from trade with the British East and West Indies. The United States should be required to give a guarantee against acquisition of the Floridas. Great Britain would take New Orleans and thus ensure its domination of the

Mississippi. America should acknowledge British rules on neutral rights and impressment. And finally, the old project of an Indian border state should be revived, the area to be carved out of the American Northwest.

The Duke of Wellington warned, however, that it would take the reconquest of Lake Champlain and two years of conflict to subdue the Americans, even if he and much of his European army were transferred to North America. The debt-ridden British government thought the cost of such sweet revenge was more than its rewards, and feared that a continuing American war might weaken its position in the European negotiations at the Congress of Vienna. The cabinet decided to accept a compromise peace rather than fight to the finish.

When serious negotiations between the United States and Great Britain began at Ghent in Belgium in 1814, the British still thought it possible to secure adjustments on the Canadian border and an Indian buffer state. Twice negotiations nearly broke off on these issues, and the Americans finally convinced the British they would never accept the buffer state. The British foreign minister, Castlereagh, ordered abandonment of the demand rather than see the negotiations founder. The British negotiators insisted on a more secure Canadian border, however, claiming it was necessary to protect against American invasion. The American delegation, which included Albert Gallatin, Henry Clay, and John Quincy Adams, ingenuously professed no interest in Canada, claiming the province had merely served as a target of convenience. Meanwhile the Americans hoped anxiously that the British would not discover that their original instructions had indeed requested the cession of Canada.

When Wellington made known his opinion of the difficulties involved in an all-out invasion of the United States, the British finally decided to settle for the *status quo ante bellum.* The issues of the fisheries and British navigation of the Mississippi were to be decided later by a neutral commission, while the combatants agreed to disagree about neutral rights and impressment in the hope that the absence of world war would leave the issues moot. The war, then, had been at best a draw for the Americans. But there was reason to rejoice even at this, for British troops in occupation of American territory along the Great Lakes and in Maine would have to be removed. Certainly the terms looked good in comparison to the extensive concessions the Federalists in the Hartford Convention would have offered the British to guarantee immediate peace.

Unfortunately for the Federalists, the demands of the Hartford Convention arrived in Washington almost simultaneously with the news of General Andrew Jackson's spectacular victory over a powerful British invasion force at New Orleans, and the report from Ghent that peace had been made without major sacrifice. Jackson's victory actually was won after conclusion of the Treaty of Ghent and had no effect on the peace terms.[2] But Americans heard

---

[2] If the British had won this battle, however, they might have refused final ratification of the treaty and extracted significant concessions, so the victory was not totally meaningless.

of both at the same time, and many linked them indelibly in their minds. They felt they had won the war decisively, and the Federalists now appeared fainthearted if not treasonous in comparison with the Republicans.

Americans abandoned the Federalists in droves to rejoice in their apparent victory. "We have stood the contest, single-handed, against the conqueror of Europe; and we are at peace, with all our blushing victories thick crowding on us," crowed Joseph Story. To Americans, the war's end vindicated their righteous views on neutral rights and secured respect for America's honor, independence, and sovereignty. The war seemed to prove that free men, "fresh from the plow," could defeat the hired guns of European tyranny. Europeans would finally respect America's dominance in the Western Hemisphere and its right to remain unentangled in the politics of the Continent. No longer could the British or French treat Americans as underlings or dictate where and how their ships would travel and trade. The last vestiges of colonial dependence had been cast off. The war seemed a second American Revolution.

The euphoria of victory was all the greater for the depths of humiliation and incompetence that had preceded it. "Our character has been retrieved from ignominy and instead of an insulted and pusillanimous people, we rank exalted in the opinion of the surrounding world," rejoiced one pamphleteer. Nationalistic fervor reached such heights that almost no piece of furniture seemed complete without a gilt eagle perched on top of it. Europe no longer need be the center of America's diplomatic attention. The people who looked to the Atlantic as America's source of wealth and power gave way to those who faced west. The United States could pursue territorial expansion with far less concern that the major powers of Europe would interfere. Neutrality and expansion would continue to be the twin themes of American foreign policy, but their priorities were now decisively reversed.

CONTROVERSIAL ISSUES AND FURTHER READING

During the nineteenth century, the War of 1812 was popular among the general public, yet most prominent historians criticized it. This was because the historical community of that time had its roots in New England and held fast to Federalist sympathies long after they had all but disappeared from most of the country. Some Federalist histories, such as Theodore Lyman's *The Diplomacy of the United States* (1826–1828), skirted public disfavor by hinting rather gently that the war should have been avoided. If avoidance had proved impossible, Lyman said, it would have been better to have fought in 1808, immediately after the *Chesapeake* affair had united the country. By 1812, Republican mistakes had permitted the navy and army to decay, had split the nation with the embargo, and had sabotaged America's moral position by resting its challenge to Britain on the fraudulent Cadore letter. Richard Hildreth, however, the most prominent historian of this issue before the Civil War, disdained any equivocation and asserted blatantly that the war should have been avoided entirely by acceptance of the Monroe-Pinkney Treaty of 1806. [Richard Hildreth, *The History of the United States* (1849–1852).]

After the Civil War, Hildreth's Federalist view was fortified by the endorsement of the prestigious German scholar, Hermann Eduard Von Holst, in his *The Constitutional and Political History of the United States* (1876–1892). In response, Henry Adams decided to correct the view of the historical fraternity. In a review of Von Holst's work jointly written with Henry Cabot Lodge, he informed the German that Americans were not now and never had been hostile to the War of 1812. Then, in his classic *History of the United States During the Administrations of Jefferson and Madison* (1889–1891), Adams endorsed the war fully but excoriated the Republicans for being too slow to embrace it.

These historians might dispute the virtues of the Republican diplomacy that led to the war, but they did not disagree over whether maritime issues were the major causes of it. Shortly before World War I, however, historians inspired by the frontier thesis of Frederick Jackson Turner began to wonder whether western desires for Canada and Florida might not have been more influential. The most significant of these works, Julius Pratt's *The Expansionists of 1812* (1925), transformed the ideas of the majority of historians in the 1920s and 1930s. The principal debate in this era focused on whether land hunger or fear of Indian depredations most influenced the desire to conquer Canada and Florida. Regardless of this dispute, the shift to a western explanation of its causes made the War of 1812 appear far more aggressive than defensive.

Modern revisionist historians have continued to view the war as an aggressive pursuit of territorial expansion. But they have added to this a condemnation of the war as a search for commercial expansion as well. They point out that the Americans intended not just to protect the trade in their own products, but to profit from others' trade thrown their way by the war. [See, for example, William Appleman Williams, *The Contours of American History* (1961). The best discussion of this point, however, is in Burton Spivak's *Jefferson's English Crisis: Commerce, Embargo, and the Republican Revolution* (1979), which is not written from the radical perspective.]

Most recent historians have deemphasized the expansionist aspects of the War of 1812 and returned to the maritime causes. In the process, they have welded the older Federalist critiques of Jefferson and Madison to the newer realist framework which denounces the Republicans for inept, unrealistic, and partisan diplomacy that brought on an unnecessary war. [The major work initiating this trend was A. L. Burt, *The United States, Great Britain, and British North America* (1940). Bradford Perkins continued the approach in the finest work on 1812 diplomacy, *Prologue to War: England and the United States, 1805–1812* (1961) and its sequel, *Castlereagh and Adams: England and the United States, 1806–1823* (1964). Roger Brown's *The Republic in Peril: 1812* (1964) best describes the division over the war as one of parties rather than sections. Reginald Horsman's *The Causes of the War of 1812* (1962) is another outstanding realist critique. Irving Brant's biography *James Madison* (6 vols., 1941–1961) is a passionate defense of Madison and the diplomacy of the war. A more balanced defense is the recent detailed survey encompassing the most recent research, J. C. A. Stagg, *Mr. Madison's War: Politics, Diplomacy, and Warfare in the Early American Republic, 1783–1830* (1983).]

The standard portrayal of the Louisiana Purchase is that it fell into American hands like manna from Heaven. This is apparent in both E. Wilson Lyon's *Louisiana in French Diplomacy, 1759–1804* (1934), and Arthur P. Whitaker's *The Mississippi Ques-*

tion, 1795–1803 (1934). But recently Alexander De Conde has supported the revisionist view by portraying the purchase as the product of American aggressiveness and acquisitiveness in *This Affair of Louisiana* (1976). [Samuel Flagg Bemis's biography *John Quincy Adams and the Foundations of American Foreign Policy* (1949) provides the best coverage of the acquisition of Florida, but see also Arthur P. Whitaker, *The United States and the Independence of Latin America, 1800–1830* (1941), and I. J. Cox, *The West Florida Controversy* (1913). On the Barbary pirates, see Ray W. Irwin, *The Diplomatic Relations of the United States with the Barbary Powers, 1776–1815* (1931), and H. G. Barnby, *The Prisoners of Algiers: An Account of the Forgotten American-Algerian War, 1785–1797* (1966).]

CHAPTER 4

The Diplomacy of Expansion: Florida and the Monroe Doctrine

MANIFEST DESTINY

For nearly half a century after the War of 1812, the issue of territorial expansion dominated American diplomacy. Certainly this was not a new concern for the United States. Franklin, Jay, and Adams had maneuvered to increase the nation's border claims during the revolution. Jefferson had purchased Louisiana. Frontiersmen had pushed aside the Indians while the United States government abetted them with military support and coercive treaties. Jefferson and Madison had nibbled at Florida and, during the War of 1812, the United States had at least squinted at Canada.

The primary force behind American expansion throughout the early history of the United States was its enormous population growth. The American people increased at an annual rate of 3 percent, which more than doubled the population every twenty-five years. This burgeoning populace moved steadily westward. Ohio had only 45,000 people within its borders in 1800; by 1820 it had ten times as many. In 1810 no more than one-seventh of America's people lived west of the Appalachians; by 1840 one-third of the population was there.

After the War of 1812, several new factors helped make territorial expansion even more central. A revolution in transportation and communication was the most important of these. Without this revolution, much of the West would have remained remote and forbidding, doomed to isolation and poverty. The area would have supported only a few scattered subsistence farmers, and it would have been impossible to protect or govern them from Washington. But in the 1820s and 1830s Americans built many new roads. The best of these were private turnpikes that cut freight prices in half. Numerous canals were built at the same time, and their impact was even more dramatic. Water transportation was far cheaper than overland transportation, and canals cut freight costs from 20 cents per ton-mile to 2 cents. Steamboats made water transportation even more practical, since they could carry goods upstream as well as down. By the 1840s even areas that canals and steamboats were unable to reach could look forward to cheap, rapid, and safe transportation for the first time in human history. Finally, the telegraph provided almost instant communication throughout the land.

The transportation revolution made possible the territorial expansion that the population boom made desirable. American citizens could profitably bring lands within the orbit of their commercial-agricultural economy that they might otherwise have left to the subsistence economy of the Indians. White Americans increasingly coveted remote territories such as Oregon and California, which Jefferson and many of his contemporaries had considered beyond the effective reach of American governance and destined at best to be independent republics.

America's growing and increasingly mobile population exerted powerful diplomatic leverage against the thinly populated and static colonies on the nation's borders. America's performance in the War of 1812 emboldened it to shift its attention from Europe to concentrate on westward expansion. At the same time, the Europeans were on notice that they would have great difficulty defending their North American colonies from the United States. The Spanish, the British, and later the Mexicans, like the Indians, watched with apprehension as time eroded their defenses against the voracious Americans. Threats against American expansion, especially from Great Britain, now spurred rather than retarded the westward movement, for American politicians could urge that the United States had to take new territories immediately or risk losing them to British interlopers.

Moral considerations posed even fewer obstacles to American ambitions than the declining threat of European intervention. Americans found easy rationalizations for acquiring territory long claimed and occupied by others. They pointed first to the relative emptiness of the lands. What right had so few Indians, Spaniards, Britons, or Mexicans to such vast expanses of good soil? They could never make proper use of them. Cultivated properly by industrious American farmers, those lands could furnish a livelihood for millions of people. It was wrong, Americans said, that such lands should languish unused in the hands of a few backward savages or lazy Europeans. How much better that they should be brought under the sway of a people that would not only use them properly, but also give them the blessings of free institutions—democratic government, individual liberty, and Protestant Christianity.

Governor William Henry Harrison of the Indiana Territory thus defended displacement of the Indians by asking rhetorically, "Is one of the fairest portions of the globe to remain in a state of nature, the haunt of a few wretched savages, when it seems destined by the Creator to give support to a large population and to be the seat of civilization, of science, and of true religion?" He and others took care to distinguish their expansion into "empty, unused" land from European imperialism, which conquered and oppressed densely settled areas. As one newspaper put it:

> What has Belgium, Silesia, Poland or Bengal in common with Texas? It is surely not necessary to insist that acquisitions of territory in America, even if accomplished by force of arms, are not to be viewed in the same light as the invasions and conquests of the States of the old world. No American aggression can stab

the patriot to the heart . . . ; our way lies not over trampled nations, but through desert wastes, to be brought by our industry and energy.within the domain of art and civilization. We are contiguous to a vast portion of the globe, untrodden save by the savage and the beast, and we are conscious of our power to render it tributary to man.

Few Americans of the early nineteenth century dissented from this view. They differed only over the pace and tactics of the westward movement. The parties of the so-called cosmopolitans, the Federalists and later the Whigs, generally favored a slower pace. The constituency of these parties included many merchants and commercial farmers who feared the disruption of their trade that might result from serious conflict with the European colonial powers. Cosmopolitans also did not want the frontier to outrun the transportation infrastructure of roads, bridges, and canals that would tie the western fringes of the country to the national commercial nexus. Remote subsistence farms and communities would do the cosmopolitans no good economically, and politically would most likely produce votes for their "localist" party opponents, the Jeffersonian Republicans and later the Jacksonian Democrats.

Excessively rapid expansion threatened the cosmopolitans culturally as well. The cosmopolitan parties generally appealed to Americans of old British stock and conservative Protestant religion who placed great store in public morality and disciplined education and who favored a strong, active government to enforce their cultural norms. They feared that remote settlers would be beyond the reach of the civilizing influences of proper churches and schools, and they often complained that the frontier was producing white savages.

Thus most cosmopolitans believed that population pressure would bring the western territories into the United States soon enough. They thought it best to wait for these lands to fall into America's lap rather than to pursue them aggressively. Let the American population flow into the borderlands, outnumber and dominate the original inhabitants, then request admission to the Union. Perhaps the colonial nations would see the handwriting on the wall and sell the borderlands to the United States peacefully, as had occurred with Louisiana. Perhaps the Indians, left alone for a time, would also move of their own accord to escape the pressures of white civilization. The Whigs could be convinced to support more aggressive expansionism if the territorial targets contained harbors, navigable rivers, or obvious commercial resources, but generally they counseled greater restraint than did their political opponents.

The "localist" parties led by Jefferson and Jackson appealed more to the subsistence farmers and those less involved in the commercial economy. Their constituencies also were composed of religious dissenters and ethnic outgroups, including such disparate people as Scots-Irish Protestants and Irish and German Roman Catholics. These people disliked strong governments with potential power to impose the cultural norms of the old stock British and conservative Protestants. They saw no reason to slow the pace of expansion to protect the trade of their political opponents, to ensure communication with the government and commercial elites in the east, or to establish "proper" schools and churches. Disliking the British, their empire, and their descendants in America, they could be aroused easily by claims that if America did not take what it wanted on the frontier quickly, the British would get it. They also had fewer compunctions about trampling on the rights of the Indians.

Another political factor increasingly affected the basic American desire for expansion—slavery. Both political parties tried desperately to keep this issue out of politics, knowing it would shatter them and divide the nation geographically rather than on a cosmopolitan-localist axis. Consequently, in the earlier years of the nineteenth century, both parties tried to avoid bringing the slavery issue into the expansionist debate. If a potential annexation stirred too much agitation over slavery to ignore, both parties generally agreed to delay the acquisition. The slave issue was powerful enough to modify the pace and tactics of American expansion, yet not powerful enough to thwart it entirely. And if even the slave issue did not stop American expansion, could anything else?

Some Americans thought geography would provide "natural" boundaries for the United States. Jefferson and many of his followers, for instance, regarded the Rocky Mountains as the natural western border of the nation. As ardent an expansionist as Senator Thomas Hart Benton once grandiloquently proclaimed that an immovable statue of the great god Terminus should be placed on the highest peak in the Rockies. The Jeffersonians visualized Oregon not as a territory of the United States, but as an independent, sympathetic republic free of European influences.

Yet if geography could erect "natural barriers" it could also provide a rationale for expansion. Americans claimed that foreign territories such as Florida and Texas were on the American side of those geographical divisions, part of America's "natural" domain. The progress of American population and transportation also expanded the perceptions of natural boundaries. As an opponent of Benton's plans for the god Terminus put it: "Gentlemen are talking of natural boundaries. Sir, our natural boundary is the Pacific Ocean. The swelling tide of our population must and will roll on until that mighty ocean interposes its waters, and limits our territorial empire." Many Americans saw the entire continent of North America as an integral unit obviously shaped by God to be ruled by a single people, and they had no doubts as to which people He had chosen to occupy it. John L. O'Sullivan, editor of the *Democratic Review*, captured this vague but powerful sense of America's supposedly predestined expansion in a vivid phrase he coined in 1845. He proclaimed that it was America's "manifest destiny" to spread over the continent allotted it by Providence.

The presence of a dense foreign population in a target area deterred American expansion more effectively than natural boundaries. If the aliens were too numerous for America's own growing population to overwhelm them, the nation would face two unpleasant alternatives. The United States could incorporate the aliens as equal voting citizens and offend the cultural and racial prejudices of most Americans. Or it could rule them as a conquered people, which had grave implications for constitutional principles. Either course would undermine America's insistence that its expansion was different from European colonialism because the United States took only "empty" areas. This conceit may have been largely rationalization, but on one level Americans devoutly believed it. For instance, after the American army conquered Mexico City during the Mexican War and gave the United States the chance to annex the entire nation, the country turned away from its brief temptation and kept only the less populated areas of the Southwest.

The power of America's neighbors set another limit to American expansion. Canada itself might be weak and relatively unpopulated, but Britain was not to be taken lightly. Americans kept their eyes on the British colonies in North America, leaving the door open for eventual acquisition, pressing successfully for portions of Oregon and some other border concessions, dabbling with revolutionary elements in Canada, but shying finally from confrontation and ultimately accepting a permanent barrier to the north.

America's other colonial neighbor, Spain, had no such power to compel respect, and its feeble hold on East and West Florida presented the most promising arena for America's territorial ambitions in the aftermath of the War of 1812.

THE ACQUISITION OF FLORIDA

The United States had long coveted Florida to round out its possessions east of the Mississippi. Florida seemed a pistol with the barrel pressed against the mouth of the Mississippi. Florida also controlled the outlets of other navigable rivers that reached up into the American South, such as the Pearl, the Perdido, and the Chattahoochee. East Florida's peninsula extended deep into the Caribbean Sea, threatening the vital shipping routes from New Orleans and other Gulf ports to the eastern coast of the United States. Florida also presented an increasing nuisance to the adjacent American territories. Escaped slaves found refuge across the Spanish border. So did marauding bands of Indians who raided American settlements, often in conjunction with some of the escaped slaves. The moribund Spanish government in the Floridas had neither the power nor the inclination to eliminate these sanctuaries, despite numerous American protests.

The United States had been nibbling at Florida since well before the War of 1812. Jefferson originally had tried to purchase Florida rather than Louisiana when negotiating for New Orleans in 1803. Then he and James Madison had begun a long series of maneuvers to extort Florida from Spain. The most decisive of these came in 1810, when Madison used the invitation of some American settlers who had revolted against Spanish rule at Baton Rouge to proclaim the occupation of West Florida up to the Perdido River. (Actually Madison sent troops only as far as the Pearl River, and thus avoided a confrontation with the Spanish garrisons at Mobile and Pensacola.) Madison feared that Great Britain, then fighting Napoleon in Spain, might preempt the

United States by taking the Floridas. The British stirred those fears further when they protested Madison's occupation of parts of West Florida.

Madison appealed to Congress, and Congress announced its "No Transfer" principle, that the United States "cannot, without serious inquietude, see any part of [Florida] pass into the hands of any foreign power." (Since it was to America's advantage that all Western Hemisphere territories either become independent or remain in the hands of a weak Spain rather than pass to a greater power, the United States later extended this "No Transfer" principle to all of Latin America as an unofficial corollary to the Monroe Doctrine.) In pursuit of this principle, Congress authorized Madison in 1810 to occupy all of Florida if necessary to thwart foreign occupation, and on the eve of the War of 1812 actually declared both Floridas annexed.

Such ringing affirmations did little to alter the fact that the United States controlled only a small portion of Florida. Nevertheless, congressional bombast gave Spain and the rest of Europe warning that the United States intended to acquire the entire territory once circumstances were favorable. Immediately after the Peace of Ghent freed America from the War of 1812, Spain made a desperate appeal to the European powers to help it preserve Florida and reclaim Louisiana. The British minister refused, with the comment that an exhausted Europe required some time for repose, and the other powers followed suit. Consequently, when Spain ordered Luis de Onís, the Spanish minister to the United States, to open negotiations with the American government, it knew there was no hope of holding Florida much longer. Spain could only stall, wear the Americans down, and extract as many reciprocal concessions as possible.

Unfortunately for Onís, the American secretary of state he hoped to wear down was John Quincy Adams, one of the most intelligent, learned, experienced, and aggressive diplomats ever to serve the United States. Adams had been minister to the Netherlands, Prussia, and Russia, had served as one of the five commissioners to negotiate the Treaty of Ghent, and then had been minister to Great Britain until James Monroe appointed him secretary of state.

Short, stout, and balding, John Quincy Adams looked much like his father and had many of the same virtues and shortcomings. An unbending integrity accompanied his learning and intelligence, but so did a strange mix of personal vanity, insecurity, and morbid suspicion of all human motivations. Unfortunately, John Quincy lacked the earthiness and humor that leavened his father's self-righteousness. John Quincy Adams, who analyzed his own failings as unsparingly as he did those of others, compared himself to Henry Clay in the following terms: "There is the same dogmatical, overbearing manner, the same harshness of look and expression, the same forgetfulness of the courtesies in society." Actually this described Adams far better than it did Clay. Clay could be arrogant, but he was also genial and outgoing, while Adams was cold and remote. Adams, for instance, was apoplectic that during the negotiations at Ghent, when he would rise before dawn to pray and read Greek and Latin, the click of poker chips and scraping of chairs from Clay's

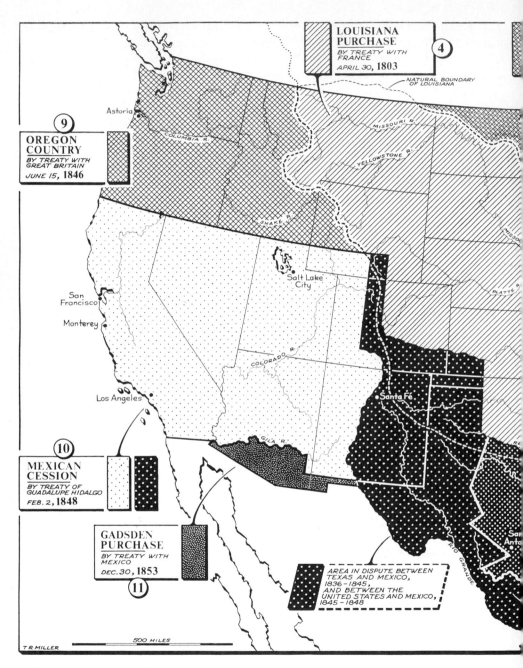

**LOUISIANA
PURCHASE**
*BY TREATY WITH
FRANCE*
APRIL 30, **1803**

④

*NATURAL BOUNDARY
OF LOUISIANA*

⑨

**OREGON
COUNTRY**
*BY TREATY WITH
GREAT BRITAIN*
JUNE 15, **1846**

Astoria

COLUMBIA R.

MISSOURI R.

YELLOWSTONE R.

SNAKE R.

PLATTE R.

MISS

Salt Lake
City

San
Francisco

Monterey

COLORADO R.

Los Angeles

Santa Fé

⑩

**MEXICAN
CESSION**
*BY TREATY OF
GUADALUPE HIDALGO*
FEB. 2, **1848**

GILA R.

**GADSDEN
PURCHASE**
*BY TREATY WITH
MEXICO*
DEC. 30, **1853**

⑪

RIO GRANDE

Sa
Anto

*AREA IN DISPUTE BETWEEN
TEXAS AND MEXICO,
1836-1845,
AND BETWEEN THE
UNITED STATES AND MEXICO,
1845-1848*

500 MILES

T.R.MILLER

Map 3   Continental Expansion, 1775–1867

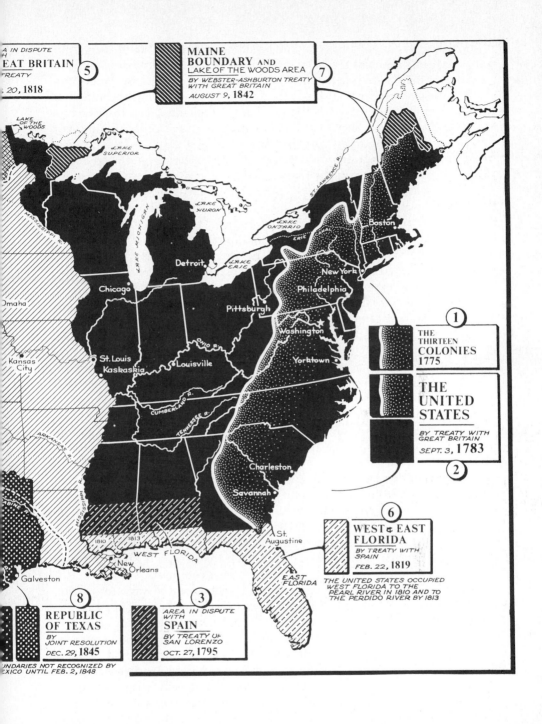

AREA IN DISPUTE
~~~~ EAT BRITAIN ⑤
~~~~ TREATY

~~~~ 20, 1818

MAINE
BOUNDARY AND ⑦
LAKE OF THE WOODS AREA
BY WEBSTER-ASHBURTON TREATY
WITH GREAT BRITAIN
AUGUST 9, 1842

① THE
THIRTEEN
COLONIES
1775

THE
UNITED
STATES
BY TREATY WITH
GREAT BRITAIN
SEPT. 3, 1783 ②

⑥ WEST & EAST
FLORIDA
BY TREATY WITH
SPAIN
FEB. 22, 1819

THE UNITED STATES OCCUPIED
WEST FLORIDA TO THE
PEARL RIVER IN 1810 AND TO
THE PERDIDO RIVER BY 1813

⑧ REPUBLIC
OF TEXAS
BY
JOINT RESOLUTION
DEC. 29, 1845

~~~~ NDARIES NOT RECOGNIZED BY
~~~~ EXICO UNTIL FEB. 2, 1848

③ AREA IN DISPUTE
WITH
SPAIN
BY TREATY OF
SAN LORENZO
OCT. 27, 1795

LAKE OF THE WOODS
LAKE SUPERIOR
LAKE HURON
LAKE MICHIGAN
LAKE ONTARIO
ERIE
LAKE ERIE
ST. LAWRENCE R.
MISSISSIPPI R.

Detroit
Chicago
St. Louis
Kaskaskia
Louisville
Pittsburgh
Washington
Yorktown
New York
Philadelphia
Boston

Omaha
Kansas City

OHIO R.
CUMBERLAND R.
TENNESSEE R.
ARKANSAS R.
MISSISSIPPI R.

Charleston
Savannah
St. Augustine

1810
1813
WEST FLORIDA
New Orleans
Galveston
EAST FLORIDA

all-night card games in the next room would disturb him. One foreign diplomat described Adams as the most grim, unsociable, and venomous minister he had ever met, a "bulldog among spaniels" at the court of St. Petersburg.

Onís began his negotiations with Adams by demanding the return of Louisiana as the price of the Floridas. Spain still claimed that the purchase had been illegal, since Napoleon had violated the provision of the retrocession that forbade him to sell the province to a third party. Adams brushed this claim aside. He not only said that the United States would keep Louisiana, but claimed the distant Rio Grande River as Louisiana's western border. This would have given Texas to the United States. He indicated immediately, however, that he intended to bargain this border for the Floridas by hinting that he would accept a border at the Colorado River. Onís's instructions anticipated such a maneuver and empowered him to retreat from his demand that the United States give up Louisiana. In turn, however, he was to extract a promise from the Americans to refuse aid or recognition to Spain's rebellious Central and South American colonies.

Onís did not retreat precipitately. He put pressure on Adams by getting a reluctant Britain to offer mediation—which, of course, the American secretary refused. The Americans in turn applied even greater pressure to Spain. In 1818, President Monroe ordered General Andrew Jackson to cross the Florida border in pursuit of marauding Indians. Monroe cautioned Jackson, however, to avoid direct conflict with the Spanish garrisons if the Indians took refuge there. Jackson immediately proposed a more aggressive course. "Let it be signified to me through any channel (say Mr. J. Rhea) that the possession of the Floridas would be desirable to the United States, and in sixty days it will be accomplished." Jackson later claimed that he had received such a signal from John Rhea and had burned the message for the sake of discretion. Monroe insisted that he had never seen Jackson's letter and denied he had authorized a conquest. Whatever the truth of all this, Monroe had taken few steps to restrain Jackson's well-known pugnaciousness, and Jackson did more than merely attack the Indians. He executed two British subjects who had been suppliers to the Indians and captured the Spanish garrisons of St. Marks and Pensacola. Jackson then asked ingenuously what the president would like him to do with his new conquests.

John C. Calhoun and William Crawford, secretaries of war and treasury, advised President Monroe to disavow Jackson and recall him. They expected the British to be furious over the execution of their subjects, and they were afraid Britain might join Spain in a war to protect Florida and punish the United States. John Quincy Adams insisted that America should make no apology. He even argued that the United States might keep Pensacola until Spain could guarantee control of the Indians and escaped slaves. In the end Monroe did recall Jackson, but he permitted Adams to justify Jackson's actions to Spain, England, and the American public on the grounds that they were a consequence of Spanish dereliction. Adams and Monroe may not have instigated Jackson's capture of the Spanish posts, but they were happy to make use of the foray to force Spain into a final favorable settlement.

Urged on by Monroe and the cabinet, Adams then offered to set the border of Louisiana at the Sabine River, in effect trading all of America's claim to Texas for the Floridas. Adams might have gotten more, for Onís's instructions permitted him to accept a boundary west of the Sabine if necessary to gain a firm border for Texas. But while Adams gave up some American claims in Texas, he acquired compensating concessions on the northwestern boundary of Louisiana. Onís agreed to accept a northern border to Spanish territories at 41° latitude, thus abandoning Spanish rights to the Oregon territory. The United States still faced competing claims to Oregon from Great Britain and Russia, but it was now considerably more likely that the United States would stretch from sea to sea. Thus the treaty has been dubbed by historians the Transcontinental Treaty of 1819.

Spain, on the other hand, gained little except a firm recognition of the border between its North American colonies and the United States, which it hoped rather forlornly would serve as a barrier to further American encroachment. Onís even failed to get a direct acknowledgment from the United States that Florida had been rightfully Spain's to turn over to the United States. Adams evaded any recognition that America's former declarations of annexation had been hot air by phrasing the Spanish cession as follows: The Spanish king would cede "all the territories which belong to him, situated to the Eastward of the Mississippi, known by the name of East and West Florida." By omitting a comma between "territories" and "which," Adams left open just which of those territories actually had been the Spanish king's property. Adams also managed to evade the Spanish demand that the treaty contain an American promise to refuse recognition of the independence of Spain's Latin American colonies.

THE INDEPENDENCE OF LATIN AMERICA

The recognition of the independence of the Latin American republics had become a very touchy issue for Monroe and his cabinet. Naturally, most Americans saw these infant nations as following nobly in the footsteps of the United States, battling colonialism and monarchy to establish free republics. Practical-minded Americans also saw commercial and strategic advantages. The ex-colonies would open their markets to the ships and goods of the United States and no longer would be potential military and naval bases for major European powers in the Western Hemisphere. Still, Monroe and Adams could not afford to grant immediate recognition to the Latin American rebels so long as the Florida negotiations were pending. Not only would recognition derail those negotiations, but it might induce other European powers to help Spain resist American pressure. In the wake of the victory over Napoleon and the French Revolution, the major European continental powers—Russia, Spain, Austria, and Prussia—had formed the so-called Holy Alliance to defend "legitimate governments" against the virus of republicanism and anticolonialism. Until the agreement with Spain was safely done, the United States could not risk defying these powers.

Monroe regretted the delay in recognition more than John Quincy Adams. Adams regarded South Americans as ignorant, racially inferior, numbed by years of ecclesiastical and military tyranny, and unlikely to form lasting republics on the model of the United States. He did not think trade with Latin America would be important, because the Latin Americans did not need the agricultural products of the United States and the United States could not afford to purchase many of Latin America's specialties. Great Britain had dominated the Latin American trade since the Spanish colonies had broken away and would continue to do so. While Adams wished the cause of Latin American independence well, he saw no reason to risk much to aid the movement. He was ready to extend the policy of neutrality to South America as well as to Europe.

Adams, however, was under great pressure to recognize the republics. Henry Clay made the issue the centerpiece of his campaign for the 1824 presidential nomination. Senator Clay embarrassed his rivals in Monroe's cabinet with continuous oratorical appeals for them to join the cause of world liberty by recognizing the republics, even though he knew the Florida negotiation required their silence.

The prospect of recognition tempted Monroe. At the president's request, John Quincy Adams dutifully sounded out the British to see if they might reduce the risks of such a policy by joining the United States in opening formal relations with the republics. The British refused. Adams judged that despite this refusal, British interests in the Latin American trade would induce them to oppose any attempt by the Holy Alliance to help restore Spain's political and commercial monopoly of the area. Still, he thought it best to delay recognition, and the British refusal helped him convince Monroe.

Once Adams concluded his treaty, everyone, including Adams himself, expected that the United States would recognize the new republics in short order. Even Clay shifted his attack away from what he thought was no longer a vulnerable flank for Adams and began bewailing the sacrifice of Texas in the treaty. But all did not go as expected. The usually punctilious Adams had overlooked a dispatch from America's minister to Spain warning him that the king had granted much of Florida's unclaimed lands to two nobles. These grants went into effect only days before the treaty made any further land distribution illegal.

The mortified Adams demanded that Spain repeal this shady proceeding, but the Spanish used the grants as leverage to gain amendments to the treaty. They again demanded that the United States promise not to recognize Spain's former colonies, and added a request for a formal guarantee of all of Spain's remaining empire in the Western Hemisphere. Clay gleefully called for Monroe and Adams to scrap the whole treaty and conquer Texas and Florida. Adams threatened Spain with just that, even though Monroe did not really want Texas because he feared that its acquisition would reopen the debate over slavery that had just been concluded with the Missouri Compromise of 1820. Under Adams's pressure, Spain finally succumbed, revoked the land grants, and ratified the treaty in 1821, two years after it had been concluded.

To help gain Spanish cooperation, Adams gave private assurances to the Spanish minister in the United States that recognition of the Latin American republics would not be immediate. So it was not until 1822 that the United States became the first nation outside South America to recognize the nations of Chile, the United Provinces of the Plata, Peru, Colombia, and Mexico. As Adams expected, Europe stood by without significant protest despite the wounded outcries from Spain. Yet no European nation joined the United States in recognition. Did Spain and Europe still harbor some hopes of regaining control of the republics?

THE MONROE DOCTRINE

That question came to a head in 1823 when France, with the support of the Holy Alliance, sent its armies into Spain to restore the authority of King Ferdinand VII over a too-independent Spanish legislature. There were fears in England and America that the French might not stop there, but mount joint expeditions with Spain to restore "legitimate" monarchical control of the lost provinces in the Western Hemisphere. As French troops poured across the Pyrenees, Richard Rush, the American minister to England, commented hopefully to George Canning, the British foreign minister, that even if France overthrew the constitutional government of Spain on behalf of Ferdinand VII, there was at least the consolation "that Great Britain would not allow her to go farther and stop the progress of emancipation in the colonies." He was startled by Canning's response: "What do you think your Government would say to going hand in hand with England in such a policy?"

A significant improvement in the relations between the two countries after the War of 1812 made possible Canning's proposal of a limited Anglo-American alliance. Trade between the two nations had become increasingly valuable. Great Britain purchased two-fifths of American exports, mostly cotton, while the Americans provided a vital market for British manufactured goods. American vessels carried almost 90 percent of Anglo-American trade, so it was especially important to the American merchant marine. Great Britain also had an added incentive to cooperate with the United States, for it was becoming clear that Canada was more a hostage to America's growing power and population than a potential staging area for a British invasion of the United States. Some hostile feelings between England and America remained, exacerbated by vituperative quarrels carried on in the newspapers and magazines of the two countries, but even confirmed British-haters like John Quincy Adams came to see the benefit of dampening Anglo-American tensions. On the British side, Canning and his predecessor, Lord Castlereagh, more than matched the growing American amicability. In this atmosphere, the United States and Great Britain settled several nagging conflicts during the years immediately preceding Canning's offer of a joint policy on Latin America.

In 1817, the Rush-Bagot Agreement established severe limits on naval forces sailing the Great Lakes. Since land fortifications remained, this was a minor step, but it was significant in showing the willingness of the two sides to reach agreements. That same year, an arbitration commission established by the Treaty of Ghent settled the dispute over the portion of the Canadian-American border running through Passamaquoddy Bay in Maine. A few months later, the Convention of 1818 adjusted several other boundary controversies. The convention confirmed the border between the Louisiana Purchase and Canada at 49° latitude from the Lake of the Woods to the crest of the Rockies. The Oregon Territory to the west of the Rockies, however, remained a subject of argument. England insisted that the border should be the Columbia River, while the United States wanted the 49° line extended to the sea. Since the territory was so remote and unpopulated, the two sides finally agreed to defer the border settlement and allow the citizens of both nations to live there freely.

The Convention of 1818 also brought compromise on the issue of the Canadian fisheries. The British claimed that the War of 1812 had ended the American "liberty" granted by the Peace Treaty of 1783 to fish and cure their catch in Canadian waters; the Americans said that this "liberty" was equivalent to a perpetual right and could never be abridged. The convention limited slightly the areas where Americans could fish and cure, but confirmed the "liberty" forever. (The agreement would break down a decade later, but worked well for the time.) Finally, the Convention of 1818 called for arbitration of the controversy over the American slaves carried away by British troops at the end of the War of 1812.

Several issues remained to plague Anglo-American relations. The United States and Great Britain could not reach agreement on impressment, and both sides assumed that this issue would drag the United States into any future European war on the side of England's enemies. Fortunately, no general European war broke out for a century. The United States and Great Britain also continued to dispute the northern boundary of Maine. They squabbled over British prohibitions against American ships trading with the West Indies as well. The British finally opened several West Indian ports in 1821 after the United States enacted retaliatory regulations, but the United States refused to repeal all its discriminatory duties until Great Britain removed all its imperial preferences in the West Indies. This stalled the agreement until 1830. Fortunately, the breakdown of negotiations did not create a crisis because by the 1820s direct commerce between the United States and Great Britain had come to dwarf the West Indies trade.

Finally, controversy continued to swirl over the desire of Great Britain to visit and search American ships suspected of carrying on the slave trade in violation of the laws of both countries. The issue of visit and search was too sensitive even for antislavery Americans to agree readily to British visitations, although the British were willing to grant American ships reciprocal rights to search suspected British vessels.

Despite the number of these remaining quarrels, most of them seemed relatively minor in 1823, and Americans and Britons alike were impressed with the growing amity between the two countries. This allowed Canning, previously one of the most anti-American of British statesmen, to approach Richard Rush with his proposal for a joint policy on Latin America.

Britain's increasing estrangement from its erstwhile allies among the reactionary regimes of Europe also encouraged Canning to make his offer. The so-called Holy Alliance of these regimes had defied British disapproval to encourage Austrian intervention in Naples and Piedmont, along with the French invasion of Spain on behalf of Ferdinand VII. The Holy Allies had even announced that they would come to the aid of France if Great Britain interfered on the side of the Spanish legislature against Ferdinand. The pressures of Britain's estrangement from its continental allies drove Canning's predecessor, Lord Castlereagh, to commit suicide by slashing his throat with a penknife. Canning accepted the estrangement with greater aplomb. He publicly warned that Britain would fight if France tried to make its occupation of Spain permanent and added ominously that he assumed France would not try to acquire the Spanish colonies in South America. To bolster Britain's increasingly isolated position, Canning then turned to the United States. He would later brag that he had called the New World into existence to balance the Old.

Canning suggested that Great Britain and the United States jointly announce their opposition to the transfer of any of Spain's colonies to another empire. Rush was much impressed with this opportunity to enlist the British navy in defense of the "no transfer" principle, a doctrine the United States had long favored but lacked the power to enforce. Canning's proposed statement, however, coupled endorsement of the "no transfer" principle to several other assertions Rush found disturbing. For instance, Canning wanted the statement to say that the United States and Great Britain sought none of Spain's colonies for themselves. Such a self-denying pledge would prevent American acquisition of Texas and Cuba.

Cuba was the primary issue as far as Canning was concerned. In 1822, Cuban underground leaders had offered to mount a rebellion against Spain if the United States would annex the island. Americans, especially southerners, had long coveted Cuba. But President Monroe and his cabinet had not risen to the underground's bait because Cuba, like Texas, could reawaken the controversy over slavery in new territories. On the other hand, they certainly did not want a major naval power like Great Britain to take it, and they were very suspicious when the British cabinet in late 1822 sent a squadron into Cuban waters to protect commerce against the island's pirates. Monroe was ready to offer a mutual self-denial pact to Britain at this point. John Quincy Adams turned him away from it, however, because Adams wanted the acquisition of Cuba left open in case the slave issue became less volatile. Naturally the British suspected America's intentions toward Cuba as well, although they knew there were no immediate plans for American annexation. This was why Canning included the mutual self-denial in his proposed joint statement.

In addition, Canning wanted the statement to say that, although Britain and America thought Spain's hope of recovering the colonies hopeless, they would pose no obstacle if Spain sought to regain them by amicable negotiations. Britain would not join the United States in recognizing the colonies' independence, but would leave that decision for time and circumstance to determine. Rush and the United States wanted the former colonies to be free from interference by Spain as well as the Holy Allies, and so Rush renewed the former appeals to join the United States in recognizing the independence of the republics, thereby foreclosing any chance for Spain to regain them.

Rush told Canning that if Great Britain would recognize the revolutionary regimes, he would accept Canning's joint statement in the name of the United States without even asking permission from his government. He thought the benefits of committing Britain in this way would be worth the statement on Cuba, and he was willing to risk disavowal and ruin if his superiors in the United States disagreed. Nevertheless, Canning refused to risk the greater estrangement from his European allies that would result from British recognition of the revolutionary regimes. He turned instead to unilateral action. He bullied the French government into a pledge, known as the Polignac Memorandum, that France had no intention of interfering in the quarrel between Spain and the Latin American colonies. Recent research into the European archives has demonstrated that there never was a danger of such intervention, but whatever crisis there might have been was clearly ended by the Polignac Memorandum. The memorandum was not published until considerably later, however, and the American government continued to deliberate Canning's earlier offer in ignorance that the crisis was over.

When Canning refused immediate recognition of the revolutionary regimes, Rush sent Canning's original offer on to Washington, expecting that Monroe might choose to accept it anyway. Indeed, that was Monroe's first reaction. Upon receiving Rush's dispatches, he sought the advice of his predecessors, Thomas Jefferson and James Madison, and he told them "We had better meet the proposition fully, & decisively." Jefferson and Madison agreed, even though it meant giving up Cuba. "Great Britain is the nation which can do us the most harm of any one, or all on earth," Jefferson wrote; "and with her on our side we need not fear the whole world." Secretary of War Calhoun supported the inclination of the two elder statesmen. But John Quincy Adams urged that the United States make an independent statement of its policies to France and the Holy Alliance. He thought a joint statement would make the United States appear a "cock-boat in the wake of a British man-of-war."

As Adams saw it, a unilateral declaration of policy would not tie America's hands on Cuba and Texas should the inhabitants of those areas later choose to join the Union. Besides, a warning against all European interference in the Western Hemisphere would apply to Great Britain as well as Spain and the rest of the continental powers. Adams dismissed the threat of an actual European invasion of Latin America. Still, the ominous rumblings from the Holy Alliance deserved a timely response. Russia had only recently shown an aggressive posture in North America, warning foreign citizens and ships away from a huge swath of territory stretching from Alaska to the tip of

Vancouver Island, including coastal waters a hundred miles out to sea. The Russians had retreated quickly enough when Britain and the United States had protested, but the Russian minister had followed this retreat with a warning that Russia would never recognize the Latin American rebels. He had coupled this warning with smug and perhaps meaningful congratulations to the United States for maintaining its own neutrality toward them. Adams was convinced that the Russians were bluffing, but he felt that, if by some grotesque chance the Holy Allies did make a move against Latin America, Great Britain would stop them with or without the support of the United States.

Monroe accepted Adams's advice. Further dispatches from Rush confirmed him in his decision. These dispatches indicated that Canning had already cooled to the project and led Monroe to speculate correctly that Canning might have received private assurance from France. (Neither Rush nor the other Americans yet knew of the Polignac Memorandum.) In any case, Monroe decided to include a unilateral pronouncement of America's foreign policy in his upcoming message to Congress.

It was these statements of diplomatic principles scattered through Monroe's message of December 2, 1823, that later generations came to call the Monroe Doctrine. The first of these principles declared that while the United States would not interfere with European colonies already existing in the Western Hemisphere, the hemisphere was no longer open to European colonization. Adams had drafted this statement previously to apply to the Russian claims in the Northwest, but now Monroe addressed the admonition

Figure 4 James Monroe (left) and his secretary of state (later president) John Quincy Adams, the principal formulators of the Monroe Doctrine. Portraits courtesy of the National Archives.

to all of Europe. Monroe had wanted to follow this warning with a vivid declaration of American support for the Greek revolutionaries fighting their Turkish overlords and for the Spanish constitutionalists opposing Ferdinand VII. Adams talked him out of this, so the Monroe Doctrine became instead a restatement of American neutrality: "Our policy in regard to Europe, which was adopted at an early stage of the wars which have so long agitated that quarter of the Globe, . . . is, not to interfere in the internal concerns of any of its powers." This promise of abstention, which formed the second major point of the doctrine, led naturally to the third and boldest assertion—Europe must keep its hands off the independent nations of the Western Hemisphere. Any attempt to extend the European system into the Americas would be regarded as "dangerous to our peace and safety." These three points, along with the No Transfer principle that John Quincy Adams was reasserting at the same time in his diplomatic correspondence, became holy writ for later generations of Americans and ranked alongside Washington's Farewell Address as a statement of foreign policy.

Part of the Monroe Doctrine was no more than a restatement of Washington's neutralist dictum and required no further explication. But what exactly was meant by the "hands off" warning to Europe? Did the United States seriously mean to fight to protect the independence of Latin America? Was it ready to abandon neutrality toward nations in the Western Hemisphere, staying neutral only toward Europe? The answer quickly became apparent. Shortly after John Quincy Adams succeeded Monroe as president, he recommended to the Senate that it confirm two delegates to attend a conference of the newly independent Latin American republics at Panama. Those republics were considering a formal alliance against any attacks on them by outsiders. They hoped that the United States, on the strength of the Monroe Doctrine, might join. John Quincy Adams's communication to Congress made clear he had no such intention. The United States would lend moral support to the Latin Americans and would seek to enlist them on behalf of the neutral rights the United States had long championed, but it would not depart from neutrality toward all foreign nations, European or Latin American. The United States might join an all-American pact to implement the noncolonization principle, but each nation would be expected to guard its own borders.

Adams's opponents in Congress used this opportunity to attack him by insisting even more strongly than he had that the United States avoid entanglements abroad. They were not about to fight for the "hands off" policy; that policy would be a verbal warning only. They quoted Washington to Adams and delayed matters so that the American delegates, when finally confirmed and sent off, were too late for the conference. With Congress demonstrating in this way that it was even more antagonistic to entanglements in Latin America than Adams, it was clear that the United States would remain neutral toward that area for the foreseeable future unless there was an immediate threat to the United States' own territory and interests.

Yet even at this, the United States had expanded its territory and interests greatly since the War of 1812. It had acquired a transcontinental domain from Florida to Oregon. It had proclaimed unilaterally its interest in the independence of Latin America and left open the possibility of acquiring Texas and Cuba. It had backed away from a full commitment to Latin American independence and relied on the British fleet for any real enforcement necessary, but it had risked considerable embarrassment by demanding hands off Latin America. If the Holy Alliance had undertaken a Latin American invasion, the resentful British could have stood aside and let the United States put up or shut up. At the very least, the United States had laid out a path for its future ambitions as a great power.

CONTROVERSIAL ISSUES AND FURTHER READING

Until the mid-twentieth century, nationalist historians were almost unchallenged in praising the Monroe Doctrine as the outstanding example of a proper American foreign policy. The Monroe Doctrine idealistically protected republican liberty in the Western Hemisphere against European monarchy while realistically diminishing the ability of another great power to threaten the United States from a close proximity. But if early American historians could agree that the Monroe Doctrine ranked with Washington's Farewell Address as the supreme guide to American diplomacy, they agreed far less on what the doctrine meant. Isolationists argued that the Founding Fathers who formulated it intended it as reinforcement for Washington's policy of abstention. Activists argued that the Founding Fathers obviously meant the United States to intervene vigorously in Latin America to keep the Europeans out.

Although for years the histories of the doctrine's origins were among the most emotional and polemical of all diplomatic histories, for the first two decades after Monroe's message, the doctrine was almost forgotten. Only one major history or textbook mentioned it at all, and the author of that one refused to include the doctrine on his list of the major achievements of the Monroe administration. [George Tucker, *History of the United States* (1856–1857), Vol. III, pp. 361–364, 407–408.] James K. Polk revived the doctrine in the 1840s to justify American expansion against Mexico, and inspired the rebuke of one historian who insisted that the Founding Fathers had not intended to assert America's right to oppose European colonization in the Western Hemisphere if such colonization took place by "purchase, treaty, or lawful conquest," however the doctrine might have come "to be regarded in these latter days." [James Clarke Welling, "The Monroe Doctrine," *North American Review* (1856).]

When Ferdinand de Lesseps tried to build a French canal across Panama in the early 1880s, it inspired a spate of polemical historical articles debating whether the originators of the Monroe Doctrine intended the United States to intervene to prevent such a foreign intrusion into the Western Hemisphere. [John A. Kasson called for intervention in his two-part history of the doctrine, "The Monroe Declaration," and "The Monroe Doctrine," in the *North American Review* (1881). So did George F. Tucker in *The Monroe Doctrine* (1885). Arguing for restraint was H. C. Bunts, "The Scope of the Monroe Doctrine," *Forum* (April 1889).] The Venezuela Crisis of 1895 renewed the debate [Interventionist: William L. Scruggs, *The Venezuelan Question: British Aggressions in Venezuela, or the Monroe Doctrine on Trial* (1894). Restraint: William F. Reddaway, *The Monroe Doctrine* (2nd ed., 1905).]

At this time, the arguments for a restrained interpretation of the doctrine seemed to predominate in historical circles. But the pendulum swung to the interventionists after the turn of the century, when Theodore Roosevelt initiated two decades of overt military interventions in the Caribbean under the rubric of the so-called Roosevelt Corollary. [Interventionist: Albert Bushnell Hart, *The Monroe Doctrine: An Interpretation* (1916). Restraint: Hiram Bingham, *The Monroe Doctrine: An Obsolete Shibboleth* (1913).]

In the process of debating the intentions of the doctrine's originators, historians began to pit the various contributors to the doctrine's formulation against one another. The interventionist John Kasson, using John Quincy Adams's recently published *Memoirs* (1874) to discover the internal cabinet debates over the issue, insisted that Adams, along with Jefferson, had wanted a doctrine that would enlist American power for all time against European intervention in the Western Hemisphere. Monroe's caution unfortunately had brought him to make a limited declaration designed only for his own time. Kasson's opponent, Bunts, conceded that Adams had been the primary inspiration for and author of the doctrine, but argued that Adams too had wanted a limited doctrine. Credit for authorship of the doctrine was granted to Adams even more convincingly by Worthington C. Ford at the turn of the century. With access to Adams's formerly closed papers, Ford tried to demonstrate that Adams had been responsible not only for the noncolonization doctrine, but also for the renewal of America's dedication to isolation from European quarrels. It had been Adams who had insisted on a unilateral doctrine rather than a joint policy with England and had warned Monroe away from statements in support of European revolutionaries. [Worthington C. Ford, "John Quincy Adams and the Monroe Doctrine," *American Historical Review* (July 1902).] James B. Schouler insisted that Monroe should receive equal credit for the unilateral, isolationist character of the doctrine. Monroe had not needed Adams to turn him from accepting Canning's offer; Monroe had only told Jefferson he intended to "meet it fully," not accept it as it stood, and after his message had been delivered, he informed Jefferson that he had made his policy unilaterally because Rush had informed him that Canning had already cooled to the project. [James B. Schouler, "The Authorship of the Monroe Doctrine," *American Historical Association Report* (1905).]

World War I embarrassed historians who had been trying to elevate the stature of Monroe or Adams by attributing to them the doctrine's statement of noninvolvement in Europe. Albert Bushnell Hart, an avid exponent of intervention, handled this by saying that Adams had been right for his time, but America had since outgrown neutralism. John Holladay Latané, however, claimed that Adams's isolationism had been wrong from the outset, and Monroe and Jefferson had been correct in their willingness to accept the British entanglement. [John Holladay Latané, *From Isolation to Leadership: A Review of American Foreign Policy* (1918).]

After World War I, the Good Neighbor Policy made open military interventions in Latin America on behalf of the Monroe Doctrine less popular, and the immediate relevance of the doctrine faded. At this time, better researched and less polemical historical works on the doctrine appeared. The classic study of the origins of the doctrine is still that by Dexter Perkins, *The Monroe Doctrine, 1823–1826* (1927). Perkins dismissed the authorship question by crediting Adams and Monroe rather equally, and it has not been a major historiographical issue since. His research in the European archives demonstrated that there never had been any real danger of France or the Holy Alliance intervening in Latin America in 1823, and so he also dismissed all claims that the United States had saved the revolutionaries.

Walter Lippmann revived historical controversy over the doctrine by making it a centerpiece of his realist critique of the history of American foreign policy. He proclaimed that the formulators of the doctrine had been supreme realists because they had balanced their goal of security for the United States with the means available. Knowing the United States was not powerful enough to defend the Western Hemisphere alone, they devised a tacit agreement with the British to have the fleet protect against intruders despite America's unilateral pronouncement in the Doctrine. Lippmann only bewailed the fact that the formulators had not made the British alliance "permanent and binding," for later generations of Americans forgot the role of the British in the Monroe Doctrine and deluded themselves that America had defended the hemisphere unaided. This misjudgment of the nation's power and influence had led to further far-flung commitments unsupported by military force, ultimately inviting World War II. [Walter Lippmann, *U.S. Foreign Policy: Shield of the Republic* (1943).]

Many historians accepted Lippmann's realist outlook on the doctrine and America's later delusions, but disputed his specific assertion that there had been a tacit British alliance behind the doctrine. Some pointed to Edward Tatum's study, which argued that the real target of Monroe's message had been Great Britain itself rather than the Holy Alliance, since it was Great Britain which seriously threatened Cuba and Latin America. [Edward Howland Tatum, Jr., *The United States and Europe, 1815–1923: A Study in the Background of the Monroe Doctrine* (1936).] Arthur Whitaker, however, argued learnedly and persuasively that John Quincy Adams did actually pursue cooperation with the British at this time and that his desire for a unilateral declaration was simply his way of warning against an Anglo-American crusade. [Arthur Whitaker, *The United States and the Independence of Latin America* (1941).] Samuel Flagg Bemis and his student, William W. Kaufmann, then argued that Lippmann was dead wrong about the existence of a tacit British alliance, but because the British rather than the Americans had spurned the formation of a "satisfying Anglo-American entente worthy of the rights of man." Bemis condemned Lippmann for glossing over the British failure "as if it were necessary to support the cause of 1940 by a perverted historical dialectic." [Samuel Flagg Bemis, *John Quincy Adams and the Foundations of American Foreign Policy* (1949), pp. 399–401; William W. Kaufmann, *British Policy and the Independence of Latin America, 1804–1828* (1951).] Later realist works have agreed that there was no tacit British alliance, that the British had actually denounced the doctrine, but indeed had used their influence to prevent any great power other than themselves from intruding too much into the Western Hemisphere. [Bradford Perkins, *Castlereagh and Adams: England and the United States, 1812–1823* (1964); Harry Ammon, *James Monroe* (1971).]

No revisionist has written a complete study of the Monroe Doctrine, but broader revisionist surveys have emphasized its expansionist implications. They have pointed especially to the desire of the United States to win Cuba, Texas, and Latin American trade from Great Britain as the reason for rejecting the British initiative and declaring the doctrine unilaterally. Meanwhile, the only recent new interpretation of the doctrine has been that of Ernest R. May, who claimed that the doctrine was almost entirely directed at domestic partisan issues rather than the nonexistent foreign crisis. [Ernest R. May, *The Making of the Monroe Doctrine* (1975). He is disputed by Harry Ammon, "The Monroe Doctrine: Domestic Politics or National Decision?" *Diplomatic History* (Winter 1981).]

The acquisition of Florida has not been so significant a historiographical issue. For the first half-century following the Transcontinental Treaty, American historians saw little to criticize in America's expansionist course except its failure to take Texas as well as Florida. Theodore Lyman, for instance, berated the Spanish for refusing "to deliver the country" despite America's proper claim to West Florida. [Theodore Lyman, *The Diplomacy of the United States* (1826–1828).] Then Henry Adams opened criticism of America's Florida diplomacy by ridiculing the claim that the Louisiana Purchase had included West Florida. It was only the dishonesty, however, not the belligerence of America's conduct that bothered Adams. He thought the United States should have taken Texas, to which the Louisiana Purchase had given better title. Then, if Spain had resisted, America could have conquered Florida as an indemnity. Adams convinced most major historians of his era that the West Florida claim had been fraudulent, but twelve of the fourteen history textbooks of the time still insisted it was legitimate.

After the turn of the century, both the belligerence and the conniving of America's Florida diplomacy came under fire from Herbert Bruce Fuller, *The Purchase of Florida: Its History and Diplomacy* (1906), and Isaac Joslin Cox, *The West Florida Controversy, 1798–1813: A Study in American Diplomacy* (1918). The best modern work defending America's course is Samuel Flagg Bemis's biography of John Quincy Adams, mentioned above. [See also Phillip Coolidge Brooks, *Diplomacy and the Borderlands* (1939), and Charles Carrol Griffin, *The United States and the Disruption of the Spanish Empire* (1937). For a general history of American territorial expansion, see William H. Goetzmann, *When the Eagle Screamed: The Romantic Horizon in American Diplomacy, 1800–1860* (1966). For the intellectual rationales offered by Americans to justify their expansion, see Albert K. Weinberg, *Manifest Destiny: A Study of Nationalist Expansionism in American History* (1935).]

CHAPTER 5

Territorial Expansion: Texas, Oregon, California, and the Mexican War

THE UNITED STATES AND THE TEXAS REVOLUTION

Spain did not have long to enjoy the secure possession of Texas it had won in the treaty of 1819. The Mexican Revolution of 1821 ended Spanish rule in all of North America. Mexico, however, was no better able to populate, govern, and protect Texas than Spain had been. Much of the Mexican population consisted of Indians who were disaffected from the government. The Mexican people were concentrated in the central highlands, where they were surrounded by rugged mountains, malarial coastal plains, and deep gorges. This made communication with outlying territories like Texas extremely difficult.

The year before the Mexican Revolution, Spain had tried to compensate for these disadvantages and protect its recently confirmed border with the United States by establishing new settlements in Texas. Unhappily, its only reasonable source of immigrants was the United States itself, so Spain invited an American adventurer, Moses Austin, to form a community in Texas. Austin did not have time to establish his settlement before the Mexican revolutionaries had seized power, but the new government confirmed the concession. Like Spain, Mexico feared that otherwise Texas would remain an empty and inviting target for acquisition by the United States, regardless of America's treaty commitments.

In 1824, Moses Austin's son Stephen took over the colonial concession and began to settle Americans in several small municipalities in eastern Texas. Although Austin seems to have made a loyal effort to work with the Mexican government, it was probably inevitable that the American settlements would gravitate toward the United States. The American immigrants formed exclusive communities, maintained their own language and culture, and remained quite separate from the few Mexicans in the surrounding area. Although Mexican law required that the immigrants be Roman Catholic, they remained Protestants. The Mexican Constitution also implied the illegality of slavery by stating that all men were equal. Yet the American immigrants brought in their slaves to try to reproduce the cotton plantation economy of the neighboring American South. The Mexican government by and large winked at these transgressions and gave the provincial government of Texas wide latitude to deal with the American communities.

Then, in 1827 a local Texas uprising known as the Fredonian revolt frightened the Mexican government into taking measures that would lessen the danger of American settlers usurping power and joining the United States. The Mexican Congress passed a series of laws that barred further American immigration into Texas, abolished slavery, and placed high tariffs on the imports Texans required from the United States. Mexico did not strictly enforce these laws, but to many Texans they seemed ominous portents of things to come. Stephen Austin and other Texas leaders urged the Mexican government to make Texas a separate state within Mexico and thus guarantee its special privileges. The distracted Mexican government responded instead with further centralization. Even more frightening, Mexican troops under General Antonio López de Santa Anna used extreme brutality to put down a rebellion in Zacatecas against this centralization. Alarmed Texans organized militia forces, and inevitably Santa Anna marched northward to quell the uprising. In the wake of news that Santa Anna intended to repeat his Zacatecas performance, Texans met in a special convention in 1836 and declared Texas an independent nation.

Santa Anna's army of five thousand wiped out the American garrison in San Antonio at the Alamo. It then captured the defenders of the town of Goliad and executed them as traitors. But it was defeated and dispersed by Sam Houston's surprise attack at San Jacinto. Some Texan troops captured Santa Anna when he tried to slip away in disguise, and Sam Houston forced him to sign a treaty recognizing the independence of Texas. Of course Santa Anna disowned the treaty once he was out of the hands of the Texas army. He claimed Mexico had a sovereign right to reconquer its rebellious province any time it wished. Meanwhile, the Mexicans protested against the aid Americans had given the Texas rebels and warned that any attempt by the United States to annex the province would result in the severing of diplomatic relations and war.

Mexico understandably suspected the United States of complicity in the rebellion. Immigrants of American descent fomented it; American sympathizers crossed the border in droves to help Houston and his army. Large funds were collected in the United States for support of the rebels. Sam Houston was a close friend and political protégé of President Andrew Jackson. Yet there is no evidence that Jackson and Houston plotted the revolution. Jackson certainly wanted Texas. Twice before he had tried to purchase it from Mexico by pressing the claims of several American citizens against Mexico for losses they had incurred during the Mexican Revolution. He implied that the United States would assume those obligations in exchange for the cession of Texas. Still, he had shown considerable caution. He was aware of the problem Texas would pose for the slavery issue in American domestic politics, and he had advised John Quincy Adams and James Monroe to give up Texas by accepting the Sabine River border during the Adams-Onís negotiations of 1819.

When he became president, he agreed ultimately to submit the claims of the American citizens against Mexico to international arbitration rather than fight when Mexico refused to cede Texas as compensation. He also kept the American government officially aloof from the Texas rebellion, although he did nothing to discourage private American citizens from aiding Houston's rebel army, since he had neither the resources nor the desire to stop them.[1] Even after Texas defeated the Mexican army at San Jacinto, Jackson advised Congress to delay recognition of Texas as an independent nation, and he waited until the last day of his lame duck period as president to grant that recognition.

The Texas revolutionaries, however, wanted more; they wanted annexation. Thousands of Americans supported their annexation petition. Many Americans had purchased land scrip sold by the Texans to raise money for their revolution. Such speculators expected the value of their lands to rise significantly if Texas joined the Union and thus received American protection against renewed Mexican invasion. Many southerners also supported annexation because they believed they could carve several slave states out of Texas. But the issue of slavery cut both ways, as demonstrated by Jackson's uncharacteristic caution. Leaders of the political parties saw the slave issue as sure to divide the nation on geographical lines. This would shatter the party system and with it the leaders' electoral prospects. On the other hand, these leaders could not afford to oppose annexation outright. Expansion was a popular issue with Whigs as well as Democrats, so most of the party leaders hedged. They tried to cater to supporters and opponents of Texas by advocating annexation, but in the future.

Another factor complicating the Texas issue was the determination of Mexico to fight if the United States annexed the province. Antislavery northerners might accept Texas if it were acquired quickly and cheaply, but they were certain to oppose fighting Mexico on behalf of a new slave territory. Jackson's Democratic successor, Martin Van Buren, followed Old Hickory's example by rejecting Texas's repeated requests for annexation. The opposition Whigs were even more in favor of delay, and the issue temporarily receded into the political background. Rebuffed by the United States, Sam Houston and the Texans considered other expedients. One alternative was for Texas to remain an independent nation and perhaps expand its territory to the Pacific.

For the present, however, these dreams seemed grandiose even to Texans. The population was growing rapidly, but by 1840 Texas still had only 60,000 scattered inhabitants and its treasury was bankrupt. It had difficulty even maintaining its claim to the Rio Grande border, and it could mount only a few hit and run raids into that desolate area. The most important of these

---

[1] There was one exception to this. General Edmund P. Gaines did cross the Texas border with some American troops when he heard that Indians were marauding eastern Texas settlements and that neither the Mexicans nor Texans could stop them. The rumors proved false and Gaines returned to the American side of the border without having affected the Texas rebellion one way or the other.

raids, a military trading expedition of some three hundred Texans which had set off to acquire Santa Fe, ended in an ignominious surrender, the immediate execution of its leaders, and the deportation of the rest in chains to Mexico City.

Fortunately for the Texans, Mexico itself was so debt-ridden and crippled by internal disputes that it could manage only a few minor raids into its distant former province. But Houston and his fellow citizens never could be quite sure that the Mexican efforts at reconquest would continue to be ineffectual, and they had to be uneasy at the treatment meted out by the Mexicans to captured rebels. As long as Mexico posed even a distant threat, the Texans preferred American annexation to independence.

The British saw this and urged Mexico to recognize the independence of Texas. Then the Texans might abandon their desire for American annexation, benefiting Mexicans and British alike. Texas would buffer Mexico's northern border from American aggression, while the British would have in Texas a separate source of cotton, along with a potential check to American expansion. An independent Texas also would contribute to a balance of power in North America, undermining United States hegemony. With abolitionist sentiments running high in Great Britain following the outlawing of slavery in the British West Indies in 1833, some of Britain's leaders also had hopes that an independent Texas might forswear slavery.

In 1842, the British officially offered to mediate between Mexico and Texas. The British foreign minister, Lord Aberdeen, did not press his case very hard. He even gave assurances that Britain would not interfere improperly against slavery in Texas. Nevertheless, an American agent in London named Duff Green instantly wrote back to the United States that the British had concocted a plot to threaten the South by establishing an independent abolitionist Texas on its flank. He urged immediate annexation. John C. Calhoun picked up the cry and accused Great Britain of being ready to foment slave rebellions to undermine the competitive economic edge the South had acquired over Britain's West Indies since slavery had been abolished in the British Empire. Green and Calhoun induced the aged but revered Andrew Jackson to write letters warning of the British plot, which the Texas advocates used to maximum effect. The annexation issue was alive again.

GREAT BRITAIN AND AMERICAN EXPANSION

Supporters of annexation saw in the British bogey the ideal lever to revive their cause against the apathy and caution of the major political parties. There was always a generous fund of latent hostility in the United States against the former mother country, and anyone who could be portrayed as defending British interests was at a terrific political disadvantage. There were real conflicts of interest between the United States and Great Britain, but those issues were more important to the United States. The British were far more concerned with the high volume of Anglo-American trade than with peripheral areas like Texas, so many British leaders, among them Lord Aberdeen himself, were quite willing to compromise. Unfortunately, Great Britain had its own blusterers. The most powerful of these was Lord Palmerston, the great rival of Aberdeen and Aberdeen's prime minister, Robert Peel. Politicians like Palmerston were perfectly happy to exploit the British public's dislike of Americans as ignorant bullies. Such politicians helped keep Anglo-American relations in an almost constant state of agitation and made it easy for any American demagogue to further a favorite cause by linking it with an anti-British crusade.

Trivial issues had dragged America and England close to war several times in the years just preceding 1842. The most volatile of these had been the longstanding dispute over the border between Canada and Maine. The Treaty of Paris of 1783, which ended the revolution, described the border as running due north from the source of the St. Croix River to the highlands that divided the rivers flowing to the Atlantic from those flowing to the St. Lawrence, then along those highlands to the northwestern head of the Connecticut River. Unfortunately, there was no St. Croix River in the area, the term "highlands" was too vague, and no one knew which stream was the northwestern head of the Connecticut. Naturally, both the British and the Americans interpreted this description to their own best advantage, and their rival claims left some 7.5 million acres in dispute. Great Britain and the United States referred the issue to the king of the Netherlands for arbitration in 1831, but Andrew Jackson rejected the line suggested by the king because the inhabitants of Maine were adamantly opposed to any concession and Jackson's political advisers urged him to avoid alienating those voters. The issue became dangerous in 1839 when a quarrel over the control of the area around the Aroostook River brought first a posse of 200 Maine lumbermen to march on the area, followed by 10,000 Maine militia. The so-called Aroostook War ended without bloodshed after Britain offered to share control of the area, but some final settlement was necessary.

The interests involved in the Maine border dispute were not vital ones. The British did have a strategic interest in keeping the border as far south as possible to enable them to build a convenient military road from New Brunswick to Quebec for use when the St. Lawrence was frozen. The United States, on the other hand, wanted title to Rouse's Point, on which it had built a key fort to guard Lake Champlain, but which a careful survey belatedly showed to be on the British side of the border along the 45th parallel. These issues could have been settled quite easily, however, if it had not been for the violent emotions of the local inhabitants. Many of the Canadian settlers in the disputed area were descendants of loyalist refugees from the American Revolution, and they had no wish to find themselves on the American side of the border. The inhabitants of Maine were even more anxious to secure the best agricultural and timber lands available, and they rallied general American support for their cause by trumpeting that the border issue was one of national honor against British rapaciousness.

Another emotional issue between England and America concerned

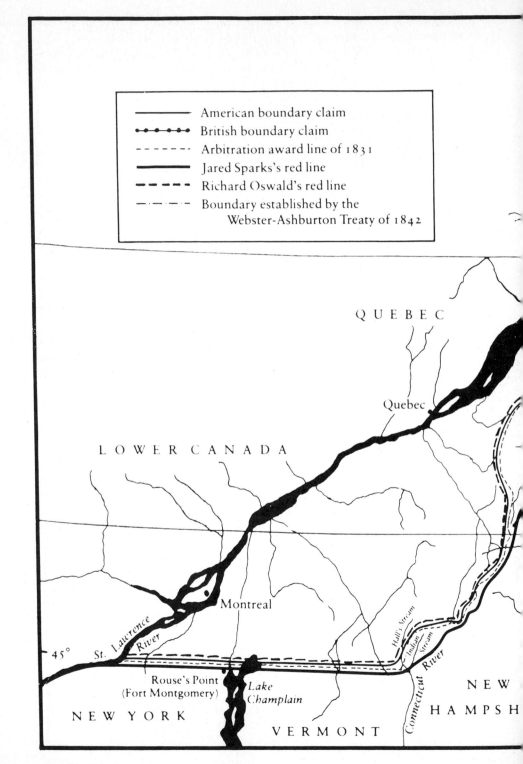

Map 4 Northeastern Boundary Problem, 1783–1842

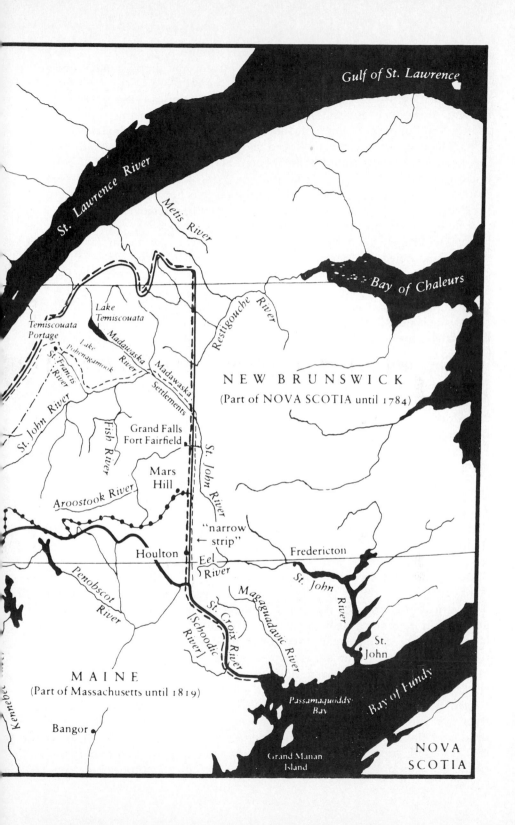

Gulf of St. Lawrence

St. Lawrence River

Metis River

Bay of Chaleurs

Temiscouata Portage

Lake Temiscouata

Lake Pohenagamook

Madawaska River

St. Francis River

St. John River

Restigouche River

Madawaska Settlements

NEW BRUNSWICK
(Part of NOVA SCOTIA until 1784)

Fish River

Grand Falls
Fort Fairfield

Mars Hill

St. John River

Aroostook River

"narrow
← strip"

Houlton

Eel River

Fredericton

St. John

Penobscot River

Magaguadavic River

St. Croix River
[Schoodic River]

St. John River

St. John

MAINE
(Part of Massachusetts until 1819)

Kennebec River

Bangor

Passamaquoddy Bay

Bay of Fundy

Grand Manan Island

NOVA SCOTIA

American aid to Canadian rebels in the area around Niagara Falls. In 1837 the *Caroline*, a ship owned by an American citizen, was supplying the rebels lodged on Canada's Navy Island just above the falls. Canadian volunteers commanded by two British officers crossed to the American side and burned the ship at its dock. An American bystander was killed in the fracas, and Martin Van Buren sent General Winfield Scott to the area and demanded redress. The British government delayed taking responsibility, which left open the possibility that the raiders had not been soldiers acting in the line of duty, but private citizens subject to trial in New York if caught. The issue died along with the Canadian rebellion when the famous Lord Durham Report to the British Parliament started Canada on the road to self-government. But it revived in 1840 when one Alexander McLeod was arrested on American territory after bragging in a tavern that he had participated in the raid and fired the shot that killed the American spectator. The British insisted that McLeod be freed, since no individual could be tried for participating in what the British now claimed as a public act for which only the British government itself could be held responsible. With local passions still high over the *Caroline* incident, the state of New York insisted on trying McLeod for murder anyway. Fortunately, the New York court acquitted him, and again the threat of war blew over.

Another issue that troubled Anglo-American relations in the 1830s and 1840s was the slave trade. Great Britain urged that the United States permit British ships off the African coast to visit and search suspected slavers flying the American flag. The United States consistently refused, remembering the humiliation of searches, seizures, and impressment that had triggered the War of 1812. The search and seizure issue was exacerbated when slaves being carried from Virginia to New Orleans aboard the American ship *Creole* killed their owner, overpowered the captain, and steered the ship into Nassau harbor in the British-owned Bahamas. The British refused to extradite the escaped slaves as mutineers or murderers, and the South joined the inhabitants of Maine and the Great Lakes area in harboring resentment against the British.

In 1842, Secretary of State Daniel Webster managed to reach agreement on these issues with a special British envoy, Lord Ashburton. The Webster-Ashburton Treaty settled the Maine border by giving the United States the best agricultural land and the fort at Rouse's Point, while at the same time keeping the border far enough south to give the British their route for the New Brunswick military road. Webster secured Maine's consent to the compromise by using government money to publish newspaper articles in favor of a settlement. He also showed Maine legislators a map discovered by historian Jared Sparks in the Paris archives on which the Maine boundary supposedly drawn by Benjamin Franklin in 1783 conformed to the British rather than the American claim. (Webster had not shown the map to Ashburton until after the settlement had been negotiated. Since there was no evidence that Franklin's supposed line was the final one rather than a preliminary proposal, the map did not mean much anyway, except as a propaganda tool.)

The Webster-Ashburton Treaty resolved several less knotty problems as well. It defined the border between Lake Superior and Lake of the Woods. It also agreed to joint British and American slave patrols in African waters. To avoid the touchy issue of visit and search, only the American ships would search suspected slavers flying the American flag. An extradition agreement in the treaty responded to the fears aroused by the *Creole* affair. It omitted any British commitment to return escaped slaves, but Ashburton signed a note promising no officious interference with American ships driven into British West Indian ports, even if they carried slaves. The British also offered an implied apology for the burning of the *Caroline* on American soil. Finally, since improved conditions aboard British naval ships made desertions less likely than in earlier years, Ashburton could afford to give private assurances that impressment was obsolete.

Although the Webster-Ashburton Treaty solved many of the problems between England and America, it did not much assuage the emotional antagonisms of the British and American peoples. These antagonisms continued to furnish a fertile field for ambitious politicians. Political opponents subjected both Webster and Ashburton to merciless criticism. Senator Thomas Hart Benton led the attack on the treaty for disenchanted American Democrats. He claimed that a map in the Library of Congress given by Benjamin Franklin to Thomas Jefferson demonstrated that America's extensive claims to Maine had been justified. When the map was brought before the Senate, the embarrassed Benton found that the line on it corresponded to the line of Sparks's map, supporting the British claim. Benton recovered to say that Webster then should not have tricked Ashburton, but the Senate overrode him and consented to the treaty.

Ashburton faced a similar attack from Palmerston, who claimed that Ashburton had given up too much, as demonstrated by the now public Sparks map. Ashburton deflated Palmerston's criticisms when he discovered still another map, this one hidden by Palmerston himself in the Foreign Office because it supported the American claim. The successful maneuvering of Webster and Ashburton saved their treaty, but Anglo-American relations remained tenuous.

Oregon

The passions that emerged in these treaty ratification debates made more ominous the failure of Webster and Ashburton to agree over the division of the Oregon Territory. Webster and Ashburton had stumbled over an obstacle to a fair division of Oregon that had plagued Anglo-American negotiations since 1818. During the 1818 negotiations the American representatives, Albert Gallatin and Richard Rush, had offered to divide the territory at the 49th parallel and thus extend the boundary between the Louisiana Purchase and Canada right through the Rocky Mountains to the Pacific. The British refused because that line would have given the United States the two most important geographical features of the Oregon territory—the mouth of the Columbia River and the Straits of Juan de Fuca. The British mistakenly thought that the Columbia River would be to the Pacific Coast what the Mississippi system was to the trans-Appalachian region, the key to the commerce and control of the whole area. Later they realized that the sand bar at the mouth of the Columbia limited the commercial value of the river.

The Straits of Juan de Fuca were another matter. They led to Puget Sound, the only decent port on the Pacific Coast outside Spanish control, and a potentially invaluable window to Asia. In addition, Great Britain's Northwest Company, soon to be merged with the powerful Hudson's Bay Company, saw the Columbia River Valley as a cornucopia for its fur-trading operation. To put all these features on the Canadian side of the border, the British proposed to divide the Oregon territory along the 49th parallel only as far as the Snake River, then go down the Snake and the Columbia to the sea. Unable to agree, the negotiators decided to share control of the entire Oregon territory for ten years.

The United States improved its claim to the Oregon Territory in 1819 by acquiring Spain's claim in the Transcontinental Treaty. The British improved theirs even more by the activities of the Hudson's Bay Company. The Americans and British tried twice more, in 1823 and 1826, to divide the territory. In those negotiations, both sides flirted with a compromise that would split the disputed rectangle between the Columbia and the 49th parallel in half. The Americans would acquire the mouth of the Columbia and several minor harbors along the Olympic peninsula, the British would get the Straits of Juan de Fuca, Puget Sound, and the right to navigate the Columbia River. The compromise failed because the Americans valued Puget Sound too highly to surrender it. On the other side, the Hudson's Bay Company pressed the British government to keep the Columbia River and valley. Consequently, despite a brief flurry of emotional rhetoric in the American Congress about establishing military forts to make good America's claim to Oregon, the British and Americans extended the joint occupation agreement indefinitely in 1826 and put the issue on the back burner.

By the time of the Webster-Ashburton negotiations in 1842, conditions in Oregon had begun to change. The British position was weakening. The Hudson's Bay Company had trapped out the Columbia basin and was planning to move its headquarters from Fort Vancouver on the Columbia to Vancouver Island. The company acknowledged in making its decision that the sand bar at the mouth of the Columbia nullified the value of the river for trade or defense. Simultaneously, thousands of Americans began to arrive in Oregon to reinforce the small contingent of some five hundred American settlers which the British fur traders had long dominated.

These immigrants were lured down the Oregon Trail by reports from American missionaries who had arrived to work among the Indians. Despite the changing balance of power in Oregon, Ashburton's hastily drawn instructions for the 1842 negotiations with Webster permitted no concessions north of the Columbia, so the joint occupation agreement was continued.

Neither envoy realized that the issue might be coming to a head in the near future.

California

During the Webster-Ashburton negotiations, Webster had suggested that if Great Britain could obtain San Francisco from Mexico for the United States, America might concede Puget Sound to the British. Ashburton offhandedly turned the suggestion aside, but Webster's proposal showed that California was joining Oregon and Texas as an arena of Anglo-American contention. Like Texas, California was a distant, weak, and disaffected part of Mexico. At the time of the Mexican Revolution in 1821, it had had a population of only 30,000, nine-tenths Indians tied tenuously to Mexican authority by the disintegrating mission system. Mexico tried to increase immigration to California by breaking up the missions and replacing them with secular *ranchos*. These ranchos soon developed a relatively profitable trade in hides with ships bound for the Far East, but the business attracted few Mexican immigrants. Instead, a handful of American and British merchants arrived to participate in the trade. Several of them became involved with disputing factions among the Californios and were deported to Mexico City on suspicion of plotting rebellion.

Like Oregon, California seemed very remote to the United States and Great Britain. Although each kept a wary eye on the other, fearing its rival might exploit the vacuum of power, neither made concerted plans to take California for itself. In 1840, Aberdeen rejected a proposal from his minister to the United States to make California a formal colony, although the United States did not know this. The United States itself had tried unsuccessfully to purchase California in 1835, and the Americans regarded the Hudson's Bay Company outpost on Yerba Buena Island in the middle of San Francisco Bay with great suspicion. Then Thomas ap Catesby Jones, the commander of America's Pacific squadron, took the British threat so seriously that in 1842 he forced the surrender of the Mexican garrison at Monterey. He did so on the basis of rumors that war was breaking out between the United States and Mexico and that the British squadron in the Pacific had moved to California to take advantage of the imbroglio. The embarrassed Jones had to haul his flag back down when the rumors proved untrue. Even the surprisingly amicable banquets he gave his former captives could not erase the suspicions his conduct had aroused among the Mexicans and British.

The Annexation of Texas

In this atmosphere of distrust arising from Anglo-American rivalry in Oregon and California and from the Webster-Ashburton Treaty, the British offer to mediate between Mexico and Texas in 1842 ignited a renewed American campaign for the immediate annexation of Texas. The leader of the campaign was President John Tyler. Unlike his predecessors, Tyler could afford to promote the Texas issue, for he had become a man without a party. Democrats detested him because he had joined his fellow southerner John C. Calhoun in deserting to the Whigs out of hatred for Andrew Jackson. The Whigs had nominated Tyler to be vice-president under William Henry Harrison as a gesture to the Calhoun rump of the party because they did not anticipate that the avid states-righter and slavery advocate could cause much trouble for the Whigs' nationalist program from that impotent office. Harrison upset their calculations by dying after only a month in office, and President Tyler promptly vetoed the Whig bill to reestablish a national bank. This veto inspired the Whigs to detest Tyler as much as the Democrats did.

With no chance of winning renomination from either major party, Tyler had no compunctions about endangering the internal unity of the parties by annexing Texas. Only by destroying the party system and reassembling a majority around himself as the hero of American expansionism could he have any hope of reelection. With this in mind, Tyler decided to negotiate a treaty of annexation with Texas. He whipped up patriotic sentiment by praising American expansion at the expense of British imperialism and Mexican degradation, and he played down the fact that annexation would increase the number of slave states in the Union.

Unfortunately for Tyler's plans, a cannon exploded aboard the battleship *Princeton* while a presidential inspection party was aboard. Tyler was below decks at the time and was spared, but the accident killed his obedient secretary of state, Abel Upshur. Tyler replaced Upshur with his old mentor, Calhoun, and charged him with completing the annexation of Texas. Calhoun did negotiate the annexation treaty, but shortly before he submitted it to a closely divided and highly emotional Senate, he sabotaged Tyler's political strategy. Inexplicably, Calhoun replied publicly to an old dispatch from Lord Aberdeen that expressed Britain's hopes for a truce between Mexico and Texas and for the abolition of slavery. Calhoun proclaimed that Britain's meddling made it imperative for the United States to annex Texas to save slavery throughout the United States. Thus, instead of portraying annexation as an expansionist issue, desirable whether slavery was affected or not, Calhoun succeeded in making slavery the primary issue. As a consequence, northern senators united against the treaty of annexation and defeated it by a two-thirds margin.

The fiasco naturally reinforced the caution of the leading candidates for the Whig and Democratic nominations, Henry Clay and Martin Van Buren. Apparently they had agreed a year earlier to avoid the Texas issue in their campaigns. On the eve of the Texas treaty vote and the party nominating conventions, both wrote public letters expressing support for eventual but not immediate annexation. A faction within the Democratic party, however, was unwilling to let the Texas issue go. These expansionists succeeded in deadlocking the Democratic convention by denying Van Buren the two-thirds vote he needed under the new party rules for nomination. They persuaded the exhausted delegates to nominate James K. Polk instead.

Polk and his expansionist Democrat supporters believed they had a way to annex Texas without arousing controvery over slavery and disrupting the unity of their party and the nation. Instead of putting off further expansion to avoid the issue, as Clay and Van Buren proposed, the United States should expand simultaneously to the north and south, bringing in slave and free territory in relatively equal measure. Their Democratic party platform called not only for annexation of Texas, but for occupation of *all* of Oregon. This included the area above the 49th parallel, presently known as British Columbia, which had been implicitly recognized as British since 1818. Polk seemed unworried that this would inevitably mean war with England. (The platform actually called for the "reannexation" of Texas and the "reoccupation" of Oregon, as though neither had ever been legitimately in the hands of anyone else.)

Running on this bold platform, Polk narrowly defeated Henry Clay for the presidency. Modern analysts of the election doubt that Polk's victory was a clear mandate for his expanionist ideas. They think it probably resulted from the natural swing back to the Democratic party of many who had voted for the Whigs in the wake of the depression of 1837, a depression many had blamed on Jackson and Van Buren. But Polk considered his election a mandate, and so did John Tyler. Tyler was now a lame duck president, but he wanted to finish the annexation of Texas. Knowing he would be unable to get two-thirds of the Senate to vote for Texas, even in the wake of Polk's electoral victory, Tyler tried to circumvent the treaty-making provisions of the Constitution and have Congress vote for annexation by a joint resolution of both Houses. This would require only 51 percent of the vote in each branch of the Congress.

The House of Representatives quickly voted for Tyler's proposal. The Senate was more wary. It was particularly worried about a potential war with Mexico over annexation. Thomas Hart Benton proposed that   annexation be delayed to allow time for negotiations with Mexico. He was persuaded to water down his proposal to require only new negotiations with Texas, which might permit time for pacifying Mexico. Benton also agreed to allow the president to choose whether to annex immediately under the House resolution or delay matters under the Senate proposal.

Benton assumed that Polk rather than the lame duck Tyler would be the one to decide how to annex Texas, and he thought he had an agreement with Polk to use the Senate plan. But Tyler fooled Benton. On his last day in office, he sent messengers to Texas to annex immediately under the House resolution. Polk could have salvaged the situation by recalling the messengers and beginning negotiations for a new treaty of annexation, but he denied he had any such agreement with Benton. Mexico immediately declared the annexation an act of war and broke diplomatic relations with the United States. The Mexican government also began reinforcing its army in the north and ordered it to prepare for war with the United States.

Even then there was some chance for a peaceful settlement. Mexico was indeed deeply offended. Any Mexican government that suggested concessions on the Texas issue would face severe internal opposition and possible revolution. But Mexico's finances were in complete disarray, and the army was in terrible shape. Its commanders were more interested in taking power in Mexico City than in fighting the United States. American patience and quiet attempts to assuage Mexico's offended sense of honor might have led ultimately to an acceptance of annexation as a fait accompli, especially since Mexico itself had finally recognized the independence of Texas just before American annexation.

Polk, however, was not inclined to be gentle or patient. He was a flinty, narrow, pious man, totally lacking in charm, and known to some of his associates as Polk the Plodder. Sam Houston said the problem was that he drank too much water. Polk had only one style of diplomacy—take a hard line and extract concessions from the other side. He avowed that the only way to deal with John Bull was to look him straight in the eye. Unfortunately, he decided to look John Bull and the Mexican eagle in the eye at the same time and found himself on the brink of war with both powers simultaneously.

The Oregon Compromise

Polk began his administration with a belligerent inaugural address in which he rejoiced at the "reannexation" of Texas and demanded all of Oregon. But he followed up his Oregon bluff by renewing the old American offer to divide the territory at the 49th parallel. Lord Aberdeen had ordered his minister to the United States, Richard Pakenham, to seek a compromise. Pakenham was to accept the 49th parallel if the United States would agree to bend the border southward and run it through the Straits of Juan de Fuca. This would give Great Britain equal access to the straits, all of Vancouver Is-

Figure 5   President James K. Polk. Portrait courtesy of the National Archives.

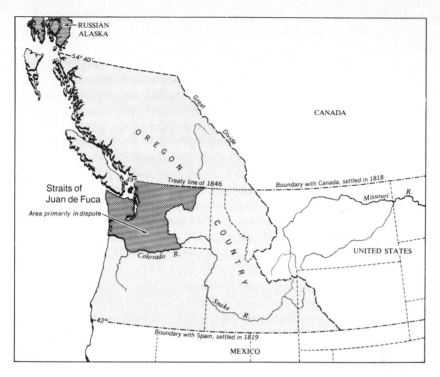

Map 5   The Oregon Settlement, 1846

land, and a decent mainland port in the lee of the island to compensate for American control of Puget Sound. Aberdeen also told Pakenham to secure Britain's right to navigate the Columbia River to its mouth.

Because Aberdeen faced domestic opposition to his proposed concessions to the United States, he asked Pakenham to get the Americans to make the compromise offer. Polk's belligerent inaugural and patronizing border proposal so angered Pakenham, however, that he forgot his instructions and rejected Polk's offer out of hand. The British rejection outraged and embarrassed Polk, since he already had betrayed his platform promises by offering a border at the 49th parallel. Polk's natural response was to become more adamant yet. He demanded 54° 40′ and insisted he would offer no more compromises.

The majority of the House and Senate was not willing to play such a risky game. Congress did give Great Britain notice that the United States was terminating the joint occupation agreement, but it couched the notification in terms that invited the British to submit a compromise plan for dividing the territory. Meanwhile, Polk let it be known with a great show of reluctance that if the Senate insisted, he would consider a British request for a compromise.

Polk's blustering actually made a settlement with Britain less rather than more likely. Aberdeen was thoroughly ready to compromise. Great Britain was undergoing a severe food shortage and needed American trade. Aberdeen even secured the agreement of Lord Palmerston to abstain from attacking an Oregon compromise. Polk gravely risked this tenuous British consensus for restraint by making any British concession seem a humiliating surrender. Fortunately for Polk and the United States, Aberdeen swallowed hard and offered the 49° border that would dip to exempt Vancouver Island. Polk referred the offer to the Senate without comment, and the Senate accepted it after insisting that the British right to navigate the Columbia be only temporary. This Oregon Treaty of June 1846 saved the United States from a perilous two-front war. For by the time the British and Americans reached agreement, the armies of the United States and Mexico were already in combat.

THE MEXICAN WAR

With the danger of war looming over the Oregon issue, one might have expected Polk to operate very prudently in his dispute with Mexico. Instead, Polk moved aggressively on this southern flank as well. Prior to his election, he had pledged to protect Texas from possible Mexican retribution if it accepted annexation, even if this involved sending troops before Texas was legally a part of the United States. When Polk's agents in Texas, some of whom seem to have been bent on inviting a war with Mexico that would provide an excuse for further American conquests in the Southwest, reported that a Mexican invasion seemed imminent, Polk ordered General Zachary Taylor and three thousand troops to take a position along the "frontier of Texas . . . on or near the Rio Grande del Norte." By thus endorsing Texas's claim that its border lay on the Rio Grande rather than on the Nueces River, the acknowledged border during the time of Spanish and Mexican control, Polk was making it all the more difficult for Mexico to live with the annexation. Of course, using pressure tactics rather than restraint was Polk's natural posture in diplomatic bargaining. Besides, he wanted more than mere Mexican acceptance of the fait accompli; he wanted to compel Mexico to pay the longstanding if inflated claims it owed American citizens. He also wanted California.

According to George Bancroft, the great historian who served as Polk's secretary of the navy, Polk had confided to him at the very outset of his term of office that he intended acquisition of California to be one of the four great measures of his administration. Polk seems to have wanted California because he knew he was going to have to betray his promise to take all of Oregon. An Oregon compromise would enrage many western and northern Democrats who had seen 54° 40' as the *quid pro quo* for their support of a slave Texas. Polk may have sought a free California as compensation for his abandonment of British Columbia. Ironically, Polk later would be accused by these same Democrats of seeking California as a slave state in a plot to extend slavery throughout the United States, a charge disproved by Polk's diary.

In any case, Polk hoped to bargain with Texas's claim to the Rio Grande border and with the financial claims to pry California loose from the Mexicans. He also considered letting the inhabitants of California, many of whom had little sympathy for the central government of Mexico, revolt and invite American annexation. He preferred such pressure diplomacy to an outright war of conquest, especially since the Oregon controversy opened the possibility that Great Britain would support Mexico in a two-front war on the United States. In the last resort, however, Polk would not shy from war if necessary to accomplish his purposes.

At the same time that Polk ordered Taylor and his troops into Texas, he sent the son-in-law of Senator Thomas Hart Benton, Lieutenant John C. Frémont, on his third exploring expedition into California. Frémont took sixty soldiers and a few cannon with him. Since the Mexicans in California already were in open rebellion against their governor, Micheltorena, Polk also ordered Commodore John Sloat, commander of America's Pacific squadron, to seize San Francisco and other California ports if war broke out between the United States and Mexico. Finally, he sent instructions by way of Marine Lieutenant Archibald Gillespie to an American merchant and agent in Monterey, Thomas O. Larkin, and to Frémont, to be on guard against any attempts by the British to exploit the troubles in California.[2]

Polk then was ready to negotiate. Mexico had reluctantly agreed to accept an American "commissioner" to settle the "present dispute" between Mexico and the United States. Presumably, the "present dispute" referred to the annexation of Texas. But for Polk, the annexation was an accomplished fact; he wanted to negotiate about all outstanding issues, including the Rio Grande border, the claims, and California. He appointed John Slidell as a regular minister rather than a commissioner and empowered him to exchange the claims and $5 million for the Rio Grande border. Slidell could offer $25 million more if Mexico would sell California. Polk seemed confident that his combination of pressure and diplomacy would work. He told Slidell not to break off negotiations even if California proved unobtainable, and he wrote private letters predicting there would be no war. On the other hand, he may simply have been delaying an all-out confrontation until the Oregon issue was safely resolved.

The unstable Mexican government was under enormous internal pressure to refuse negotiations and hold firm on Texas to the point of war. It found reason to reject Slidell because of Slidell's title, "minister." To negotiate with a minister as opposed to a special commissioner implied that the diplomatic relations Mexico had broken off were now restored and that the annexation of Texas was a fait accompli. Yet even the rejection of Slidell

---

[2] Controversy still surrounds the orders Polk gave Gillespie and what Gillespie actually told Frémont. Some of Gillespie's contemporaries said he encouraged American rebellion in California. But since Polk was negotiating for California at the same time and still seemed to expect success, it is doubtful that Polk gave him such orders.

failed to save the Mexican government from rumors that it intended to abandon Texas. A coup brought in a still more adamant regime.

True to form, Polk responded aggressively. General Zachary Taylor, in response to his earlier orders to camp on or near the Rio Grande, had stopped short at Corpus Christi, just across the the Nueces River. Polk now ordered him specifically to march across the disputed territory to the Rio Grande itself. Polk followed this by telling Slidell to throw the blame for any broken negotiations on Mexico, and warned that America then would take the redress of its injuries into its own hands. At this point Polk was visited in Washington by a Mexican, Colonel Alexander Atocha, bearing a message from the exiled Santa Anna. According to Atocha, Santa Anna was ready to take power again, and for $30 million he would give California to the United States. Atocha noted, however, that no Mexican government could appear to offer such terms freely. He suggested more American pressure and threats to give Mexico an excuse to make the necessary concessions. Polk did not take Atocha's revelations at face value, but he did decide to have Slidell retire to an American naval vessel and from there issue an ultimatum. Under pressure from his cabinet, Polk delayed sending this instruction while the Oregon controversy was still in a dangerous phase. He did not know that Slidell had anticipated him and had broken off his mission.

When Polk learned that Slidell had broken negotiations, he prepared to request Congress to declare war on the grounds that Mexico had rejected Slidell's mission and had not paid America's monetary claims. He did this even though he knew Congress might well find his reasons insufficient, especially with the Oregon crisis still in limbo. Polk was rescued from his gamble by news from General Taylor that elements of the Mexican army had attacked an American scouting force north of the Rio Grande. Polk immediately told Congress that war was already underway by act of Mexico, which had shed American blood on American soil. A divided Congress finally obliged the president by declaring war on Mexico, and Polk had his excuse to acquire California.

Mexico was not blameless in this affair; there seems to have been as much war fever in Mexico as in the United States. Mexico rather than the United States broke relations and warned that the annexation of Texas was an act of war. When Taylor began his move from Corpus Christi to the Rio Grande, the Mexican president ordered two of his generals to initiate hostilities against the United States immediately. Nevertheless, Polk's pressure tactics destroyed whatever chance there might have been of settling the issue without war. Clearly he intended to get California at all costs, whether by aggressive diplomacy and purchase or through war. Polk probably did not seek war from the outset of his administration, as some historians have charged; his original instructions to Slidell contained no ultimatum. His subsequent hesitation and the obvious danger of a two-front war also indicate that he preferred other means. But he would accept war rather than forego his plans, even if there remained a risk of simultaneous war with Great Britain.

Victory and the Treaty of Guadalupe Hidalgo

Within a year after the first shots of the Mexican War, American troops had obtained everything Polk had wanted out of the conflict. California fell easily. Frémont lent support to the American residents in northern California who initiated the Bear Flag Rebellion. After the rebels took Sonoma and imprisoned the Mexican leaders, they moved on to the San Francisco Bay Area where Frémont took formal command. They then joined forces with the American naval squadron that occupied San Francisco and Monterey under Commodore Sloat. Sloat reined Frémont in somewhat, treated the Mexicans in the territory mildly, and found little opposition from them when he declared California annexed to the United States. Unfortunately, Commodore Robert Stockton replaced Sloat and issued a bombastic declaration that American military forces would crush the "boasting and abusive" Mexican leaders. Such anti-Mexican sentiments, along with the arrogance of Frémont, Lieutenant Gillespie, and some of the American troops, roused greater opposition to American occupation than necessary in a province so long alienated from Mexico. The combined forces of Frémont, Stockton, and Gillespie conquered Los Angeles, but a revolt forced their retreat. General Stephen Kearny finally pacified California in January 1847 after he had marched with an American regiment from Fort Leavenworth through Santa Fe.

While Kearny was taking California and New Mexico, General Zachary Taylor was pushing the Mexican army beyond the Rio Grande and occupying the northern Mexican towns of Monterrey and Saltillo. Once Texas and California were secure, Polk was ready to make peace. He offered a liberal payment if Mexico would concede the Rio Grande border of Texas and a line to the Pacific that would give the United States New Mexico and California as far south as San Diego. Santa Anna, who had returned to Mexico with the connivance of the Americans, forgot his offers through Atocha, rejected Polk's offer, and took command of the army fighting Taylor.

Naturally Polk exerted more pressure. He sent General Winfield Scott and an army of some 12,000 troops to occupy Vera Cruz. The troops could not stay there through the summer because of the presence of yellow fever, so Scott had to attack inland toward Mexico City. Polk hoped that Mexico would make peace before this became necessary. He sent Nicholas P. Trist, the chief clerk of the state department, to accompany Scott and negotiate a peace whenever that became possible. Polk ordered Trist to try to obtain Lower as well as Upper California and authorized him to make a cash settlement of several million dollars.

Despite Scott's victorious march toward Mexico City, the Mexican government refused to deal seriously with Trist, perhaps in part because Trist and Scott distrusted one another so openly they were not even on speaking terms. Only when Scott's army camped outside Mexico City did Santa Anna consent to a truce and begin serious negotiations. Trist was conciliatory. He agreed to accept a compromise border somewhat north of that required by his instructions if the Mexicans would propose it. The Mexican cabinet refused, and Scott's conquest of Mexico City began.

Trist's compromise offer pleased Polk even less than the Mexican government. As American victories had mounted, so had popular demands for more conquests. Some even called for the annexation of all of Mexico. Polk never committed himself to the all-Mexico movement, but he was tempted to take more than he originally had intended. He was angry that Trist had conciliated the Mexican delegation rather than confronted it. He also was suspicious when he heard that Trist had reconciled with the Whig General Scott and believed that Trist might have come under the influence of anti-expansionists. Polk recalled Trist and told him to break off negotiations.

When Trist received notice of his recall, however, he was on the verge of negotiating a reasonable peace with the fractured but moderate new Mexican government. He was afraid that if he let this chance escape, there would soon be no Mexican government left with which to deal. The United States would have to occupy and bring order to a shattered, hostile nation. He defied his orders and negotiated the Treaty of Guadalupe Hidalgo. It gave the United States the Rio Grande border of Texas, the New Mexico Territory as far south as the Gila River, and a California border that put San Diego on the American side. The United States would assume responsibility for the old monetary claims and pay Mexico $15 million.

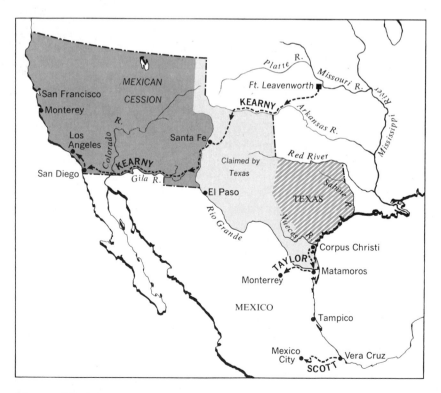

Map 6 The Mexican War, 1846–1848

Polk was indignant that Trist had defied his orders, but he could not afford to reject the unauthorized treaty out of hand. Although many Americans had been swept up in the enthusiasm of the war to demand all of Mexico, many others had remained adamantly opposed to the conflict. The Whig party, in which commercial groups who feared the impact of the war on overseas trade were very influential, opposed the war, and that party commanded a majority in the House of Representatives. Many antislavery advocates also opposed the war, including some northern and western expansionist Democrats who felt betrayed by Polk's compromise on Oregon. Ironically, these opponents were joined by some southerners who believed, along with John C. Calhoun, that any territory taken from Mexico except for Texas itself would be inhospitable to the plantation system.

Opponents of the war had never been able to defeat appropriations for the army, but they had indicated their strength and disapproval in other ways, especially in their support for the Wilmot Proviso. The Wilmot Proviso called for a prohibition of slavery in any territories conquered from Mexico in the war. If Polk were to refuse to submit Trist's treaty to the Senate, this opposition might be able to unite sufficiently to block military appropriations and undermine the war effort. Polk submitted the treaty without comment, and the Senate accepted it.

With the Treaty of Guadalupe Hidalgo, the United States had rounded out its continental empire. By annexing Texas, acquiring full control of the southern half of the Oregon territory, and conquering California and the Southwest, it had vastly increased the nation's size. To many, it seemed that the United States had reached its natural geographic limits. British Canada lay athwart any projected expansion northward, and Americans had considered and rejected further expansion into Mexico with the Treaty of Guadalupe Hidalgo.[3] Any further territorial expansion would have to be directed at territory separated from the United States by water or by other foreign territory. Many such areas were also densely inhabited by peoples of different cultures and races, making it difficult to regard acquisition as the incorporation of "empty" land and raising the specter of racial amalgamation and American colonialism in an unavoidable way.

There were some Americans willing to defy such inhibitions. They would seek further acquisition if their consciences could be assuaged by pointing to requests from the inhabitants of valuable lands for American annexation, or if the bogey of British intervention could be raised plausibly. But the only areas that seemed open to such expansion lay in Latin America, and they would undoubtedly come to the Union as slave territories. The Mexican War and the Wilmot Proviso had raised too much opposition to the spread of slavery to make such acquisitions possible.

President Polk was one of those who was thwarted. Some inhabitants of the Yucatan Peninsula who were rebelling against Mexico in the wake of the

---

[3] In 1853, the United States did purchase from Mexico an additional strip of territory on the southwestern border to facilitate the building of a transcontinental railroad, but this Gadsden Purchase was a minor exception.

Mexican War requested annexation to the United States. Polk considered the invitation and invoked the Monroe Doctrine to warn the British away, but nothing came of his interest. Polk also toyed with the idea of buying Cuba from Spain, but neither Spain nor Americans fearful of the slavery question would hear of it. Some southerners decided to take expansion into their own hands. "Filibusterers" like William Walker and Narciso López led private military expeditions to conquer Cuba, Nicaragua, and Lower California. Most of these filibusterers came to a bad end. Walker and López both were captured and executed in the lands they had come to "liberate."

This did not discourage the administrations of Polk's successors—Millard Fillmore, Franklin Pierce, and James Buchanan. They continued America's not-so-subtle attempts to acquire Cuba. Fillmore warned that the United States would oppose any attempt by another European power to relieve Spain of Cuba. When Havana seized the American ship *Black Warrior* for customs violations, Pierce unsuccessfully used the crisis to press Spain into disgorging its colony. Pierce's ministers to Great Britain, Spain, and France, James Buchanan, Pierre Soulé, and John Mason, met in Ostend, Belgium, to plot further strategy for annexing Cuba. They agreed that if Spain would not sell it, the United States would be justified in taking the island forcibly. Their confidential written conclusions, which came to be known as the Ostend Manifesto, leaked to the press and stirred a storm of controversy that destroyed any realistic hopes of annexation. Buchanan continued to agitate the question throughout his own administration, but the issue of slavery checkmated expansion until after the Civil War.

CONTROVERSIAL ISSUES AND FURTHER READING

Since the Mexican War aroused more domestic opposition than any other war in America's history with the exception of Vietnam, it is not surprising that historians have argued over it since the 1840s. In the immediate aftermath of the Mexican War, most historians treated America's diplomacy favorably. They blamed Mexican intransigence and duplicity for the outbreak of hostilities. [See, for example, R. S. Ripley, *History of the War with Mexico* (1849), and Nathan Covington Brooks, *A Complete History of the Mexican War, 1846–1848* (1849).] However, there were some dissenting histories. William Jay blamed the war on a slaveholders' plot to expand slave territory in *A Review of the Causes and Consequences of the Mexican War* (2nd ed., 1849). Albert Gallatin agreed with Jay that the United States was more at fault than Mexico, but attributed the war to the aggressive expansionism of all sections, not just that of the slaveholders. [Albert Gallatin, *Peace with Mexico* (1847). For a similar view, see Charles T. Porter, *Review of the Mexican War* (1849).]

The Civil War brought significant changes to the historiography of this question. Many northerners, led by the Republican party, blamed the expansionism of the slaveholders for the Civil War, and saw the Mexican War as early evidence of the southern conspiracy against the free northern states. The views espoused in the antebellum period by William Jay, very much a minority opinion at that time, were endorsed by every major historical study of the Mexican War written in the post-Civil War era. [Hermann Von Holst, *The Constitutional and Political History of the United States* (1876–1892); Hubert Howe Bancroft, *History of Mexico* (1883–1888); James Schouler, *History of the United States* (rev. ed., 1892–1913); James Ford Rhodes, *History of the United States from the Compromise of 1850* (1893–1906).] Even after one of these historians, James Schouler, gained access to Polk's diary, which showed that Polk was willing to see California come into the Union as a free state, Schouler did not abandon his opinion that Polk had demanded expansion because he had seen what southerners coveted. [James Schouler, *Historical Briefs* (1896).]

As the passions of the Civil War and Reconstruction subsided, younger historians challenged the slaveholder conspiracy theory. Not only did they cite Polk's diary, they also noted that some southerners like John C. Calhoun had opposed the Mexican War, fearing that the territory to be acquired in the Southwest was unsuitable for the plantation system. After 1900, little was to be heard of the slavery expansion theory, causing Hermann Von Holst to bewail the "tendency in the younger historical students to look upon the expansion of the country as the important consideration, and the slavery question as incidental." Ever since, the debate has been over whether the United States was justified in going to war and taking so much territory from Mexico.

This has blended naturally into the modern debate among nationalists, realists, and revisionists. Nationalists generally have defended American policy and blamed Mexican intransigence on the Texas issue for the war. Realists are not so likely to defend the abstract justice of the war or to deny the aggressiveness of Polk and the Americans. They see no need, however, to attribute the expansion to the capitalist ethic or extraordinary greed and rapaciousness, as revisionists do, or to try to gloss over the moral transgressions of Polk and the United States, as the nationalists do. Instead, they portray American expansion into the Southwest as the inevitable result of a growing nation on the border of a vacuum of power. Hard realists even defend Polk's tactics and credit him and a conservative coalition in Congress with harnessing the frenzy for expansion into all of Mexico to limited, realistic goals. Soft realists are inclined to believe that America could have acquired the territory with more restrained tactics.

The pendulum of historical approval and disapproval about the Mexican War has swung back and forth several times since 1900. Between 1900 and 1920, when the United States was acquiring the Philippines, intervening blatantly in Latin America, and finally participating in World War I, most significant histories supported the American side of the war. [See especially Justin Smith, *The War with Mexico* (1919), and the more moderate defense, George L. Rives, *The United States and Mexico, 1821–1848* (1913). For opposition to the American course, see Jesse S. Reeves, *American Diplomacy under Tyler and Polk* (1907).]

In the post-World War I reaction to the more blatant aspects of American imperialism, historians were more willing to see the Mexican side of the war. [N. W. Stephenson, *Texas and the Mexican War* (1921), and Richard Stenberg, "The Failure of Polk's Mexican War Intrigue of 1845," *The Pacific Historical Review* (1935). Eugene Irving McCormac's biography, *James K. Polk* (1922), supported the American side.] After 1941, America's struggle against the Axis and the succeeding Cold War brought more favor to policies that had enhanced and used American power. Polls of historians placed James K. Polk in the top ten American presidents, and Allan Nevins told the *New York Times* that "The general view of historians used to be that the war was wrong; more recently they have taken the opposite view."

Those historians who did criticize the war in the post-World War II era did not condemn American expansion per se, but criticized the tactics used and the attempts of historians to cover those tactics with a veneer of morality. [Defenses of the justice and morality of American actions can be found in Bernard DeVoto, *Year of Decision: 1846* (1943); Alfred Hoyt Bill, *Rehearsal for Conflict: The War with Mexico, 1846–1848* (1947); and Otis Singletary, *The Mexican War* (1960). Frederick Merk, *Manifest Destiny and Mission in American History* (1963), criticizes Polk's tactics. Norman Graebner wrote the best realist analyses of the war in *Empire on the Pacific: A Study in American Continental Expansion* (1955), and *Manifest Destiny* (1968). He emphasizes the importance of the Pacific ports as opposed to agricultural land in the motivation of Polk and his contemporaries and praises Polk for restraining American expansionist fever to encompass only those lands truly valuable to the United States. See also Richard W. Van Alstyne, *The Rising American Empire* (1960), for a realist view of American imperialism.]

Finally, Vietnam swung the pendulum back toward a more critical view of American policy. A good example of a moderate revisionist critique written in this era is Glenn W. Price, *Origins of the War with Mexico* (1967). The best and most balanced work on the Mexican War is David H. Pletcher, *The Diplomacy of Annexation: Texas, Oregon, and the Mexican War* (1973). [Another excellent modern work is Charles Sellers, *James K. Polk: Continentalist, 1843–1846* (1966). Nationalist defenses of America's course are Seymour V. Connor and Odie B. Faulk, *North America Divided: The Mexican War, 1846–1848* (1971), and William H. Goetzmann, *When the Eagle Screamed: The Romantic Horizon in American Diplomacy, 1800–1860* (1966).]

Other important books on special topics covered in this chapter are Frederick Merk, *The Oregon Question: Essays in Anglo-American Diplomacy and Politics* (1967); Frederick Merk, *The Monroe Doctrine and American Expansionism, 1843–1849* (1966); Howard Jones, *To The Webster-Ashburton Treaty: A Study in Anglo-American Relations, 1783–1843* (1977); Ephraim D. Adams, *British Interests and Activities in Texas, 1838–1846* (1910); J. D. P. Fuller, *The Movement for the Acquisition of All Mexico, 1846–1848* (1936); and John H. Schroeder, *Mr. Polk's War: American Opposition and Dissent, 1846–1848* (1973).

CHAPTER 6

The Civil War and Its Diplomatic Aftermath

ANGLO-AMERICAN RELATIONS ON THE EVE OF THE CIVIL WAR

The Webster-Ashburton Treaty, the Oregon compromise, and America's final victory in Texas and California had removed many of the issues disturbing Anglo-American relations in the decades before the Civil War. But serious rivalry continued between the two powers over Central America. Both England and the United States wanted an isthmian canal through Central America to facilitate trade between the Atlantic and the Pacific, and each wanted to control the vital waterway.

Nicaragua and Panama furnished the two best routes for the canal. The United States had the advantage in the contest for the Panama route, having signed a treaty in 1846 with New Granada (later Colombia) granting America transit rights in exchange for protection of the neutrality of the isthmus and of New Granada's sovereignty over it. Great Britain was in a strong position to control the Nicaraguan route, which seemed more practical than Panama in that era. Britain dominated the Caribbean side of the Nicaraguan route with colonies in Belize (later British Honduras) and the Bay Islands, along with a claimed protectorate over the Mosquito Islands. It enhanced its position in 1848 by seizing Greytown, which lay at the very mouth of the river that would serve as the Caribbean entrance to the canal. The United States responded by signing two treaties with Nicaragua. The first gave America the exclusive right to build the canal, the second permitted an American naval base on Tigre Island at the Pacific end of the canal route. The angry British made plans to preempt the United States by seizing Tigre Island before the Americans could establish their base there. With war in the offing, both sides decided a compromise was necessary.

In 1850 they negotiated the Clayton-Bulwer Treaty. They agreed that neither country would maintain exclusive control over a Central American canal nor fortify it. Each side also promised vaguely not to colonize or dominate any part of Central America. But this did not immediately end the Anglo-American contest. After the treaty was signed, the British asserted that the prohibitions against colonies did not apply to those already in existence.

They also refused any clear definition of their present possessions and set out to expand their holdings. The United States protested loudly. An American ship actually bombarded Greytown, and American filibusterers injected a further note of violence into the quarrel. The British drew back, however, partly because the Crimean War chastened them and partly because it was becoming clearer that construction of a canal would be a very difficult project. The British ceded the Bay Islands to Honduras and the Mosquitoes to Nicaragua in 1859. This laid to rest a major source of friction between the United States and Great Britain.

A revival of trade also improved Anglo-American relations in this period. The United States absorbed a quarter of Britain's exports, while the British took fully half of America's. In the meantime, the Marcy-Elgin Treaty of 1854 resolved the running quarrel over the Canadian fisheries and navigation of the St. Lawrence River. As a result, there was something of a détente between England and America on the eve of the Civil War. But this détente did not long survive the secession of the southern states.

THE DIPLOMACY OF THE CIVIL WAR

The Civil War greatly endangered Anglo-American relations, because British intervention on the side of the Confederacy was the South's great hope for survival and the greatest threat to the North's victory. For the North to win the war, it had to conquer the South; for the South to win, it had only to keep from being conquered. A key factor in the North's strategy to force the surrender of the South was a naval blockade of all southern ports. This would work a hardship on the British as well as the Confederates, however, because the British textile industry relied heavily on southern cotton. The interruption of the cotton supply would mean severe economic hardship for the owners and workers of British textile mills and for the many other enterprises whose prosperity was at least partly dependent on those mills.

The Confederates counted on Britain's need for cotton to bring British naval help in breaking the Union blockade. They also assumed that their King Cotton diplomacy would be abetted by Britain's interest in replacing United States hegemony in North America with a balance of power system. With British support, Canada and the Confederacy could check the expansive tendencies of the United States. To encourage the British in such strategic thinking, the South studiously avoided mention of its previous efforts to expand toward British interests in Central America and the Caribbean islands. Finally, the Confederates assumed that the conservative aristocrats who governed Great Britain would sympathize more with the genteel southern planters than with the supposedly money-grubbing Yankees of the North.

British sympathies assumed added significance because Napoleon III of France took his cues on American policy from the British. Napoleon inclined toward intervention on behalf of the Confederates. He detested the United

States and the Monroe Doctrine, which stood as a barrier to his ambitions in Mexico. He hoped to put a French puppet on the throne of Mexico and had just given Spain a free hand to conquer Santo Domingo in return for Spain's consent to his Mexican project. But Napoleon had to be cautious. He had just alienated the British and much of the rest of Europe by supporting Italy in a war against Austria and then, to reward himself for this effort, annexing the strategic Mediterranean provinces of Nice and Savoy. Not only had his war and annexations made Anglo-French relations delicate, they had disrupted the French economy and revived domestic liberal sentiment against him. In this tenuous economic and political situation, Napoleon would want to make sure the game was worth the candle before risking France's export trade to the United States in silks, china, wine, lace, and clocks. Unilateral French intervention would endanger Anglo-French relations and the domestic economy; joint Anglo-French intervention would avoid these problems and guarantee the intervention's success.

Actually the British were considerably more cautious than the Union, the Confederacy, or Napoleon expected them to be. British leaders certainly saw the benefits of an independent Confederacy, a secure cotton trade, and a North American balance of power. But the British people were in a wary mood because of the dangers and sacrifices they had endured during the recently ended Crimean War. The disarray in the British party system strengthened their guarded mood. Sir Robert Peel's successful leadership of the movement to repeal the Corn Laws had split his Tory party and disrupted the Whigs as well. The two parties became little more than loosely confederated factions. This required bipartisan support before any major foreign policy initiative could be undertaken.

It was difficult to get agreement on policy toward the American Civil War because the British had strong interests in the North as well as the South. British subjects were heavy investors in American canals, roads, railroads, banks, and public securities, all of which would be endangered by a vindictive policy toward the North. Also, much of Britain's trade in foodstuffs was with the North. As further incentive to caution toward the Confederacy, not only was the increasingly diversified British economy becoming less dependent on cotton textiles, but at the outset of the war Britain's warehouses were oversupplied with raw cotton.

The Confederates were overly sanguine in expecting rapid British intervention. While the British economy was still more dependent on southern cotton than on the trade of the North, the balance was closer than the Confederates acknowledged. British leaders were more sympathetic toward the genteel South than toward the Yankee North, but antislavery elements in Britain provided some counterweight to that. Thus, although the British tilted their policy slightly toward the South in the early years of the war, this owed less to their pro-Confederate sympathies than to their judgment that the North could not conquer the South. They feared that the war would drag on as an interminable stalemate, destroying the cotton trade and other American resources to the detriment of the British economy and at the continuing risk of an incident that might drag Britain into the war. Once it became clear that the North could win, British leaders abandoned all thoughts of intervention.

The Union government resented the early British tilt toward the South and dreaded the prospect of British intervention. The primary figure in shaping the Union's foreign policy to counter the possibility of British intervention was Secretary of State William H. Seward. President Abraham Lincoln maintained a general supervision of policy, but gave Seward broad authority over major decisions as well as the day-to-day activities of the State Department. Seward was a man of strong passions and flamboyant rhetoric. He was a fervent supporter of American expansion, and although he insisted that expansion be peaceful, his ambitions reached far into the Pacific and South America. He was particularly eager for naval bases and trade routes that could extend American foreign trade. His nationalism and expansionism naturally had brought him into conflict with British ambitions, and he was regarded at home and abroad as virulently anti-British and anti-European. Actually, there was a caution and hard pragmatism in Seward. Occasionally he could be carried away by his rhetoric and overreach himself, but Lincoln generally reined him in when that happened, and on the whole Seward was an effective and realistic secretary of state.

Lincoln had to restrain Seward twice early in his administration. First, Seward suggested to Lincoln a harebrained proposal to reunite the country by provoking war either with Spain, then engaged in the conquest of Santo Domingo, or with Britain and France, who were interfering in Mexico. Seward offered to take charge of the project and the government itself, since he thought Lincoln was not up to it. Some historians have seen a shred of realism in the plan, because it would have required the United States to station troops at Fort Pickens in Florida for the assault on the Caribbean, thus avoiding reinforcement of Fort Sumter. This would give some hope for a reconciliation with the Confederacy while positioning troops for an attack on the South if negotiations failed. Nevertheless, Lincoln quickly deflated Seward and his plans and saw that no mention of them leaked to the press.

Seward's second overreaction came in response to Great Britain's decision to recognize that a state of war existed in the United States and to declare British neutrality. In effect, this resolution acknowledged that the Confederates were belligerents rather than pirates or criminals. Naturally the British declaration encouraged the southerners and strengthened their determination. But it was difficult to see what else the British could have done: The North had declared a blockade of the South, which was an acknowledgment that a state of war existed. It should have been far more important to Seward and his fellow American officials that the British neither recognized the Confederacy as an independent nation nor announced any intention to disrupt the blockade. The British had warned strongly against a blockade, but had decided for the time being to respect it and to store up the precedent for use against the United States in later years when America should resume its habitual protests against British maritime practices. Britain also had taken heed of Seward's warning that recognition of the Confederacy would be an act of war.

Nevertheless, Seward took great umbrage at Britain's Declaration of Neutrality. Perhaps he did so because the British recognized Confederate belligerency before the new minister to England, Charles Francis Adams, had arrived to make the Union's case, and just shortly after the British foreign minister received a Confederate delegation. Charles Francis Adams actually considered returning home and breaking relations immediately. In the end, he decided to stay on to work against British interference with the blockade or recognition of the Confederacy's independence, but Seward threatened that any further communication whatever between the British government and the Confederacy, let alone recognition, would mean the end of Anglo-American diplomatic relations. Lincoln blue-penciled some of Seward's more strident threats, and Adams softened the dispatch even further by reading the relevant parts aloud to the British foreign minister rather than turning over the written message in its entirety. The intensity of the American reaction astounded the British minister, Lord John Russell, and he became more cautious in his policymaking, so the crisis blew over for the moment.

A far more serious crisis erupted shortly afterward in November 1861. Captain Charles Wilkes, an American naval officer, stopped a British ship and removed two Confederate diplomats on their way to Europe. These diplomats, James Mason and John Slidell, had run the Union blockade on a chartered steamer and arrived in Havana, where they boarded the British mail packet *Trent* to continue their journey. Captain Wilkes and the *San Jacinto* were in Havana harbor at the time, and Wilkes decided to capture the Confederates. Once the *Trent* had put to sea, Wilkes's boarding party removed Mason and Slidell, but disobeyed the captain's order to take the ship itself as well, so that it could be brought to a prize court and the issue adjudicated. Great Britain erupted in indignation. The cabinet composed an ultimatum demanding return of the envoys, a disavowal of Wilkes, and an apology. Prince Albert, consort of Queen Victoria, softened the ultimatum by getting the cabinet to add reminders of past Anglo-American friendship and an acknowledgment that Wilkes might have acted without instructions. Still, the British minister in America, Lord Richard Lyons, was ordered to break relations if the Americans did not bow to the ultimatum within seven days.

The British were willing to negotiate a bit further on the issue if necessary. But England was mobilizing rapidly, and a British war would ensure the victory of the South. After some soul searching, Lincoln, who had balked at releasing the envoys and was considering arbitration instead, accepted Seward's advice and released Mason and Slidell. Seward put the best face on the surrender. He announced the release in a note that blatantly defended the capture of the diplomats and asserted a wide range of belligerent rights. Seward apologized only for the failure to bring the entire ship in for adjudication by a prize court. Despite Seward's peremptory tone, Britain was glad to see the end of the crisis. The cabinet accepted Seward's half-hearted expressions of regret and noted America's defense of belligerent rights for future use.

The danger of British intervention was still not completely dispelled. The failure of Union General George McClellan's campaign against Richmond, followed by Robert E. Lee's brilliant counteroffensive in 1862, seemed to confirm the Confederacy's ability to survive and portend an unending war unless the North could be brought to see reason. Napoleon III suggested joint recognition of the Confederacy to England. The British cabinet hesitated, but several headstrong members of Parliament introduced a resolution that Britain offer its mediation. Palmerston and Russell finessed the effort by suggesting that Parliament leave the issue to them, and they began to consider intervention seriously. Then news of the Union quasi-victory at Antietam turned Palmerston away from his brief flirtation with intervention. Russell continued to mull the idea, but he too was put off when Chancellor of the Exchequer William E. Gladstone exaggerated the cabinet's inclinations toward intervention in a public speech and raised a storm of parliamentary and newspaper opposition. While Russell quietly shelved the whole project, if further southern victories had given firmer proof of the Union's inability to conquer the Confederacy, Palmerston and Russell might have revived the idea of intervention. As it turned out, however, the crisis for Union diplomacy had passed.

For years afterward, British and American popular historians attributed the cabinet's decision largely to the influence of the British mill workers, whose supposed devotion to the antislavery cause had brought them to ignore their own economic interests in the restoration of the cotton trade and protest the aristocracy's Confederate sympathies. Recent historians have put that myth to rest. Some leaders of liberal thought like John Bright and Richard Cobden had indeed been in the forefront of the protest, but the mill workers themselves, where they did express themselves in political meetings, seem to have favored the Confederacy and the restoration of the cotton trade more than the Union and antislavery. In any case, workers had little influence on parliamentary politics or cabinet decisions.

Troubles between England and Lincoln's government soon erupted again over the construction of ships for the Confederacy in British shipyards. The British cabinet was unsure of its interests and recourse in this situation. Private enterprises were building the ships. Confederate agents who commissioned the vessels carefully concealed their ownership. The ships were to leave England unarmed and be fitted out by the Confederates as armed cruisers beyond British waters. A Union agent, Thomas Dudley, spent much effort and money ferreting out information about Confederate involvement in building these ships, and he turned it over to Charles Francis Adams for use in pressuring the British government to step in. Adams insisted that the British themselves should detain the ships and investigate when there were legitimate suspicions of the intent of the builders and owners, since only the British government had access to the information necessary to prove such intent. While the British cabinet debated the issue, the recently constructed *Alabama* fled from Liverpool, fitted out in the Azores, and began a two-year campaign of fearful destruction against the Union's blockade and shipping.

Adams and the Americans howled, made dire threats, and began adding up the damages caused by the *Alabama* with the idea of suing the British government for compensation. The greatest fear of the Americans was that several other cruisers then being built in British shipyards, including two ships with metal prows for ramming Union blockaders, would follow the *Alabama* to sea. Adams went so far as to write Russell, "It would be superfluous in me to point out to your Lordship that this is war." Many historians later praised Adams for forcing the British to back down with his threat. Actually, Russell had decided to detain the rams two days before he received Adams's letter. He had been inspired less by American threats than by the fears of his cabinet and naval officials that in permitting neutrals to build ships for belligerents, they were setting a precedent that would work against their usual naval supremacy in future wars. In any case, the British government got around the legal issues involved by simply purchasing the vessels for its own use.

British concern for neutral precedents also helped defuse potentially explosive issues surrounding the later conduct of the Union blockade. The British islands of Bermuda and the Bahamas served as primary jumping off points for blockade runners trying to reach Confederate ports, and Union blockade vessels often intercepted suspect ships right outside the ports of those islands. Union ships also intercepted British ships carrying goods to Matamoros, Mexico, on the grounds that these supplies were then smuggled across the border to Brownsville, Texas, in what amounted to a continuous voyage. The British were indignant, but they were increasingly occupied by quarrels among the continental powers over Poland, Schleswig-Holstein, and Italy which threatened the European balance of power. A growing string of northern victories, accompanied by Lincoln's Emancipation Proclamation, also deterred them from intervention against the Union. The British muted their protests and took careful note of America's endorsement of doctrines favoring belligerent over neutral rights.

The events in Central Europe also distracted Napoleon III from intervention in the Civil War. Nevertheless, he continued his interest in a Confederate victory because he had undertaken a semi-permanent occupation of Mexico to which a reunited America would pose a serious threat. Napoleon began his Mexican adventure by sponsoring a joint Anglo-French-Spanish expedition to punish President Beníto Juárez for suspending debt payments to his European creditors. Napoleon's army then left the troops of his erstwhile allies in Vera Cruz and marched to Mexico City to join conservative Mexican clerics and landowners in establishing a new government. Subsequently Napoleon offered the throne of Mexico to Archduke Maximilian of Austria and promised to prop him up with the French army. To protect Mexico's northern flank, Napoleon urged the British to lead the way in recognizing the Confederacy. At the same time, he was assuring the Union of his friendliness and hoping the British would bear the brunt of the American government's anger.

As hopes for a Confederate victory dimmed, he began searching for a face-saving way out of Mexico and began to withdraw some of his troops. After Appomattox, when the United States stationed on the Texas border a substantial portion of what was now the largest army in the world to protest the French presence, Napoleon abandoned Maximilian. Maximilian stayed on, however, foolishly expecting that his good intentions and support from his Mexican followers would save him. His confidence was rewarded by a firing squad at the hands of the victorious armies of Beníto Juárez.

BRITAIN AND AMERICA IN THE AFTERMATH OF THE CIVIL WAR

The attitudes and actions of Napoleon and the British government during the Civil War left Americans even more embittered and distrustful toward Europe than they had been in the antebellum years. That bitterness affected America's relations with Great Britain more than with the other European powers because American and British interests clashed more directly. Britain's presence in Canada was a constant annoyance. It also was a standing temptation to Americans and their politicians, who continued to think vaguely that North America should be the preserve of the United States. Canadian border quarrels and disputes over fishing and sealing rights in adjacent waters kept the English and Americans embroiled throughout the late nineteenth century. There were also interminable wrangles over the damages the British owed for Union losses caused by Confederate ships built in British shipyards. These damage claims served as constant reminders of the rancorous years of Civil War diplomacy. Besides, everywhere the United States turned beyond its borders—toward the Caribbean, the Pacific, the Orient, or the canal routes of Central America—it found the British Empire its predominant rival.

Many of these Anglo-American quarrels seem petty today, but they dominated the diplomatic activity of the United States at the time. Politicians searching for issues to win votes could always count on a hard line toward Great Britain to be popular—"twisting the lion's tail," they called it. Perhaps the most difficult and emotional of these Anglo-American issues was that of the damages caused by the British-built Confederate raiders. America claimed that the *Alabama* and other such cruisers had cost the Union millions of dollars worth of destroyed ships and cargoes. The British were willing to pay a moderate sum so they could use the precedent to prevent America from building ships for Britain's enemies during a European war. They signed an agreement with Seward to arbitrate the amount of damages, but Charles Sumner, chairman of the Senate Foreign Relations Committee, denounced the accord because it did not include a British apology. Sumner also insisted that the scope of the arbitration be expanded to include the costs of the last few months of the war because he figured the British-built cruisers had lengthened the conflict. He thought the British should pay $2 billion, but he hinted broadly that the United States might accept Canada in lieu of that sum. The Senate, tempted by Sumner's reasoning and looking for a way to punish President Andrew Johnson for his unpopular reconstruction policies, rejected Seward's arbitration agreement with the British.

Ulysses Grant's secretary of state, Hamilton Fish, revived the arbitration of the *Alabama* claims in 1870, when the congressional atmosphere had improved. The British attitude had softened as well because of the dangers posed by the Franco-Prussian War and other European embroilments. Fish himself helped chances for agreement by abandoning the attempt to extort Canada from the British. Fish realized that the British would never agree to Sumner's inflated figures, and he saw that the Canadians themselves had grown increasingly hostile to American absorption. They had formed themselves into a dominion in 1867 largely to protect themselves from the United States. They were embittered by the raids into Canada from American soil by the Fenians, Irish revolutionaries who hoped to free Ireland by provoking a war between Britain and the United States. Quarrels over the fisheries also alienated the Canadians. These quarrels began immediately after the Civil War, when the Americans abrogated the Marcy-Elgin agreements on mutual fishing rights and extended their fishing activities into Canadian waters. Several American fishermen had clashed dangerously with British patrol boats.

Finally, the British and Americans argued over the exact placement of the border that dipped from the 49th parallel through the Straits of Juan de Fuca to give Canada Vancouver Island. The United States insisted that the border ran north of the San Juan Islands and that those islands were therefore American. The British and the Canadians argued otherwise. The United States and Great Britain stationed rival garrisons on San Juan Island to assert their claims, and shortly before the Civil War these garrisons nearly came to blows over which had jurisdiciton in a legal case that involved a rampaging pig.

This so-called Pig War, along with the *Alabama* claims and the fisheries, were the subjects of the Treaty of Washington which high commissions from each side negotiated in 1871. The treaty referred the border issue to the arbitration of the German emperor, who gave the San Juan Islands to the United States in 1872. The Treaty of Washington also referred the *Alabama* claims to arbitration. After some tension over whether the arbitrators could consider the costs of the lengthened war, Fish devised a face-saving formula that would deny all such indirect claims (thereby protecting the United States against similar demands from the British in future wars) and would award the United States $15 million in damages.

The Treaty of Washington also gave the United States the right to purchase fishing privileges from the Canadians. But that agreement broke down over the price Canada demanded, and the fishery issue continued to roil Anglo-American relations. In the 1880s, a dispute over seals in the Pacific exacerbated the issue of the fisheries. The fur seals bred in the Pribilof Islands of the Bering Sea, which were American by virtue of the Alaskan Purchase of 1867. Congress had sold an American company the exclusive right to kill 100,000 seals annually under regulations that preserved the herd, but Canadian ships were taking the seals in open waters (a practice called pelagic sealing). This was wasteful, since the killed seals were often lost in the water before they could be dragged aboard, and the toll of pelagic sealing, when added to the land slaughter by the Americans, endangered the species. President Grover Cleveland, in righteous anger, ordered the seizure of Canadian sealing ships on the high seas. This was a flagrant violation of international law and embarrassingly similar to British seizures of American ships fishing off the east coast of Canada.

With passions running high, the Americans and British worked out a *modus vivendi* under which both sides would cease ship seizures. The agreement almost came unglued when Benjamin Harrison defeated Cleveland for reelection. One cause of Cleveland's defeat was an indiscreet letter from British minister Lionel Sackville-West recommending Cleveland over his Republican opponent. This had led to charges that Cleveland was too pro-British, and the angered lame duck president tried to prove otherwise by ordering seizures of pelagic sealers to resume. Naturally his Republican successors found it politically difficult to revoke the order. Ultimately, in 1892 the Americans and British referred the issue to arbitration, and the arbitrators, while finding the United States guilty of violations of international law, set limits on pelagic sealing that would preserve the herd.

None of these Anglo-American controversies led to the brink of war; most were minor enough to be resolved by arbitration. But they kept reminding Americans of their long and bitter rivalry with the British, and Anglo-American anger remained at a fairly high pitch throughout the later nineteenth century.

CONTROVERSIAL ISSUES AND FURTHER READING

The diplomacy of the Civil War has stirred considerable controversy. Historians writing in the aftermath of the war shared the general public's outrage at the supposedly unneutral attitudes and actions of Great Britain during the conflict. They ignored an erudite defense of British policy by Oxford don Montague Bernard, and concluded that England had been "by active sympathy favorable to the South," even to the point of grasping for "the pretext for making war." [Montague Bernard, *A Historical Account of the Neutrality of Great Britain during the American Civil War* (1870); John G. Nicolay and John Hay, *Abraham Lincoln: A History* (10 vols., 1886–1890); George Bemis, *Hasty Recognition of Rebel Belligerency: And Our Right to Complain of It* (1865); Thomas L. Harris, *The Trent Affair* (1896).] The only saving grace for Great Britain was that while the upper classes that controlled the government were "gloating" over the prospect of a divided republic, the lower classes remained staunchly Unionist because they recognized that the Civil War was a struggle against slavery. [James Ford Rhodes, *History of the United States from the Compromise of 1850* (7 vols., 1893–1906).] But by the turn of the century, America and Great Britain were drawing closer together, and historians reconsidered. Now they portrayed the attitudes of the British government and upper classes as neither particularly unfriendly nor friendly toward the Union, noting that the Confederates had regarded Lord John Russell as hostile. Also historians were not just happy but ecstatic about the support the North supposedly had received from antislavery liberals and the lower classes. [Frederic Bancroft, *The Life of William Seward* (1899–1900); James Morton Callahan, *The Diplo-*

matic History of the Southern Confederacy (1901); James Kendall Hosmer, *The Appeal to Arms, 1861–1863* (1907).]

After World War I, this trend toward sympathetic portrayals of British policy continued with two outstanding books based for the first time on thorough research in British and French archives: Ephraim Adams, *Great Britain and the American Civil War* (1925), and Donaldson Jordan and Edwin J. Pratt, *Europe and the Civil War* (1931). A dissenting view of British benevolence was offered by the book that still stands as the best on Confederate diplomacy, Frank L. Owsley, *King Cotton Diplomacy* (1931). Owsley argued that the Union's violation of the rights of neutrals during its blockade of the South set precedents very harmful to America's own attempts to maintain its neutral rights against the British in World War I. He also claimed that Great Britain had not refused to support the Confederacy on idealistic antislavery grounds, but because the grain and trade of the Union were more valuable to its economic interests than southern cotton. Owsley's blatantly pro-southern bias led to some discounting of his opinions in his own day. But recent works have swung the pendulum of historical opinion some distance back toward his view of British policy. Mary Ellison, *Support for Secession* (1973), has effectively undermined the contentions of earlier historians that the British lower classes favored the North. D. P. Crook, author of the best modern surveys of Civil War diplomacy, has concluded that British policy was marked by cynical self-regard and moral hesitations rather than lofty and generous statesmanship: "Only the rhetoric of historians who wrote during the Great Rapprochment of 1895–1930, and the wishful thinking of the apostles of Atlantic unity since, have obscured that fact." [D. P. Crook, *The North, the South, and the Powers, 1861–1865* (1974), pp. v, 371. Crook has published a condensation of this book entitled *Diplomacy during the American Civil War* (1975). Other significant modern works on Civil War foreign policy include Lynn M. Case and Warren F. Spencer, *The United States and France: Civil War Diplomacy* (1970); Frank J. Merli, *Great Britain and the Confederate Navy* (1970); Stuart L. Bernath, *Squall across the Atlantic: American Civil War Prize Cases and Diplomacy* (1970); Wilbur D. Jones, *The Confederate Rams at Birkenhead* (1961); and Gordon H. Warren, *Fountain of Discontent: The Trent Affair and Freedom of the Seas* (1981).]

CHAPTER 7

Looking Abroad: Overseas Expansion in Mid-Century

WILLIAM SEWARD AND THE ATTEMPTED RESUMPTION OF AMERICAN EXPANSION

The triumph of the North in the Civil War confronted the world with a reunited America far more capable of extending its domain and influence than would have been the case if the South had succeeded in dividing the nation. The Union victory also eliminated slavery, which had been a major stumbling block to American expansion in the antebellum period. William Seward was quick to try to take advantage of the new opportunity provided by the end of the war.

Seward shared with many Americans of the mid-nineteenth century a broad if unsystematic vision of the directions American expansion should take. He looked toward the absorption of all of North America. He hoped that in time Canada would gravitate toward the United States and that Great Britain might finally decide to let it go. He also dreamed vaguely of Mexico, although he had no firm plans for handling the knotty problem of the large and culturally different population that would undoubtedly be hostile to American annexation. Since he was anxious to avoid conflict, however, Seward was content to leave the acquisition of these countries to time and rather mild diplomacy; he devoted his attention instead to other areas that might be valuable to the United States and easier to acquire. These were places of longtime American interest, such as the Caribbean, the Central American canal routes, and Hawaii. The fate of his expansionist efforts, however, demonstrated that America's interest in expansion into these remoter areas was not yet strong enough consistently to overcome other countervailing interests. Most of Seward's expansionist proposals were thwarted in one way or another. So were those of his successors, until the 1890s ushered in a new era of American foreign policy.

One of Seward's projects that succeeded was his purchase of Alaska. The Russians were anxious to sell the territory because the Russian-American Company, which administered it, was near bankruptcy. Russia also was incapable of defending the territory against the British navy. Finally, Russia assumed that even if it were able to hold on to the area for a few years, the burgeoning American population inevitably would swarm into it and drag it

Figure 6 William Seward, secretary of state during the Civil War and ardent expansionist. Portrait courtesy of the National Archives.

into the American orbit. When the Russians hinted that they would sell Alaska, Seward offered $7.2 million for it. The Senate quickly approved the treaty, but the House of Representatives balked at appropriating such a large sum for what several congressmen were calling Seward's Icebox. Partisan politics came into play as well, with all but two of the Republicans who had recently voted to impeach President Johnson also voting against the Alaskan project of Johnson's secretary of state.

After much debate and persuasion, including, it was rumored, some strategically placed bribes from the Russian minister, the House approved the appropriation. The House was especially gratified that Alaska was not already populated by a large, hostile, "inferior" people. The House also wished to avoid offending Russia, which Americans regarded as the only country in Europe sympathetic to the North during the Civil War.[1] Finally, Senator Charles Sumner had pointed elaborately to the pressure America's possession of Alaska might bring to bear on the British position in Canada.

The surprising strength of congressional opposition to the purchase of Alaska presaged the reception the rest of Seward's proposals for expansion would receive. His other targets were not only far removed from America's borders, but also densely populated by peoples of different races and cultures. Seward negotiated the purchase of the Danish West Indies and their outstanding harbors, only to have the Senate reject the agreement as too costly. He failed in his attempts to purchase Santo Domingo, Haiti, and Cuba. He did negotiate a new treaty of privileges with Nicaragua, but a simi-

[1] A Russian fleet had taken refuge in American ports during the Civil War, fearing an outbreak of war between Russia and England; Americans mistakenly regarded the visit of the fleet as a sign of Russian support for the Union.

lar one with Colombia was turned down by the Colombian Senate. He renewed attempts to acquire Tigre Island off the Pacific coast of Nicaragua, but
that also failed. Farther out in the Pacific, Seward got approval for a naval
captain's seizure of the uninhabited Midway Islands. But the Senate rejected
a more important reciprocal trade treaty with Hawaii which Seward regarded
as a prelude to annexation. The Senate was bent on partisan revenge against
Seward, fearful of racial amalgamation with the islanders, and anxious to
avoid the competition of Hawaiian sugar in the domestic market.

THE OLD DIPLOMACY: ISOLATIONISM VERSUS EXPANSIONISM

The forces arrayed against Seward's expansionism continued to prevail
throughout most of the rest of the nineteenth century. American politics in
the post-Civil War period revolved around domestic issues, especially those
of reconstruction. The sectional and racial passions that had fueled the war
continued to dominate party politics, even after federal troops had been removed from the South in the 1870s. The Democratic and Republican parties
remained organized around Civil War issues, with the Republicans reopening old wounds each election by "waving the bloody shirt" and calling
the Democrats the party of secession and popery. Partisan rivalries per-
meated all aspects of American politics, and neither party showed much hesitation in voting down the foreign policy initiatives of a president or secretary
of state from the opposition party. This could be done easily because the
parties were evenly balanced in the size of their constituencies. Seldom in the
late nineteenth century did a single party control the presidency and the majority of Congress simultaneously.

Economic issues generated by the rise of America's industrial economy
also had a significant impact on politics, bringing about a reorganization of
the entire party system by 1896, when William Jennings Bryan ran his famous Free Silver campaign. America's growing economy naturally had an
impact on foreign affairs. Industry was anxious to encourage overseas trade
in the hope that new markets would increase the demand for American
products. Since half the postwar years were depression years, many Americans looked toward foreign trade as something necessary to relieve the vicious swings of the domestic economy. The concern for economic expansion
would peak in the 1890s after the particularly deep depression known as the
Panic of 1893.

Between the War of 1812 and the Civil War, territorial expansion had
been a more significant force behind American diplomacy than overseas
trade. After the Civil War, the rising industrial economy, along with the lack
of any convenient, empty, contiguous territory to attract American migra-
tion, combined to make economic rather than territorial expansion the more
important force. The territories Americans sought, such as the Caribbean islands, the Central American canal routes, and Hawaii, were valued more for

their harbors than for their land or resources. They were steppingstones to markets.

The position of the two parties reflected this shift from territorial to trade expansion. Prior to the Civil War, the agrarian Democrats had been the most avid expansionists; after the Civil War, the Republican party, increasingly the party of industry, became the more expansionist. Many farmers also favored expansionist diplomacy in search of markets for surplus agricultural products, but by 1890 it was industry and the Republicans that led the way.

Nonetheless, in the post-Civil War era, industry and agriculture were more concerned for domestic than for overseas markets. The Republican party favored high tariffs to protect America's domestic market despite their harmful effect on the search for markets abroad. The Republicans tried to offset their protectionist stand and appeal to those anxious for overseas markets by calling for reciprocity treaties that would trade American tariff concessions for similar concessions by foreign countries. But the priority they assigned to the domestic market was demonstrated by the regular defeat of almost any reciprocity treaty brought before the Senate. Seward's reciprocity treaty with Hawaii was only the first of these defeats; other reciprocity treaties quashed by Congress included ones with Brazil, several Central American states, the Spanish colonies of Cuba and Puerto Rico, the British Caribbean islands, Canada, Germany, and Austria-Hungary.

Some revisionist historians have argued that the Democratic party's opposition to the Republicans' high tariff showed that the Democrats at least were concerned for overseas trade. But this traditional low tariff plank, stemming from the earliest days of the American Republic, reflected mostly a concern for party doctrine and for consumers seeking lower prices on imported products, not for industrialists hoping to win favor in foreign markets. Exports constituted only 6 to 8 percent of America's gross national product in the post-Civil War era, and well over 80 percent of these went to Canada and Europe rather than to the targets of America's attempted territorial expansion—Latin America, the Pacific, and Asia.

Further evidence of the relative lack of concern for aggressive diplomacy and overseas expansion can be seen in Congress's neglect of the instruments needed for such a policy—the army, the navy, and the diplomatic corps. At the end of the Civil War, the American army had been the most powerful in the world. Soon afterward it averaged only about 28,000 men, most of whom were scattered in frontier forts and Indian territories. None were serving outside the borders of the nation, as contrasted with the post-Spanish-American War period, when American soldiers would be found in Cuba, Puerto Rico, the Philippines, and China.

America also permitted the navy to decline. The United States did not make a rapid transition to warships of steel and steam, as the European powers did. It equipped some wooden vessels with steam engines, but permitted them to fall into disrepair. Many American ships could make only four and a half of their designed twelve knots. In 1885, the secretary of the navy considered the fleet an "alphabet of floating washtubs." He added four new steel-clad ships to the navy in the next two years, beginning a building program that would take the United States navy from twelfth to seventh in the world by 1893. By that year, the United States also had begun its transition from a defensive coastal navy to an offensive fleet with ships capable of ranging across the oceans. But prior to the mid-1890s, the navy was not strong enough to inspire or carry out major expansionist ventures.

America neglected its diplomatic corps even more than the armed forces. In the nineteenth century, most diplomats were selected not for knowledge and competence, but as rewards for partisan service. The State Department often sent uniform instructions to its ministers abroad, failing to differentiate between the problems faced by diplomats in Latin America or Asia as opposed to Europe. Scandal and contempt surrounded American representatives abroad. The U.S. minister to Ecuador attempted to annex the country and to assassinate the British ambassador. The minister to Japan whirled through Tokyo in a carriage with a pistol in his belt, cracking his whip at pedestrians. America's diplomats were woefully underpaid by a Congress that sometimes asked seriously whether the United States needed a diplomatic service at all.

Under these circumstances, it is not surprising that American foreign policy in this period was erratic, amateurish, and devoid of careful planning. Some secretaries of state, like Seward, Fish, and James G. Blaine, seem to have had a reasonably coherent long-range vision, but they did not have orchestrated planning or very specific goals. The presidents of this time were all far more concerned with domestic affairs. Most diplomatic initiatives did not come from Washington, but from foreigners. Many of Seward's expansionist projects and later ones as well came at the behest of substantial factions in Cuba, Santo Domingo, or Hawaii. At other times resident Americans in Latin America, Asia, or the eastern Mediterranean urged annexation, investments, diplomatic protection, or aid in opening markets.

When these suggested projects were expensive or dangerous, they were often thwarted in the same way Seward's had been. Nevertheless, the United States believed with the rest of the Western world that a nation owed protection to its citizens and their property abroad. American diplomats and naval captains were often involved in minor episodes overseas primarily to protect the lives and property of American merchants and missionaries. Usually these caused little stir. So long as the incidents did not involve great expense or the danger of a serious war, Americans assumed that such interventions were the proper function of diplomacy.

If most of these episodes seemed minor to an apathetic American public, they did not necessarily have a correspondingly minor effect on the weak and insular peoples who were their usual objects. American merchants and missionaries, like those of most of Europe, were convinced that their activities were beneficial to the people with whom they were dealing. They felt that the benefits of American industry, civilization, and religion could not help but improve peoples they regarded as backward and barbarian. Only a few among the American general public had any worries that American trade, missionary work, or even annexation could harm others. Most resistance to American intervention came from those who feared its effect on the United States. Americans did not regard their expansion as the equivalent of European imperialism, but feared that the expense and the military force needed for it would destroy economic and civil liberty at home. The nature and impact of American expansionist efforts in the post-Civil War period can be seen in a survey of the major areas at which those efforts were directed.

EXPANSION IN THE CARIBBEAN

When Ulysses S. Grant assumed the presidency, he indulged his dislike of Seward by letting Seward's agreement to purchase the Danish West Indies lapse. No sooner had he turned his back on one Caribbean venture, however, than he plunged headlong into another. The ruling faction of Santo Domingo offered to sell the island to the United States, and Grant seized the opportunity. He personally lobbied various senators and congressmen to appropriate the money, only to be forestalled by the opposition of Charles Sumner as chairman of the Senate Foreign Relations Committee. Sumner persuaded his colleagues that America should avoid imperialism because it was costly and because it would mean American suzerainty over large numbers of Catholics and nonwhites. Sumner was one of the few Americans who truly believed in racial equality and feared for the Cubans themselves, but many others were no doubt persuaded by his argument for less elevated reasons. In any case, Grant never forgave Sumner for destroying his dream. He fired Sumner's closest friend in the diplomatic corps, shook his fist when passing Sumner's house, and finally maneuvered the senator out of his chairmanship.

A bloody rebellion in Cuba in 1868 provided another opportunity for Grant to contemplate a Caribbean acquisition. Some of the Cuban rebels invited American annexation. Many congressmen urged that the United States at least recognize the rebels' belligerence. Secretary of State Fish opposed this, since he was in the midst of pressing Great Britain for damages caused by British recognition of Confederate belligerence. He and others also saw problems with annexing Cuba that were equivalent to those of the proposed purchase of Santo Domingo. When Grant finally ordered Fish to issue a proclamation of neutrality toward Cuba, Fish found a pretext to withhold it. Later, when Congress itself was ready to initiate a recognition of rebel belligerence, Fish threatened to resign, and in this way got Grant to throw his influence against the move.

As long as the Cuban rebellion continued, America teetered on the brink of intervention, stirred by the inevitable sensational incidents that roused popular emotions. Early in the rebellion, the Spanish captured and executed two Americans aboard a ship commandeered by the rebels. One of the captives wrote a highly publicized pathetic letter of farewell to his family. A more serious incident occurred in 1873, when Spanish authorities in Cuba executed fifty-three people aboard the rebel ship *Virginius*, including several

Americans. Only Spain's timely apology and compensation to the families of the dead men prevented American intervention. The danger of American involvement finally ended after an able Spanish General, Arsenio Martínez de Campos, brought the insurgents to yield in 1878 through a judicious mixture of concessions, bribery, and force. But Americans quickly moved in to buy up many of the sugar plantations that had been destroyed or abandoned during the rebellion, and this meant that American interests and emotions would be involved even more thoroughly in any new revolution.

EXPANSION IN CENTRAL AND SOUTH AMERICA

American interests in Central America stumbled over obstacles and domestic opposition similar to those involving Cuba. The completion of the transcontinental railroad in 1869 lessened the need for a canal and raised a powerful interest group that saw a canal as a threat to its prosperity. Grant did make unsuccessful attempts to negotiate new treaties with Colombia and Nicaragua. Earlier treaties with those nations had given Americans the right to cross the peninsula; Grant hoped to gain the right for America actually to construct a canal. Even though he failed, his administration sent survey teams to select the best route. They reported that Nicaragua was preferable to Panama, and for the next quarter-century American ambitions for a canal were focused on Nicaragua.

Nevertheless, the United States was very disturbed in 1879 when Ferdinand de Lesseps, the builder of the Suez Canal, announced that he would begin work on a French-supported canal through Panama. De Lesseps set up a $1.5 million fund for an American committee to purchase support for his canal in the United States, but failed to buy off President Rutherford B. Hayes, who insisted that any canal would in effect be part of the United States coastline and should be controlled by America. Hayes even sent American naval vessels to cruise off the Panama coast to show America's displeasure.

De Lesseps' canal stirred a new interest in the Monroe Doctrine. Except for Polk's references to it in the 1840s, Americans had almost forgotten about Monroe's insistence that Europeans make no new acquisitions in the Western Hemisphere. Suddenly in the 1880s, historians and publicists began debating whether the Founding Fathers had intended the Monroe Doctrine to be enforced by military action. Because De Lesseps' efforts bogged down in the mud and mosquitoes of Panama, the United States was not forced to make such a choice. But the public had been reminded of the doctrine and much more highly sensitized to the nation's interests in Central America.

At the same time that the French began building their canal in Panama, an American company secured the rights from Nicaragua to build a rival canal. But Congress, partly influenced by the transcontinental railroad interests, refused any help, and the project foundered. It also foundered because the provisions of the Clayton-Bulwer Treaty required the United States to share control of any isthmian canal with Great Britain. The American government had tried consistently to get the British to revise the treaty, but the British just as consistently refused. Chester Arthur's secretary of state, Frederick T. Frelinghuysen, decided to push the Nicaraguan project forward by simply ignoring the Clayton-Bulwer Treaty. He negotiated a treaty with Nicaragua providing for a permanent alliance with Nicaragua and a canal totally controlled by the United States. Again the Senate balked and frustrated the design, and Grover Cleveland withdrew the treaty when he took over the presidency.

American efforts in Mexico were somewhat more successful. For a brief time after Porfirio Díaz took power in Mexico in 1876, he and the United States argued over America's right to pursue bandits across the border into Mexico. Finally, under pressure from commercial interests seeking concessions in Mexico, the Hayes administration recognized Díaz's government and ended cross-border pursuits. American investments in and exports to Mexico rose markedly.

This sort of economic expansion in Latin America was a pet project of James G. Blaine, secretary of state to Benjamin Harrison after serving briefly in the same capacity for James Garfield. Blaine organized a Pan-American Conference in 1889 in hopes of establishing a customs union that would allow the nations of the Americas preferred treatment in one another's markets. This would give the United States a competitive edge over Great Britain and other European powers. He also hoped for arbitration agreements that would deter war among Western Hemisphere nations.

Blaine failed in this. The Latin American nations were interested in staving off the influence of both the United States and the Europeans. They asked endorsement of the so-called Calvo Doctrine, named after its Argentine originator, Carlos Calvo. The Calvo Doctrine would have prevented foreign nationals from appealing to their own nations to give diplomatic support for private economic interests. The Latin Americans argued that so long as they treated foreign nationals in the same way they treated their own citizens, foreigners should have no complaints. The United States and the other major powers insisted that their nationals were entitled to certain minimum standards of treatment regardless of how the Latin American nations treated their own citizens. These major powers were totally unwilling to give up their rights under international law to intervene on behalf of the lives and property of their citizens abroad. The Calvo Doctrine raised an issue that would haunt U.S. foreign policy in Latin America for the next century.

Blaine also sought naval bases in the Caribbean to further Latin American trade. He pressured the government of Haiti for Môle St. Nicholas, which controlled the vital windward passage between the islands of Cuba and Santo Domingo. Failing to get Haiti's consent, he refused to cut off supplies flowing from the United States to revolutionaries who had promised to give America the strategic harbor. When the revolutionary faction won, it reneged. Blaine applied some diplomatic pressure, but stopped short of using force. He was content to hope for peaceful annexation of Cuba and Puerto Rico in the next generation.

Blaine and Harrison also became embroiled in a civil war that broke out between the president and the legislature of Chile in 1891. Chile was much less strategically significant to the United States than Central America or the Caribbean, but its nitrate fields were important. Germany and other European nations supported the legislature in hopes of strengthening their commercial position in the country. The United States naturally supported the president. Harrison even intercepted an American ship carrying arms to the legislative faction. Nonetheless, this legislative faction won, and American relations with Chile were severely strained. Foolishly, the commander of an American naval vessel that arrived a couple of weeks later in Valparaiso, Chile, gave shore leave to over a hundred of his crew.

In the ensuing riot, one sailor was killed and six more seriously wounded. The United States demanded an apology. When Chile's foreign minister hesitated and made some rather uncivil remarks about the United States, Harrison sent an ultimatum and prepared for war. Blaine, ill and tired, delayed matters until Chile realized how close to the brink it stood and apologized. The matter quickly blew over, but the Valparaiso incident demonstrated that America's erratic and sometimes belligerent policymakers could rather easily get the United States involved in a war over very minor but emotional issues.

EXPANSION IN THE PACIFIC: HAWAII AND SAMOA

Hawaii had stirred America's imagination for a century. Britain's famous Captain James Cook made the first European contact with the islands while sailing with a grant of immunity from Benjamin Franklin during the American Revolution. America's Captain Robert Gray, who had helped lay claim to Oregon, paid a visit to the islands in 1789 on his way from the Pacific Northwest to China. American fur traders followed Gray's route to the Orient. They reprovisioned in Hawaii and picked up sandalwood to supplement their cargoes of furs. American and European contacts were an ecological disaster for Hawaii, depleting the forests of the islands and killing the inhabitants. Disease and alcohol affected the Hawaiians much as they had the American Indians. There were 200,000 Hawaiians when Captain Cook arrived in 1778; by 1890 this population had dwindled to some 35,000.

The sandalwood trade prompted the rise of mercantile establishments in Hawaii to supply the American and European traders. Four of these firms were American. As the sandalwood forests declined following the War of 1812, the slack was picked up by the shift of the whaling industry from the Atlantic to the Pacific, again led by Americans. Between 1824 and 1843, 1,400 of the 1,700 whaling ships that arrived at Honolulu were American. Missionaries sent out from New England after 1820 further enhanced American influence in Hawaii. Within a few years, they had converted much of the island population to their Calvinist brand of Christianity. In the process, missionaries also systematized a written form of the Hawaiian language, established an education system, and entered a long rivalry with the dissolute whalers and the European missionaries of other faiths. American missionaries and their descendants served as the primary advisors to most Hawaiian monarchs and chiefs. To a great extent, Hawaii became a cultural outpost of the United States.

But the British and French also had whalers, naval captains, and missionaries seeking influence in the islands. They were much in the minority, but some of the early Hawaiian kings, particularly Kamehameha III and IV, encouraged them as a counterweight to the Americans. American leaders were quick to recognize the value of Hawaii, and in 1842, Daniel Webster announced that the United States would not take Hawaii as a colony, but would oppose any attempt by the British or French to do so. Millard Fillmore renewed this declaration in 1851. The Democrats were willing to go even further: Franklin Pierce's administration negotiated a treaty of outright annexation in 1854. The treaty failed, however, because of the death of the Hawaiian monarch involved.

During the Civil War, sugar began to replace whaling as the primary economic activity of Hawaii, and most of the plantation owners were Americans or descendants of Americans. It was vital to their livelihood to have access to the American market, something domestic sugar producers opposed intensely. Secretaries of State Seward and Fish saw the benefit of tying the Hawaiian economy more firmly to the United States, since the increasing trade with China and Japan made Hawaii more and more important as a stopover on the route to East Asia. The advent of steam-driven warships also enhanced the strategic value of Hawaii. No fleet could attack the Pacific Coast of the United States without coaling in the islands. Nevertheless, the Senate defeated Seward's reciprocity treaty with Hawaii and Fish's suggestion to annex the islands fell dead in Grant's cabinet.

In some desperation, Hawaiian sugar plantation owners tried to purchase reciprocity by offering Pearl Harbor to the United States. King Kalakaua made a highly publicized tour of America in 1875 and got the reciprocity treaty. But agitation in the islands disrupted the process by forcing the Hawaiian government to withdraw the offer. Hawaii promised only to deny the port to any other country. The reciprocity treaty finally slipped through Congress anyway. Hawaiian sugar production boomed, and planters imported thousands of Asians to work in the fields to supplement the rapidly declining population of native Hawaiians. Although the reciprocity treaty tied Hawaii firmly to the American economy, some Americans worried that this Asian immigration might remove Hawaii from the American orbit. Faced with domestic opposition to a renewal of the reciprocity treaty in 1884 and forced to acknowledge that reciprocity cost the United States more than it brought in, the American government had to make the strategic importance of the islands clear if it hoped to get a renewed agreement through Congress. Consequently, the United States insisted on and finally received the exclusive right to use Pearl Harbor.

In 1890, however, American domestic sugar interests forced revision of Hawaii's preferred tariff status. Hawaiian planters now saw American annexation as the most promising means of restoring their former prosperity.

Their determination increased when King Kalakaua was succeeded by his sister, Queen Lilioukalani. Lilioukalani announced that she would proclaim a new constitution depriving the minority white planters of the special governing privileges they had won from Kalakaua. With secret encouragement from Benjamin Harrison's cabinet, Hawaii's planters resolved to secure Lilioukalani's acquiescence to American annexation one way or another. In 1893, in a nearly bloodless coup, they deposed the queen, set up a revolutionary government, and offered the islands to the United States. The United States minister to Hawaii ordered sailors from the American cruiser *Boston* ashore during the coup to maintain order and thus lent support to the revolution. He also granted recognition of the new government on his own authority. Harrison quickly negotiated a treaty of annexation and sent it to the Senate.

Grover Cleveland took office as president before the Senate took action, and he withdrew the treaty for further investigation. The commissioner he appointed reported that the American minister and the crew of the *Boston* had exercised undue influence in helping impose a government opposed by the majority of the islanders. As a consequence, Cleveland refused to resubmit the treaty, and even talked of restoring Lilioukalani to the throne. The provisional government pledged to resist any such attempt with force so Cleveland dropped that idea, but he continued to block American annexation.

Ironically, while the United States failed to annex Hawaii in the post-Civil War era, it did annex a Pacific island group far less significant to American interests. Samoa, with its harbor of Pago Pago, was a convenient steppingstone to the British colonies of Australia and New Zealand even though it was far more remote from America's Pacific Coast, far less valuable strategically, and provided access to a less desirable market area than did Ha-

Figure 7   President Grover Cleveland, who blocked the annexation of Hawaii for a time. Portrait courtesy of the National Archives.

waii. In 1872, an American naval commander signed an unauthorized treaty giving the United States an exclusive naval base in Samoa. The Senate rejected it, but President Grant was interested, and his successor Hayes concluded a nonexclusive naval base treaty six years later. The British and Germans also were interested in Samoa, and the American consul took it upon himself to agree to a three-way government of the powers over the islands. Although the American government never officially approved of the arrangement, the three consuls were the de facto government of Samoa for many years.

The dangerous entanglement involved in this arrangement became clear when in 1885 the Germans moved troops into the islands to quash native resistance. The American consul responded by announcing an American protectorate. President Cleveland disavowed the consul, but as the Germans fastened their grip more firmly, Cleveland detected an American moral commitment to the area and a German insult to American prestige. He ordered American warships to Samoa, where they joined British and German ships, all watching one another warily. The crisis subsided quickly when a hurricane sank all three fleets, killing 150 people. The German Chancellor Otto von Bismarck then called for a conference. The subsequent Treaty of Berlin of 1889 involved the United States in official joint supervision with the British and Germans over the Samoan king and brought American political entanglement in an area of little importance and great distance.

American expansion in the Pacific remained dubious and debatable to many Americans. Henry Adams, for instance, was at first a strong supporter of annexations in the Pacific. He turned away from the idea in 1893 after observing the effects of colonialism in Tahiti. He became convinced that America had no future in the Pacific, and urged instead that the United States look to Siberia. Siberia was "empty," and when Russia went to pieces, as Adams confidently expected, Siberia could be colonized and populated, in the manner of the American West. Thus the United States could avoid the problems inherent in colonizing remote areas densely populated by foreign and probably inferior peoples like the "worthless Malay types" Adams considered dominant in the Philippines. Adams's vacillation demonstrated how unsure even expansionists were as to the forms American expansion should take.

EXPANSION IN EAST ASIA: CHINA, JAPAN, AND KOREA

Just as merchants, missionaries, and naval captains entangled the United States in the Pacific, they likewise encouraged involvement in East Asia. Americans, however, had no ambitions for outright annexations in East Asia, as they did in the Pacific and the Caribbean.

Americans began trade with China immediately after the revolution. As an independent nation, the United States no longer had an obligation to respect the monopoly Great Britain had given the East India Company over the

China trade. The *Empress of China,* which sailed in 1784, was the first of many American ships that ultimately carried close to one-third of China's trade in the nineteenth century. Like other foreign merchants, of whom the British were the most dominant, Americans dealt with China under very strict Chinese rules historians generally call "the tribute system."

The Chinese visualized their territory as the center of the earth. They regarded any contact they allowed between themselves and outsiders as a privilege far more beneficial to the foreigners than to China. They did not think of dealings between representatives of foreign governments and their emperor as diplomacy between equal sovereign nations, but as inferiors paying tribute and requesting favors from a superior. They looked upon European merchants, missionaries, and diplomats as "overseas barbarians" bringing ideas, customs, and merchandise that were only marginally useful at best and positively harmful at worst. To protect their people, the Chinese emperors restricted European traders to the port of Canton and prohibited them or their fellow countrymen from venturing into China's interior. Those who violated the court's standing proclamation, especially missionaries, faced harsh punishment.

Under this system, Europeans found none of the trappings of trade and diplomacy to which they were accustomed. There were no treaties, no consulates, no diplomatic relations, and no protection of European lives and property by home governments. The consequences became clear to Americans in 1821, when the Chinese authorities in Canton demanded that an American merchant ship turn over one of its sailors, a man named Terranova. The Chinese claimed that Terranova, in carelessly dumping garbage overboard, had struck and killed a Chinese woman on a raft below. The Chinese authorities had Terranova strangled, after which they acknowledged the Americans' "proper submissiveness."

It was not such events as the Terranova incident, however, that brought the end of the tribute system; instead, it was the imbalance of trade. There was a far greater demand in Europe for Chinese products like tea and rhubarb than there was in China for the hides, furs, sandalwood, and ginseng the Europeans brought in exchange. The Europeans and Americans increasingly offset this imbalance by bringing opium to China from the British colony of India. The Chinese court had a standing prohibition against the importation of opium but did not enforce it strictly until 1839, when the volume of the trade began to threaten both the physical and economic health of China. Not only did opium ravage its addicts, the demand for it reversed the balance of trade. Silver flowed out of China to pay for the excess of European imports over Chinese exports.

By enforcing the prohibition against opium, the Chinese court threatened the whole structure of Europe's China trade. Great Britain resorted to naval force, and this Opium War of 1839–1842 resulted in a complete British victory. The British forced China to sign a treaty opening five more ports to European trade and to cede Hong Kong as a British naval base. A year later, a supplementary treaty limited China's tariffs on foreign goods. It also gave

Britain most favored nation status, meaning that England received any concession China gave to another foreign power. Finally, this supplementary treaty established the right of extraterritoriality, allowing British offenders in China to be tried not by Chinese courts, but by the British themselves.

As the treaty system replaced the tribute system, the United States moved quickly to share the spoils. In 1843, Caleb Cushing signed a treaty with China that gave the United States as well as Britain most favored nation status and extraterritoriality. The Chinese, in their traditional tactic of dividing their enemies, hoped to exploit the rivalry they vaguely recognized between Great Britain and the United States and to use the Americans to protect China against ambitious Europeans. Soon other nations, notably France and Russia, were clamoring for similar treaties, and each subsequent concession China made to these nations automatically accrued to all previous treaty countries under the most favored nation clause. China soon found itself whipsawed between the foreign powers.

At first, the Chinese did not regard the concessions under an obviously unequal treaty system as significant. It did not seem to matter that limits on China's tariff were unmatched by limits on European tariffs, for Chinese products would always be in demand. If Europeans were accountable for their own citizens in China under extraterritoriality, that relieved Chinese authorities of the task of disciplining the outsiders. And if Europeans did not furnish similar extraterritorial privileges to Chinese abroad, it served those Chinese right for abandoning the civilized world to reside in barbarian lands.

In the 1850s, however, a new Chinese emperor began to resist European pressures for further concessions. To his consternation, he found himself faced at the same time with an uprising known as the Taiping Rebellion, which ultimately cost China between 20 and 40 million lives. The Europeans used their navies to attack the distracted Chinese government. They destroyed the forts guarding the capital at Peking, burned and looted the Summer Palace, and forced new treaty concessions from the emperor.

The American administrations of Pierce and Buchanan supported treaty revision, but ordered no American use of force. They reprimanded two naval officers who participated in bombardments against their instructions. Nevertheless, they ordered American diplomats in China to partake of the benefits of treaty revision, and the United States joined in successfully pressing for the opening of eleven more treaty ports. Under the new treaties, foreigners, including missionaries, were permitted to travel anywhere in China, tariffs were limited to 5 percent, the legality of the opium trade was confirmed, and foreign diplomats were permitted to reside in Peking. Foreign diplomats, missionaries, merchants, and their property would be protected by European and American gunboats sailing not just on the coast, but up the major rivers into the heart of China. Subsequently, foreign soldiers, including two Americans and the famous British officer C. G. "Chinese" Gordon, served as leaders in the Chinese army that restored imperial authority over the Taiping rebels. In addition, the Imperial Maritime Customs Service, managed primarily by British subjects, took charge of collecting tariff revenues for China, giving foreigners control of what had become the Chinese government's primary source of revenue.

The United States had played a fairly passive role in the establishment of the treaty system. It avoided force by and large and acquired concessions by benefiting from the military activities of other European powers in what some have aptly called "jackal diplomacy." The Chinese thus tended to regard the United States as the best of a bad lot of European exploiters. At least the Americans had no territorial designs on China and opposed the inclination of some European powers to carve China into exclusive colonial outposts. Instead, the Americans supported a unified China open to the trade of all nations. The Chinese even sent an American, Anson Burlingame, as their emissary to the United States and the major European capitals in 1866.

Whatever goodwill might have existed toward the United States was thoroughly dissipated by the treatment of Chinese in the United States in the latter half of the nineteenth century. By 1868, over 100,000 Chinese had come to the United States in search of work. There was a great reaction against them, particularly in the West, where the completion of the transcontinental railroad threw many Chinese railway workers into competition for new jobs with recent Irish immigrants. Violence and lynchings erupted, and Congress responded by trying to outlaw all further Chinese immigration. President Hayes vetoed the bill because it violated the Burlingame Treaty, which permitted open immigration to both countries. Instead, he negotiated a new treaty in which China permitted the United States to suspend rather than prohibit Chinese immigration. Congress seized the opportunity by suspending Chinese immigration for ten years, with the obvious intention of renewing the suspension indefinitely thereafter. If the Chinese government had not previously bothered about the fate of Chinese abroad, the American breach of faith made it highly sensitive now. Americans continued to regard the Chinese patronizingly as friendly protégés, but time would prove that a silly conceit.

For the most part, merchants, missionaries, and a few independent-minded naval officers dominated America's relations with China in the nineteenth century. The American government itself paid little attention to diplomatic relations with the Middle Kingdom. In Japan, however, the U.S. government played the major role in opening relations.

Japan, like China, originally tried to isolate European influence. The Tokugawa shogunate opened the port of Nagasaki to Dutch traders but turned away the ships of all other Europeans, including Americans. The Japanese even treated shipwrecked sailors like criminals; they were killed or sent in cages to Nagasaki for repatriation. As Pacific whaling and trade with China expanded, the number of sailors receiving such treatment increased.

In the 1850s, Secretary of State Daniel Webster instructed Commodore Matthew Perry to lead an American naval squadron to Japan to seek protection for shipwrecked seamen and property, to open trade, and to gain the right to deposit coal for refueling ships on their way to East Asia. Perry was to warn Japan especially that any further acts of cruelty to American sailors would be severely punished. After two visits in force, Perry got Japan to sign a treaty permitting Americans to purchase supplies at two insignificant ports. The treaty also offered protection for shipwrecked mariners and accorded most favored nation status to the United States. The Japanese signed at least in part because they knew that other European powers were about to demand even greater concessions, and they hoped this moderate treaty might serve as a restraining precedent. Great Britain, Russia, and the Netherlands did sign similar treaties with Japan in short order.

Perry urged that the United States continue an active policy in East Asia. He occupied the Bonin Islands and asked the administration to make Taiwan (then known as Formosa) an American protectorate. But the government insisted that the United States' only interest should be the protection of American citizens and property in the area. The new American consul in Japan, Townsend Harris, managed to gain fresh concessions from Japan anyway. He reminded the Japanese that the Americans were more moderate than the European powers and induced them to sign a treaty which opened four new ports to American trade, gave Americans the right to reside in several areas of Japan and practice their religion, and set a limit on the tariffs the Japanese could charge. Since the European nations signing treaties with Japan had gained the right of extraterritoriality, Harris reluctantly sought and acquired that as well. Thus Japan was subject to an unequal treaty system similar to China's.

After Harris's agreements with Japan in 1857 and 1858, the United States reverted to the status of follower rather than leader of European influence in Japan. The United States cooperated with Great Britain and other naval powers in resisting attempts by some Japanese leaders to return to the old system and remove the foreigners. An American ship participated in the bombardment of areas of southern Japan to put down rebellious clans. When the Meiji Restoration of 1868 brought to power a number of Japanese modernizers who saw Western technology as essential to Japan, America returned happily to a policy of peaceful trade. By the turn of the century the United States even led the movement that ultimately ended the tariff limitations and extraterritoriality.

With China and Japan opened to Western trade by the 1850s, only the Hermit Kingdom of Korea remained closed. American naval ships tried unsuccessfully to open Korea in 1867 and 1871; Japan succeeded in doing so in 1876. Several Americans tried to follow in Japan's footsteps and negotiate a treaty with Korea, but they failed. Then in 1882, Commodore Robert Shufeldt realized that Korea wanted to use China to balance the influence of Japan. By approaching Korea through the Chinese government, he managed to negotiate a treaty that protected American sailors and gained the usual concessions of most favored nation and extraterritoriality. Shufeldt acted without instructions or support from home, and American influence might have dwindled rapidly except for the remarkable activities of the new American minister, a missionary named Horace Allen. Allen actually became a close advisor of the Korean rulers. Neither the American government nor

American merchants shared Allen's enthusiasm for Korea, however, and the American position faded as China, Japan, and Russia began to compete in earnest for the strategically placed peninsula.

Thus American diplomacy in the post-Civil War period was limited essentially to the protection of the lives and property of American citizens abroad, most of them merchants and missionaries. The navy, composed of outdated cruisers, was the primary instrument of this protection. It sought to free the seas of pirates and to remove obstacles to American navigation and trade, whether posed by the European naval powers or by the weaker countries of Latin America and Asia. A few ambitious expansionists serving as president or secretary of state initiated attempts to acquire areas important to navigation and trade. But in this era almost all such initiatives were aborted by countervailing power, apathy, and ideological distaste for incorporating or suppressing populated, noncontiguous, and culturally or racially different peoples. It would be different in the 1890s: Americans would then pursue expansion far more aggressively and successfully.

CONTROVERSIAL ISSUES AND FURTHER READING

The primary historiographical dispute over mid-nineteenth-century U.S. diplomacy has been whether to visualize it as a part of a continuous expansionist drive toward empire or as a relatively isolationist hiatus between the era of territorial expansion prior to the Civil War and the acquiring of an overseas empire following the Spanish-American War of 1898. Revisionist historians, emphasizing the concern in this period for expanding America's foreign trade and the attempts to acquire naval bases to defend it, portray the era as an age of imperialism. They tend to equate the expansion of trade with more overt forms of imperialism, such as formal territorial annexation or military intervention. They argue that America's economy has been so strong that its trade dominates and coerces other peoples almost as surely as political and military force. Often they refer to this economic expansionism as the new imperialism, informal imperialism, or neo-imperialism to differentiate between it and the more traditional military or political domination of colonies. Many revisionists advocate the development of self-sufficient national economies to avoid much foreign trade and the danger of such neo-imperialism. The most influential book asserting this view is Walter LaFeber's *The New Empire: An Interpretation of American Expansion, 1860–1898* (1963). William Appleman Williams added to LaFeber's interpretation by showing the concern of farmers as well as rising industrialists for overseas markets in *The Roots of the Modern American Empire* (1969).

More traditional historians agree that expanded trade can result in the dominance of one people by another and tempt nations to further overt military and political interventions to protect their markets, resources, and investments in weaker lands. But they are unwilling to accept the idea that this is truly equivalent to formal colonialism, or even similar enough to be called neo-imperialism. They portray the post-Civil War era, which saw the defeat of most attempts at annexation of further territory, as an isolationist contrast with the previous era of rapid territorial expansion. They contrast it also with the subsequent period when, following the Spanish-American War, the United States acquired several formal colonies and pursued other foreign interests far more aggresssively and purposefully. The careful reader of this book will notice that I agree more with these traditional historians than with the revisionists.

The best traditional works emphasizing the relative isolationism of this period and the contrast with later imperialism are Robert L. Beisner's thoughtful *From the Old Diplomacy to the New, 1865–1900* (1975), and the best survey of post-Civil War diplomacy, Charles S. Campbell, *The Transformation of American Foreign Relations, 1865–1900* (1976). Standing somewhere between these authors and the revisionists is Milton Plesur, *America's Outward Thrust: Approaches to Foreign Affairs, 1865–1890* (1971). Other important works on more limited topics are David M. Pletcher, *The Awkward Years: American Foreign Relations under Garfield and Arthur* (1962); David Donald, *Charles Sumner and the Rights of Man* (1970); Allan Nevins, *Hamilton Fish* (1937); Glyndon Van Deusen, *William Henry Seward* (1967); and a revisionist analysis of Seward, Ernest N. Paolino, *The Foundations of American Empire* (1973). For contrasting views of the tariff issue and its significance for American expansionism in this period, see Tom Terill's revisionist *The Tariff, Politics, and American Foreign Policy, 1874–1901* (1973); Paul S. Holbo's critiques of the revisionists, "Economics, Emotion, and Expansion: An Emerging Foreign Policy," in H. Wayne Morgan, ed., *The Gilded Age* (1970) and *Tarnished Expansion: The Alaska Scandal, the Press, and Congress, 1867–1871* (1983). See also Mira Wilkins, *The Emergence of the Multinational Enterprise: American Business Abroad from the Colonial Era to 1914* (1970), and an outstanding analysis of American business, naval, and missionary activities in the Mediterranean, James A. Field, *America and the Mediterranean World, 1776–1882* (1969).

The important part played by the navy in the diplomacy of this era can be traced in Kenneth J. Hagan, *American Gunboat Diplomacy and the Old Navy, 1877–1889* (1973); Harold and Margaret Sprout, *The Rise of American Naval Power, 1776–1918* (1939); and John A. S. Grenville and George B. Young, *Politics, Strategy, and American Diplomacy* (1967). Policy toward Latin America is best surveyed by Dexter Perkins, *The Monroe Doctrine, 1867–1907* (1937). See also Samuel F. Bemis, *The Latin American Policy of the United States* (1943); Karl M. Schmitt, *Mexico and the United States, 1821–1973* (1974); Russell H. Bastert, "A New Approach to the Origins of Blaine's Pan American Policy," *Hispanic Historical Review*, 39 (1959). On Hawaii, see Merze Tate, *The United States and the Hawaiian Kingdom* (1965), and Thomas J. Osborne, *"Empire Can Wait": American Opposition to Hawaiian Annexation, 1893–1898* (1981). On Samoa, see Paul M. Kennedy, *The Samoan Tangle: A Study in Anglo-German-American Relations, 1878–1900* (1974), and George H. Ryden, *The Foreign Policy of the United States in Relation to Samoa* (1933). On China, see John K. Fairbank, *The United States and China* (3rd ed., 1971); Warren I. Cohen, *America's Response to China* (1971); and Immanuel C. Y. Hsu, *China's Entrance into the Family of Nations* (1960). On Japan, see Charles Neu, *The Troubled Encounter: The United States and Japan* (1975); Akira Iriye, *Across the Pacific* (1967); and Edwin O. Reischauer, *The United States and Japan* (3rd ed., 1965). On Korea, see Fred Harvey Harrington, *God, Mammon, and the Japanese: Horace N. Allen and Korean-American Relations, 1884–1905* (1944).

CHAPTER 8

The Spanish-American War and the Decision for Empire

THE IMPERIAL SURGE, 1895–1917

It is doubtful that many Americans living in the early 1890s realized that they stood on the threshold of a new age in American diplomacy. National politics still revolved around internal questions. Americans regarded the economic issues stemming from industrialization and immigration as essentially domestic ones, despite rising concerns for foreign trade. The warnings of the Founding Fathers against foreign entanglements, military establishments, and colonial oppression still dominated popular attitudes toward foreign policy. Little of the nation's economic strength had been translated into the military or diplomatic power necessary for large-scale overseas intervention, and most Americans would have been aghast at any suggestion that the United States should involve itself in a major way in Europe or Asia. The balance of opinion was more tenuous on acquisitions closer to home, however, especially if they might be annexed without much fuss or expense. Rejections of treaties or petitions for the annexation of Santo Domingo, Cuba, Haiti, and Hawaii had been somewhat accidental, involving political partisanship, personalities, and fortuitous events that swung the balance against territorial expansion. The balance against overseas annexations and involvements was becoming increasingly precarious, ready to be altered by a major crisis or opportunity that could give it a substantial push.

The forces inclining the United States toward overseas expansion and intervention had developed rapidly in the post-Civil War period. Most important of these was America's growing power. The nation's population increased from 39 million in 1870 to 63 million in 1890. By the 1890s, America surpassed all nations in the production of coal, oil, and steel, the sinews of modern power until the atomic age. Popular writers and politicians made clear to the American people the strategic and economic benefits of acquiring Caribbean naval bases, an isthmian canal, and Hawaii. They helped translate hazy inclinations into systematic thought patterns.

The Spanish-American War supplied the catalyst to create a new national majority ready to intrude into the realm of great power politics and accept an overseas empire. The original rationale of the Spanish-American War, intervention to free Cuba from Spain, did not stretch the old diplomacy too much, especially when Congress declared its intention not to annex Cuba. But the thrill of military combat and victory broke down many of the barriers to overseas intervention and annexation. The United States took Puerto Rico, the Philippines, Guam, and Wake Island, completed the annexation of Hawaii, and asserted a protectorate over Cuba. It then acquired the Panama canal route, undertook wholesale military interventions in Central America and the Caribbean, and increased its diplomatic activity in Asia, as symbolized by the issuance of the Open Door Notes.

Even in this imperial aftermath of the Spanish-American War, Americans remained wary of European entanglements. They defended their Latin American interventions by claiming they were necessary to ward off European expansion and consequent conflict with the interests of the United States. They offered the Open Door in Asia as an alternative to European attempts to carve China further into spheres of interest, a process that might entangle the United States in European balance of power politics. Finally, however, World War I dragged the United States into the European arena. Americans became thoroughly enmeshed in global politics.

THE DIPLOMATIC REVOLUTION OF THE 1890s

Foreign nations seemed no more aware that the United States was on the verge of adopting a new diplomatic posture in the 1890s than Americans themselves. When the Turkish sultan sought to cut expenses in 1880, he decided to eliminate diplomatic missions in several minor powers, including Sweden, Belgium, the Netherlands, and the United States. The German envoy in Washington offered to take a pay cut if his superiors would transfer him to Madrid. Russia neglected to send a minister to the United States for two years after the old one had left.

These nations failed to realize that the Industrial Revolution had increased American strength tremendously. By the 1890s, the United States was manufacturing almost as much as Great Britain, Germany, and France combined. This gave the United States the means to expand its diplomatic role from a regional to a global power. Industry also provided a motive for such a change in American foreign policy, creating more need for overseas markets. By the 1890s, manufactures had surpassed agricultural products as America's main exports. Of all the nations in the world, only Great Britain outstripped the United States in the total value of its exports, and Britain's lead was clearly temporary. America's increasing desire for overseas markets naturally led to calls for a more active diplomacy.

Throughout the post-Civil War period there had been no lack of voices calling for a more aggressive military and diplomatic policy to accompany America's increasing economic strength and expanding foreign trade. Naval officers like Admiral Stephen Luce extolled the benefits of a larger, more modern navy. In the 1880s these officers succeeded in beginning a naval building program that produced long-range, steam-driven, steel-clad battle-ships. Otherwise, as we have seen, the United States pursued overseas markets, coaling stations, and strategically located colonies sporadically and ineffectually. Then, in the 1890s, advocates of an aggressive foreign policy took advantage of several traumatic events to propel America into a policy of global intervention and the acquisition of an overseas empire.

The economic panic of 1893, initiating a four-year depression more severe than any America faced until 1929, did much to turn influential Americans toward a more active pursuit of foreign markets. Fifteen thousand businesses failed in 1893, including several major railroads. Hundreds of banks went under. Three million people were left jobless, some 20 percent of the workforce. Farm production and prices plummeted. Violent strikes occurred in coal mines and railroads, and federal troops were called in to break up the great Pullman Strike. Discontented farmers flocked into the Populist party. They demanded currency inflation by unlimited coinage of silver, advocated a graduated income tax, and urged government control of railroads and utilities. Some leaders of government and industry feared that America stood on the brink of revolution.

The depression highlighted other disturbing trends that had seemed less ominous when the country was more prosperous. Large combinations of capital were becoming increasingly dominant in American business, threatening the older America of smaller competitive enterprises. Cities expanded tremendously, undercutting the power and prestige of the countryside and the older prototypical American, the yeoman farmer. Immigrants flowed into these cities at a staggering rate; over 500,000 arrived in America every year. Most of these newcomers were from Southern and Eastern Europe, bringing with them cultural mores and religious practices that clashed with the Protestantism and Anglo-Saxon culture of the dominant elite.

In addition to the problems posed by immigration, historian Frederick Jackson Turner startled the nation by publicizing the fact that the census of 1890 no longer recognized the existence of a frontier line in the West. Turner warned that the disappearance of this frontier would mean declining opportunities for internal territorial and economic expansion. Since he thought much of America's democracy had stemmed from the frontier, he feared its disappearance would have political as well as economic consequences.

All this produced in America what historian Richard Hofstadter called a "psychic crisis." Powerful and wealthy as the United States was, many Americans seem to have feared that the nation was close to blowing up, or at least entering a decline in wealth and political well-being. For some, this led to depression and apathy; but others sought to deny their own failure of confidence by embarking on a frantic crusade, motivated by the hope that if they could convince others of their virtue and virility, they could convince themselves as well.

The economic, political, and psychic crisis brought on by the depression of 1893 caused some soul-searching among leading figures in the Cleveland administration, Congress, and business. They argued that the depression resulted from a glut of American agricultural and industrial products. Since America's factories and farms were producing more than domestic markets could consume, the United States needed to pursue overseas markets more aggressively. Yet at the same time that exports came to seem so much more important to many American leaders, foreign markets seemed to be closing against American trade. European nations were carving up Africa, and in the wake of Japan's victory over China in 1895, were seeking to increase their spheres of influence in Asia as well. These European colonial powers generally erected discriminatory tariff barriers in their newly acquired territories. Even in Great Britain, the trend seemed to be toward closing markets to foreign competition. Joseph Chamberlain advocated preferential tariff structures throughout the British Empire, which formerly had been relatively open to exports from the United States.

While the depression frightened the United States into a more interventionist policy abroad, intellectual and religious currents provided a moral rationale for expansion. The surge of European imperialism in the 1880s and 1890s led to a wealth of literature praising the beneficence of European colonial government. Writers such as Frederick Fabri and James Anthony Froude spread these ideas to the attentive and cosmopolitan portion of the American public that was aware of and concerned for national policy.

Influential politicians also helped propagate the imperial gospel among Americans. Theodore Roosevelt, for instance, argued that peace could not be had "until the civilized nations have expanded in some shape over the barbarous nations. This means the cooperation of the civilized peoples of the earth to that end, whatever the cost or time." Naturally Roosevelt thought the United States the best of such civilized nations, but in areas outside America's interests, he was willing to support the imperialism of other European powers. For instance, he thought England would be doing "her duty as a civilized nation" by colonizing the Sudan. He also said it was in the interest of civilization that the English-speaking race be dominant in the Western Hemisphere.

Roosevelt did not believe such colonialism ran contrary to the traditions of the Founding Fathers expressed in the Declaration of Independence and the Farewell Address. In his best-selling book, *The Winning of the West,* he pointed out that the Founding Fathers had conquered and colonized the Indians. This had been perfectly justified, he thought, for it had been impossible "to avoid conflicts with the weaker race, unless we were willing to see the American continent fall into the hands of some other strong power," or "willing that the whole continent west of the Alleghenies should remain an unpeopled waste, the hunting-ground of savages."

A still more influential propagator of the imperial vision in the 1890s was Roosevelt's friend, Admiral Alfred Thayer Mahan. His world-famous book, *The Influence of Sea Power upon History,* extolled the benefits of Christianity and Western civilization and noted the role the British navy had played in establishing the British Empire for the mutual benefit of the British economy and these barbaric natives. He urged that the United States likewise build a strong, two-ocean navy, acquire bases and coaling stations in the Caribbean and the Pacific, build an isthmian canal, and thus extend protection to the extensive commerce that would carry American civilization to Asia and Latin America while enriching the United States. He pointed out that modern technology had brought within reach lands that the Founding Fathers had considered far beyond the realm of vital American interests. Conversely, he warned that the United States now was also within easier reach of foreign powers and would become increasingly vulnerable militarily if it did not build its navy and take a more active interest in overseas affairs.

American missionaries reinforced the inclination of the followers of Mahan and Roosevelt to seek a more activist foreign policy. Josiah Strong embodied this missionary spirit. His best seller, *Our Country*, proclaimed that the Anglo-Saxon race of America, a "race of unequaled energy, with all the majesty of numbers and the might of wealth behind it—the representative, let us hope, of the largest liberty, the purest Christianity, the highest civilization—having developed peculiarly aggressive traits calculated to impress its institutions upon mankind, will spread itself over the earth. If I read not amiss, this powerful race will move down upon Mexico, down upon Central and South America, out upon the islands of the sea, over Africa and Beyond. And can any one doubt that the result of this competition of races will be the 'survival of the fittest'?" Strong emphasized that this expansion need not be a "war of extermination . . . ; the contest is not one of arms, but of vitality and of civilization." Nonetheless, his description of international affairs as a competition of races culminating in the survival of the fittest could not help but contribute to a more aggressive American foreign policy.

"The survival of the fittest" was a catchword of the 1890s and a powerful intellectual support for the "large policy" of people like Roosevelt and Mahan. It derived from Charles Darwin's path-breaking work on biological evolution that portrayed natural selection as the means by which species had evolved from primitive forms to their present status. An Englishman, Herbert Spencer, adapted Darwin's idea of biological evolution to the realm of human social affairs. Spencer theorized that civilizations, like biological species, progressed by natural selection and the survival of the fittest. Spencer's Social Darwinism was translated by many imperialists into a formula for international relations. Nations and races competed with one another; the strong survived, the weak succumbed. Thus civilization progressed.

Some Americans found the Darwinian emphasis on survival of the fittest a convenient rationale for their own desire to participate in a glorious fight. Most of the generation alive in the 1890s had not experienced the blood and terror of the Civil War. That war appeared to them in retrospect as a great adventure fought for profound principles. It seemed far more exciting than the dreary economic concerns that dominated their own industrial America of the 1890s. They were like adolescents desperate to test their new power in a fight with an evil bully. Some even agreed with Theodore Roosevelt that "This country needs a war."

The depression, the "psychic crisis," the increased need for foreign markets, the rapid development of modern communications and transportation, the surge of European imperialism, and the development of powerful, systematic rationales for overseas expansion helped set the stage for the Spanish-American War and its imperial aftermath. But there were still strong voices for restraint, even from among those one might have expected to be in the vanguard of imperialism.

Two of America's most prominent Social Darwinists, William Graham Sumner and John Burgess, were nonetheless strong opponents of overseas expansionism. So was the historian James Schouler, who had written paeans to earlier continental expansion. Such people could agree that the United States housed a superior race and civilization, yet oppose overseas acquisitions. Like the older generations of Americans, who had an equally fervent if not so systematic belief in American superiority, they were convinced the United States best fulfilled its missionary impulse by serving as a model for foreigners rather than as a conquerer and reformer.

James Schouler summarized these ideas in an article opposing the annexation of Hawaii. He thought Americans did not "wish these islands thrown upon them, under a race conquest, like that of Cortes over the Astecs [sic] in Mexico, but must feel well assured that the Hawaiians themselves come toward us with open arms and of their own free accord, as well as resident foreigners who undertake to pledge their consent." For "notwithstanding our innate and earnest desire to diffuse the blessings of freedom which we enjoy over the rest of the globe, one would think that, with Indians not yet reclaimed, negroes emancipated only by the bloodiest and costliest of civil strifes, and, as the latest factor, Chinese disturbing our national peace of mind,—not to speak of the refuse of European nations cast lately upon us so constantly by the Atlantic tides,—this Union had enough of the problem of amalgamating races into one brotherhood to last at least for the rest of this century." Schouler thought America's present Hawaiian trade ties and coaling stations satisfied the national interest and that the United States should avoid territorial annexation and overt political rule.

THE VENEZUELAN BOUNDARY DISPUTE

The Venezuela crisis of 1895 demonstrated the delicate balance between the conflicting impulses for an aggressive and a restrained foreign policy. Grover Cleveland, the president who precipitated the crisis with his belligerent claims of American rights abroad, was the same man who had rejected the Hawaiian annexation treaty two years before. Thus he embodied within himself these competing urges. Perhaps he tipped toward intervention in the Venezuelan case because the issue involved opposition to British annexations rather than pursuit of American acquisitions, and Venezuela was a Caribbean nation rather than a Pacific one like Hawaii. Still, Cleveland's conduct in the Venezuelan crisis puzzles most historians.

Venezuela and the British colony of Guiana had never agreed on the boundary between them. For many years the conflict had been muted because the boundary ran through uninhabited and seemingly valueless land. Still the issue had the potential for serious conflict. Venezuela claimed that its proper border included nearly two-thirds of the territory Britain already ruled as Guiana, while the British insisted that the true boundary was a line favorable to Guiana established by Robert Schomburgk in a survey commissioned by the British in 1840.

The United States had expressed mild concern about the border controversy from time to time in the post-Civil War era, but the issue heated up in 1894 when an American agent paid by Venezuela, William L. Scruggs, published a vitriolic pamphlet accusing the British of open aggression and defiance of the Monroe Doctrine. Congress responded with a unanimous vote on behalf of a resolution, drafted largely by Scruggs himself, urging Venezuela and Great Britain to submit the dispute to arbitration. Venezuela wanted arbitration rather than direct negotiations with Great Britain because it knew that its large delinquent debt to Britain could be used as leverage against Venezuela's border claims in an open negotiation. Arbitration would supposedly limit the issue to the border alone.

The United States probably did have sufficient interest in the dispute to justify a call for arbitration. The largest gold nugget ever discovered came from the disputed area. Great Britain also was trying to bend the Schomburgk Line to include Point Barima, with its access to the mouth of the Orinoco River. This would give Great Britain a chance to control what some regarded as a vital trade artery into the heart of South America. The claim to Point Barima, which Britain made formally in 1895, came on the heels of several other international conflicts involving British territorial claims. The most important of these resulted when British marines temporarily occupied the Nicaraguan town of Corinto, close to the potential canal site. Because Cleveland had stayed aloof from these disputes, denying in particular that the British-Nicaraguan clash involved the Monroe Doctrine, he was roundly criticized by the Republicans for his "weakness."

Cleveland believed he had already lost one election for his supposed softness toward the British in the Sackville West incident of 1888. Facing the backlash from the Corinto incident as well as the fallout from the depression of 1893, he may have thought it salutary for the national as well as his own political interest to call a loud halt to Britain's creeping advance in South America. In any case, he proved receptive to a blustering note his new Secretary of State, Richard Olney, proposed to send to Great Britain. Olney and Cleveland decided to end the Venezuelan boundary dispute once and for all, and in the process defend the Monroe Doctrine. Thus they hoped to dash any ideas European nations might have entertained of extending their race for colonies from Asia and Africa to the Western Hemisphere.

Although Richard Olney was not a particularly warlike man, he was impatient, blunt, rigid, and self-righteous. (He banished his daughter from his home and refused to see her for thirty years even though she lived in the same town.) With Cleveland's approval, Olney told the British that the

Monroe Doctrine was well-established public law in America, and that England was violating it by seeking to expand its territory in the Western Hemisphere at the expense of Venezuela. The United States had a right to demand that Britain submit the entire matter to arbitration, since "distance and three thousand miles of intervening ocean make any permanent political union between an European and an American state unnatural and inexpedient. . . . To-day the United States is practically sovereign on this continent, and its fiat is law upon the subjects to which it confines its interposition."

The British did not realize how gravely Cleveland and Olney viewed what seemed to be a remote border quarrel. Olney's inflated language no doubt made the crisis seem a political ploy aimed at domestic voters rather than a serious diplomatic initiative. Besides, the British cabinet was preoccupied with the massacre of Armenians in Turkey and Russian pressure for Chinese concessions in Manchuria, both of which held the potential for a general European war. As a consequence, Prime Minister Lord Salisbury delayed the British answer to Olney's note for four months. Cleveland was especially irritated by the delay because he wanted to announce a resolution of the issue in his State of the Union message. He was even more irritated when the British response, handed to Olney a few days after Cleveland's congressional message, rejected out of hand any suggestion that the Venezuela dispute was covered by the Monroe Doctrine or that the doctrine was international law. Salisbury also said Britain could not risk arbitration of any territory that might result in the transfer of "large numbers of British subjects . . . to a nation of different race and language, whose political system is subject to frequent disturbance, and whose institutions as yet too often afford very inadequate protection to life and property."

Cleveland's response was to threaten war. In a sensational message to Congress, Cleveland asserted that the Monroe Doctrine was indeed international law and that it covered the Venezuela dispute. He announced that the United States would commission a study of the proper boundary which, when approved by the American government, would obligate the United States "to resist by every means in its power, as a willful aggression upon its rights and interests, the appropriation by Great Britain of any lands or the exercise of government jurisdiction over any territory which after investigation we have determined of right belongs to Venezuela."

For a few days war seemed imminent. Congress unanimously accepted Cleveland's recommendation for a border survey. But opposition quickly arose and helped dampen the flames, reasserting the balance between the urges for aggression and restraint. The famous Harvard philosopher, William James, said Cleveland had committed a political crime. Henry Adams's elder brother, Charles Francis Adams, Jr., joined James's opposition, causing Henry to wail that Charles had aligned himself with "all the other Harvard college 'mokes,' the professors of history, by talking out loud" against Cleveland's action. Businessmen joined the outcry against war with Britain when stock market prices plunged, while farmers expressed fears of losing their export markets in a war with England.

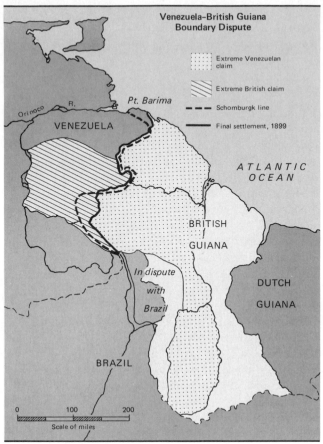

Map 7   The Venezuela–British Guiana Boundary Dispute

Britons also recoiled from war. Thousands signed petitions urging their government to arbitrate. Sentiment was so strong in both countries that the two nations agreed not only to arbitrate the Venezuela-Guiana border dispute, but to negotiate a general arbitration treaty that would cover almost all future Anglo-American disputes. Ironically, in the euphoria of their reconciliation, the United States and Great Britain excluded Venezuela from any part in the arbitration of its own border. Venezuela protested and opposed the arbitration agreement. The United States and Great Britain relented and allowed Venezuela to choose one member of the panel, although they stipulated that the member could not be Venezuelan. Venezuela reluctantly accepted the modified arbitration agreement and selected an American to serve as its representative.

The arbitration panel decided substantially in favor of the British position. It established the Venezuela border close to the Schomburgk Line, excluding only the mouth of the Orinoco and several thousand miles of trackless interior. The Venezuelans were outraged.[1] The United States and Britain, however, hailed the Venezuela arbitration with enthusiasm. Even though the Senate later rejected the general Anglo-American arbitration treaty, giving it three votes less than the two-thirds necessary for consent, the incident had clearly shocked the United States and Great Britain into a new recognition of their mutual interests.

THE ANGLO-AMERICAN RAPPROCHEMENT

In January of 1896, while the Venezuela incident still endangered the peace between Great Britain and the United States, the German kaiser sent a note of congratulation to the president of the Boer Republic of South Africa on the failure of a raid into the Transvaal by a band of Englishmen led by a Dr. Leander Jameson. This "Jameson telegram" dramatized for the British the growing challenge Germany presented to their preeminent position as a world empire and helped turn them away from the impending confrontation with the United States. Unified only two decades before the Jameson incident, Germany had rapidly become the greatest land power in Europe. The German army had beaten Austria and France in quick succession in 1866 and 1870. In the 1890s Germany began planning a navy that would threaten Britain's traditional supremacy on the seas. As a latecomer to the ranks of great powers, Germany felt left out of the earlier scramble for colonies and therefore began abrasively asserting new claims in Africa, the Pacific, and even to some extent in the Western Hemisphere.

Russia, a giant nation of immense population and potential, also was awakening to challenge British interests in eastern Europe, Turkey, and the Mediterranean. Russia was active in Afghanistan, which bordered British India, and it looked covetously toward China, where England had long been supreme. In addition, Japan demanded entrance into the exclusive club of world powers. With its policy of industrialization after the Meiji Restoration, Japan had leaped miraculously into the modern age, and it dramatized its arrival as a great power by defeating China handily in the Sino-Japanese War of 1894–95. Afterward, it too demanded a share in the exploitation of continental Asia. Russia, Germany, and France intervened and forced Japan to give up a portion of its conquests, especially the Liaotung Peninsula of China. Then they began their own scramble for new concessions from the rotting hulk of the Chinese empire. These European powers and Japan thus threatened the British position in Asia at about the same time Cleveland hurled America's challenge on Venezuela and the Western Hemisphere.

As Great Britain watched the rise of these new powers and the dangers they posed to the stability of the Pax Britannica, the British leaders decided it

---

[1] They became even more disturbed in 1949 when they discovered that the American members of the arbitration panel had made the award unanimous only because otherwise the neutral member threatened to vote for the British position. The border issue is still open and sensitive between Venezuela and the now independent state of Guiana.

was foolish to provoke the United States. Of all the rising powers, the United States posed the least danger to Britain's vital interests. The United States no longer agitated for the annexation of Canada, and the expansion of its power and interest in the rest of the Western Hemisphere did not pose an intolerable threat to Britain's growing trade and investment in Latin America. In any case, Latin America was far less important to the British than Europe, East Asia, or the eastern Mediterranean, with its Suez link to India. As Britain's policy of "splendid isolation" began to look less and less splendid, British leaders contemplated the benefits of having the United States as a friend, if not an outright ally.

Other recent events had helped pave the way for this sudden turn toward Anglo-American friendship. The British had reformed their electoral system, broadened the franchise, and brought their politics more into line with the democracy of the United States. At the same time, the new immigration into the United States had emphasized to the old stock elites of America the kinship they felt with the culture of their British cousins, as opposed to the teeming masses of Catholic Italians, Irish, and southern Europeans who threatened to displace them in the cities. The racial attitudes of the day drew attention to the shared Anglo-Saxon heritage of the two nations, and the American elites began to find attractive even the British aristocratic attitudes they had formerly so resented. They hailed the many trans-Atlantic marriages between American daughters and such British luminaries as Joseph Chamberlain, Lord Randolph Churchill, and the duke of Marlborough. Practical economics reinforced sentimental ties. Great Britain took more than half of America's exports and supplied more imports and capital than any other nation. The United States provided nearly a quarter of Britain's imports and bought more than 10 percent of its exports.

Consequently, Great Britain began to withdraw from its dominant position in the Western Hemisphere and entrust the remainder of British interests in the area to American hegemony. The submission of the Venezuelan border dispute to arbitration was only the first step in a retreat that continued through the next decade. As the British turned the Western Hemisphere over to the United States, they also sought to draw American power into East Asia. They saw in the United States a potential ally in the struggle to keep Russia, Japan, and Germany from carving China into exclusive spheres of interest that would be closed to the trade and investment of other foreigners. Britain then dominated the China trade, and left its own sphere of China relatively open to foreign trade because it was strong enough to tolerate competition. The United States was not anxious to acquire a sphere of its own, and the establishment of closed foreign spheres would hurt American trade. Noting the harmony of interests between the two nations, the British approached the United States in 1898 on a joint policy to hold the Chinese markets open. Cleveland's successor, William McKinley, refused Britain's offer.

McKinley's rejection of a limited British alliance did not stop the American movement toward cooperation with Great Britain as the United States moved toward world power. The British continued their transformation from chief rivals to best friends. Those nations that had helped America challenge British supremacy on the high seas in earlier days, such as Russia and Germany, went from friends to enemies. The United States thus played a key role in the world diplomatic revolution of the 1890s.

THE SPANISH-AMERICAN WAR

The Cuban rebellion against Spain in 1895 furnished the major catalyst for America's own diplomatic revolution. Cuba had endured nine separate rebellions since 1823, and the endemic chaos on the island worried American leaders throughout most of the nineteenth century. Americans had long coveted Cuba, and the abolition of slavery in both countries following the American Civil War eliminated the major roadblock to intervention. America's desire for Caribbean naval bases to protect an isthmian canal added to Cuba's attractiveness.

When rebellion broke out in Cuba in the 1870s, President Ulysses Grant came to the brink of intervention. Congressional opposition to the annexation of a tropical province of a different race and culture thwarted Grant for the moment, but even Grant's opponents had no wish to see a major power replace the moribund Spanish rule. Americans of both parties feared that increasing chaos in Cuba would provide an incentive for Spain to request military aid from other European powers, and the intrusion of a new European nation in Cuba would be a direct challenge to the Monroe Doctrine. The United States publicly warned Germany against acquisition of Cuba in the 1880s after rumors circulated that Germany was seeking a pretext for intervention.

By the time a new revolution erupted in Cuba in 1895, American sentiment was far readier for intervention than it had been in Grant's era. The Venezuela incident of that same year had been too ambiguous to upset the close balance between restraint and assertiveness in American foreign policy. The Cuban revolution, on the other hand, was dramatic and popular enough to swing the balance toward an aggressive, interventionist diplomacy and to help America sustain that posture for at least two decades.

Cuba certainly had enough reason to revolt against Spain. The Spanish army and civil service in Cuba were inefficient, corrupt, and arrogant. Spaniards occupied almost all positions of power and wealth. They confined most of the 800,000 white Cubans to menial labor and left the 600,000 recently emancipated blacks in conditions little better than their previous slavery. Spain monopolized Cuba's trade, and the United States compounded the problems this created by placing high duties on Cuban sugar in the Wilson-Gorman Tariff of 1894.

Americans sympathized thoroughly with the Cubans. They had regarded Spain with dislike and contempt since the early days of America's westward movement. One railroad magnate wrote his senator that "Spain is and always has been an impudent, arrogant, and barbarous nation. . . . It is quite time she was boosted out of Cuba . . . and nine out of every ten of our citizens without regard to party will agree with me." Newspapers of the time, which were just then becoming instruments of mass circulation, played on these anti-Spanish sentiments. In their battle for circulation in New York, the Pulitzer and Hearst papers tried to outdo one another with titillating horror stories about the war in Cuba. The most sensational episode in this battle of the "yellow press" was the rescue of the daughter of a former Cuban official from her Spanish cell by a Hearst reporter, who naturally made the most of his scoop. Local newspapers were perhaps even more important then the big-city yellow press in stirring American emotions. Desperate for copy, they often printed verbatim the handouts from the Cuban junta's headquarters in New York.

While the general public was enthusiastically for the rebels, the Cleveland and McKinley administrations were more interested in seeing the war come to an end regardless of the victor. They feared Spain might call in another major power to help put down the rebellion. The war was also hurting American trade and investments in the island. American exports to Cuba dropped from $20 million in 1894 to half of that in 1898. The fighting endangered some $50 million worth of American investments in Cuba. Most of these were in sugar plantations sold by frightened Spaniards during the previous revolution of the 1870s. The rebellion's impact on American business could not help but concern America's political leaders, even though most businessmen opposed military intervention in Cuba because they feared that war with Spain would threaten their far more valuable trade with Europe.

Cleveland had responded at first to the 1895 rebellion by invoking America's neutrality laws. These laws forbade organizing or recruiting men in the United States. They did not specifically bar the sale of arms, but Cleveland sought to discourage this traffic as well. Nominally this neutrality policy helped Spain more than the rebels, since only the rebels needed men and arms from the United States. Actually, neither American nor Spanish patrols could halt the aid that flowed to the revolutionaries from Cuban exiles and other sympathetic Americans, a situation which brought howls of protest from Spain.

Congress urged Cleveland to do more for the rebels. Congressional Democrats and Republicans alike saw in the Cuban issue a popular cause around which they could unite their parties. By outdoing one another in professions of sympathy for the oppressed Cubans, they hoped to paper over the deep divisions within their parties brought about by the free silver issue. Over Cleveland's protests, Congress passed a resolution urging recognition of the Cubans' belligerent status. Cleveland refused to offer that recognition and asserted that he would not use the American army in Cuba even if Congress authorized him to do so. But the situation in Cuba was becoming worse: The revolution was rapidly growing from an issue the parties could use for their own purposes to one they could not escape even if they wished.

The revolution simply demolished Cuba. The rebels saw their best chance for victory in the ruin of the Cuban economy, and with it the island's value to Spain. They burned crops and sugar refineries, tore up railroads, and made a special effort to destroy American-owned plantations. They hoped that such attacks might force American intervention and knew that America would never intervene on the side of Spain. Meanwhile, in early 1896, the Spanish appointed General Valeriano Weyler, nicknamed "Butcher" Weyler by the Hearst press, as the new commander in Cuba. Toward the end of the year, Weyler initiated the *reconcentrado* policy. People living in the country-side would be concentrated in camps where they could be defended against the rebels and also prevented from supplying or supporting them. The army would assume that all people outside these camps were rebels and would shoot them on sight.

The Spanish army had no way to supply adequate food and sanitation for these camps. By 1898, newspapers estimated that nearly 400,000 Cubans, one-quarter of the island's entire population, had died during the revolution. Later studies have shown this to have been an exaggeration. The true figure was probably somewhere between 100,000 and 200,000, but that was bad enough, and the Spaniards themselves actually believed that the number of deaths had been close to 400,000.

As reports of destruction and atrocity multiplied, even Cleveland came to believe that American intervention might be necessary. In a lame duck message to Congress, he proposed that Spain grant Cuba greater autonomy, and warned that if the war dragged on it would be the duty of the United States to halt it. His successor, William McKinley, had similar opinions. He too wished for an early end to the revolution to avoid the need for American intervention. But McKinley seems to have been somewhat more pro-rebel than Cleveland. Cleveland might have forced the rebels to accept a Spanish offer of limited autonomy; McKinley would not require the rebels to accept a settlement they thought unfavorable. Since the rebels wanted nothing less than independence, and Spain was adamant against that, the prospects for securing an early end to the war were minimal.

Despite the obstacles, McKinley hoped that through diplomatic pressure he might bring both sides to settle. He instructed America's minister to Spain, Stewart L. Woodford, to inform Spain that the United States expected notice of an "early and certain peace" by November 1, 1897. Otherwise the United States would do whatever was necessary to procure that peace. McKinley reasoned that the Spanish were at the peak of their strength in Cuba during the 1897–98 campaign season. If they were unable to settle the war by the time the tropical rains forced a halt to the fighting, the prospect was for an interminable and bloody stalemate. Perhaps an American ultimatum would force Spain to offer concessions which, along with military pressure, could bring the rebels to a settlement. Meanwhile, McKinley induced Congress to appropriate $50,000 for aid to the suffering Cubans and got Spain to admit these supplies duty-free. He personally contributed $5,000 to the Cuban relief fund.

Coincidentally, just as McKinley began to apply pressure, a new liberal

Spanish government succeeded that of the assassinated conservative prime minister. The liberals recalled General Weyler, alleviated the reconcentration policy, released American citizens imprisoned for rebel activity, and offered considerable autonomy to Cuba within the Spanish empire. Although these concessions were made as a result of Spain's domestic politics rather than American diplomacy, McKinley could portray them as a partial response to his initiative. He used his supposed success to keep Congress from demanding immediate intervention and hoped he still could force both sides into agreement.

The slim chance that Spain and Cuba could work out an agreement was shattered, however, when riots broke out among Spanish loyalists in Cuba against the recall of Weyler and the offer of Cuban autonomy. Many army personnel who were supposed to suppress the riots joined them instead. Opposition rose in Spain as well as in Cuba. The queen and her government feared they might be overthrown if they surrendered Cuba voluntarily. McKinley and other Americans wondered whether the Spanish government could come to an agreement with the Cuban rebels even if Spain negotiated in good faith. When the Americans read an intercepted letter written by the Spanish minister to the United States, Enrique Dupuy de Lôme, they had to wonder whether the government was negotiating in good faith in any case. De Lôme characterized McKinley as "weak and a bidder for the admiration of the crowd, besides being a would-be politician who tries to leave a door open behind himself while keeping on good terms with the jingoes of his party." Then de Lôme suggested negotiating with the Americans "even if only for effect."

Shortly after the de Lôme letter, the American battleship *Maine* exploded in Havana harbor. McKinley unwisely and hastily had sent the *Maine* to Havana during the Weyler riots to show American desire for order in Cuba. When it sank, killing 266 of the 350 crew members aboard, it made American intervention in the Cuban revolution almost inevitable.

While a naval board investigated the cause of the *Maine* explosion, McKinley tried one last time for a diplomatic solution. At his request, Congress appropriated $50 million for a defense fund that McKinley could use at his own discretion. Woodford said the appropriation stunned the Spanish government, and McKinley seemed to have considerable leverage to force a settlement. He lost much of his room to maneuver, however, when Redfield Proctor, a highly respected senator from Vermont, made an extraordinary speech on his return from an inspection of Cuba. In a calm and dispassionate voice, he recounted the horrendous scenes he had witnessed and confirmed the rumors that 200,000 Cubans had died in the reconcentration camps. His speech convinced many that Spain had simply lost control of Cuba; it could never win the struggle, but only draw out the bloody stalemate.

The report of the American naval board on the sinking of the *Maine* reinforced the assumption that Spain had lost control; the board concluded that an external rather than an internal explosion had destroyed the ship. A floating mine was a more likely culprit than a boiler room accident. Although some of the more lurid newspapers and excitable politicians of the time implied that the Spanish had sunk the *Maine,* neither the naval board nor most American leaders accused the Spanish of deliberate sabotage. Yet Spain was responsible for the safety of ships in its harbors, and the *Maine* incident convinced almost all Americans of Spain's impotence to control the colony over which it claimed sovereignty.

McKinley was under terrible pressure to do something dramatic. Failure would open the door for the Democrats to proclaim themselves the true advocates of Cuba and portray the Republicans as cowardly betrayers of freedom. The powerful Republican Senator Henry Cabot Lodge warned McKinley: "If the war in Cuba drags on through the summer with nothing done we shall go down in the greatest defeat ever known. . . . I know that it is easily & properly said that to bring on or even to threaten war for political reasons is a crime & I quite agree. But to sacrifice a great party & bring free silver upon the country for a wrong policy is hardly less odious."

McKinley had known for a week the results of the naval board's investigation. He could imagine the public reaction, so he tried to force a quick settlement of the Cuban revolution. His secretary of state, John Sherman, was senile; so McKinley bypassed him and communicated with Spain through his close friend, Acting Secretary of State William Day. On March 26, McKinley composed and Day signed a telegram to the American minister, Woodford, informing the Spanish that it was essential peace be made within a month. Spain should revoke the reconcentration order and offer the Cubans "full self-government, with reasonable indemnity." Woodford asked if this actually meant Cuban independence. Day responded that it did.

But after Woodford reported that Spain had made some tentative inquiries about an armistice in Cuba, McKinley and Day sent another telegram that clouded their earlier ultimatum. McKinley and Day told Woodford to get Spain to offer the rebels an armistice under American good offices until October 1, along with revocation of the reconcentration order, and to add "if possible: Third. If terms of the peace not satisfactorily settled by October 1, President of the United States to be final arbiter between Spain and insurgents."

A careful reading of this final telegram indicates that McKinley was still demanding Cuban independence. The rebels would never agree to a settlement before October 1 because they knew that after that date McKinley would arbitrate and he would grant Cuba independence. Still, the telegram said that the third demand was to be added only "if possible." Did Woodford understand that McKinley was still demanding Cuban independence? Did he make McKinley's position clear to Spain?

Those questions are important, because Spain ultimately conceded the unequivocal first two demands of McKinley's final telegram. It revoked the reconcentration order and offered a cease-fire to the rebels, although it offered the armistice only after refusing until the last minute, then claiming it made the offer because the pope had requested it, and finally asserting that the length and extent of the armistice would be up to the Spanish commander in Cuba. Spain said nothing of American arbitration or Cuban independence.

Woodford reported these concessions as the prelude to further Spanish surrenders and urged McKinley to delay the use of force. McKinley, however, regarded the concessions as too little, too late, and given with insufficient grace to indicate that Spain was willing to go still further and grant Cuba independence. He sent a long-contemplated message to Congress requesting authority to intervene with force if necessary to end the war in Cuba. He noted the last-minute Spanish concessions only as an afterthought.

There was no doubt Congress would grant McKinley the authority he wanted. The vast majority in Congress and the country were in favor of war, and many were criticizing the president for his procrastination. Even the business community, long opposed to armed intervention in Cuba, had come to feel that anything was preferable to the current lingering uncertainty. Thus, McKinley led a united and enthusiastic nation to war. After the war, however, when McKinley's telegrams and Woodford's advice that Spain would submit without war became public, it triggered a debate over the intervention that still continues among historians. Most concluded that the war indeed had been unnecessary, that a weak and vacillating president had bowed to partisan advantage and the war frenzy whipped up by an unscrupulous press. Like Theodore Roosevelt, they portrayed McKinley as a man with no more backbone than a chocolate éclair. Echoing Representative "Uncle Joe" Cannon, they said the president kept his ear so close to the ground that it had grasshoppers in it.

Some historians made more sinister accusations. They argued that imperialists like Assistant Secretary of the Navy Theodore Roosevelt and Sen-

Figure 8   President William McKinley, whose diplomacy leading up to the Spanish-American War still stirs controversy among historians. Portrait courtesy of the National Archives.

ator Henry Cabot Lodge had manipulated McKinley into an unnecessary war to give the United States a chance to acquire a colonial empire. Supposedly, Roosevelt and Lodge had arranged the appointment of Commodore George Dewey to the command of the Pacific squadron. Then, in the temporary absence of the secretary of the navy, Roosevelt had ordered Dewey to attack the Spanish fleet in Manila harbor. Dewey's victory would allow the United States to acquire the Philippines and gain access to the China markets.

The charge that Roosevelt and Lodge had maneuvered McKinley into an unnecessary war in order to acquire the Philippines is quickly enough dismissed. An attack on the Spanish fleet in Manila had long been part of the plan for war with Spain. That fleet was one of the two major Spanish naval forces, and its existence would threaten America's Pacific Coast as well as any expedition to Cuba. Manila's harbor defenses had been investigated by an American naval officer in civilian clothes as early as 1876, and an attack on the fleet was made part of the formal plan for a war with Spain in 1896. Roosevelt's telegram to Dewey was approved by McKinley himself.

The attack on the fleet, however, was not part of a concerted plan to conquer the Philippines. No troops were sent with Dewey to occupy Manila in the event he defeated the fleet. McKinley made preparations to send troops only after he received news of Dewey's victory and amid fears that Spain was sending another fleet to the Philippines. McKinley and the American navy did decide quickly that they wanted to keep Manila's great harbor as a window to the China market, but this was a consequence of Dewey's victory, not a motive for the attack in the first place.

It is also extremely doubtful that Spain was ready to relinquish its hold on Cuba, despite Woodford's opinion that it would do so. The Spanish government faced riots over declaration of the armistice, let alone Cuban independence. The queen feared she would be overthrown if she freed Cuba without a fight. While the Spanish government offered an armistice, it also looked about Europe, in the hope of getting other powers to intervene against Cuba and the United States. Thus there is little chance that Spain's compliance with American demands for revocation of the reconcentration order and an armistice presaged a grant of independence. It was more likely a delaying tactic. So long as America insisted on Cuban independence, war was probably inevitable.

Nevertheless, many historians continue to criticize McKinley for failing to pursue the slim chance for peace by making his demand for Cuban independence clearer and then delaying a while to see if Spain would extend its concessions. McKinley's defenders, and their number has increased substantially in the past decade, argue that the Spanish understood perfectly well that Cuban independence was necessary to prevent American intervention and that McKinley could not risk a categorical demand because the proud Spanish would have been sure to reject it. They see McKinley's diplomacy as the product not of weakness and vacillation, but of strength, subtlety, and realism. The evidence does seem to support their claim that McKinley was in full control of his policy and was not the spineless creature portrayed in earlier accounts, but it is still difficult to see why he avoided a clear statement of his purposes to Spain. Since war resulted anyway, it could not have made matters worse.

Even after war was imminent and McKinley announced the goal of Cuban independence to the American people, he studiously avoided recognition of the Cuban rebels as the successor government of the island. During the *Maine* crisis, the rebels had told McKinley: "We do not ask you to go to war; we only ask you for your neutrality, for the recognition of Cuban belligerent rights." McKinley rejected this plea. He did not think the rebels could win the war quickly without American assistance, he had no doubt Spain would declare war immediately if he recognized Cuban independence or belligerence directly, and he did not think the Cuban government was yet "capable of performing the duties and discharging the functions of a separate nation." While he implied that he might recognize Cuba later, he decided to try to stop the war as a neutral, and he asked Congress to authorize him to use force to do so.

The House of Representatives gave him the authorization he requested. But the Senate insisted on pushing him further than he wanted to go. It passed resolutions directing rather than authorizing McKinley to use force in Cuba, recognized Cuban independence and the rebels as the legitimate government (the Turpie-Foraker Amendment), and disavowed any intention of annexing Cuba (the Teller Amendment).

McKinley threatened to use his veto if the House accepted the Senate version. He insisted at least that recognition of the rebel government be dropped. A joint House-Senate resolution did so amid charges that McKinley and his followers opposed recognition because they feared this would invalidate Spain's Cuban bonds, some of which allegedly had been purchased by Americans. When McKinley signed the resolution on April 20, Spain broke diplomatic relations. Two days later, McKinley imposed a naval blockade on Cuba, and Spain declared war on the United States.

THE ACQUISITION OF AN OVERSEAS EMPIRE

John Hay, who became McKinley's last secretary of state, called the Spanish-American conflict "a splendid little war." The United States had clear military superiority over Spain, and it won a quick and decisive victory. Nevertheless, the war could have been far bloodier and more prolonged had it not been for considerable luck and Spanish incompetence. Dewey's fleet steamed into Manila harbor past the fortress island of Corregidor without suffering a single effective shot. The Spanish fleet fatalistically anchored in shallow water so its men could get to shore when the ships were sunk. These shallows were located out of reach of the shore guns in Manila that could have helped fight the Americans. Dewey won the battle with the loss of only a single man, and he to a heart attack.

The Americans were equally lucky in their invasion of Cuba. The ill-planned amphibious operation began only after a long wait in tropical Florida camps by soldiers clothed in winter woolens. The scramble to the ships was chaotic. Artillery and cavalry went aboard one ship, ammunition and horses aboard another. Fortunately, the invasion force landed unopposed on Cuban beaches because the Spanish foolishly abandoned their coastal defenses for inland positions. The American army cooperated tenuously with the Cuban rebels and together they moved toward Santiago, where the Spanish fleet had taken refuge. The famous charge up San Juan Hill put the Americans and their Cuban allies in a commanding position above Santiago, so the Spanish fleet made a forlorn dash from the harbor. The American blockading vessels pursued and sank them one by one. Americans won the war while losing only 379 men in combat (however, over 5,000 died from malaria and yellow fever).

While American troops were occupying Manila and Cuba, McKinley and his administration moved to expand and consolidate their hold on other territories in the Pacific and Caribbean. McKinley finally secured the formal annexation of Hawaii, partly by claiming that the islands were vital for getting troops and supplies to Dewey in the Philippines. Even so, to overcome Democratic opposition, McKinley had to resort to a joint resolution of Congress rather than the formal treaty procedure. American forces also took Spain's lesser colony of Puerto Rico without a fight, and no Teller Amendment required the United States to forego annexation of this Caribbean island.

It was a foregone conclusion by the end of hostilities with Spain that the United States would have an overseas empire. The only question was how big that empire would be. Should the United States keep the Philippines as well as Puerto Rico and Hawaii?

McKinley seems to have decided shortly after Dewey's victory to keep at least Manila. It was a fine port and naval base which provided access to China and the rest of Asia. McKinley also ordered seizure of the uninhabited Wake Islands and the Spanish island of Guam as steppingstones from Hawaii to Manila. He found it difficult, however, to decide what to do about the rest of the Philippines. It seemed intolerable to leave them in the hands of Spain, after seeing Spanish misrule of Cuba. He did not want to see great Britain, Germany, or Japan acquire them and use them to gain supremacy in the China trade.

He might have left them to the Philippine rebels, whose leader, Emilio Aguinaldo, had returned to the islands aboard an American ship. But McKinley did not think the rebels capable of governing the Philippines any more than he thought the Cuban rebels prepared to govern their island. He believed the Philippines would fall into anarchy, and then into the hands of one of the other great powers. While America might throw a protectorate over the islands to prevent this, the difficulties and frictions of dealing with a native government in such a situation had already been made clear in Samoa. Besides, McKinley's military advisers told him that Manila was indefensible without control of the entire island of Luzon.

McKinley's inclination to keep the entire archipelago was confirmed by a

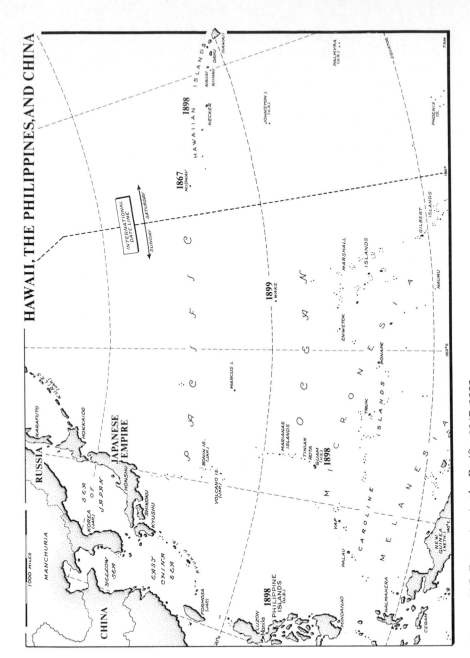

Map 8 U.S. Expansion in the Pacific, 1867–1899

campaign swing through Middle America, where mention of taking the islands drew cheers from the crowds. He returned to Washington to instruct the American peace commission negotiating with the Spaniards in Paris to insist on keeping the Philippines. After the United States assuaged Spanish protests with an offer to pay $20 million, the peace treaty was signed.

The thrill of victory brought most Americans to accept the acquisition of Puerto Rico and Hawaii, but a substantial number of influential Americans thought the Philippines were too distant, too alien, and too hostile to be annexed. Grover Cleveland, Andrew Carnegie, and Mark Twain joined the campaign againt annexation organized by the newly formed Anti-Imperialist League. They argued that America could never bring the Philippines into the Union as an equal state; the United States would have to rule the Philippines as a colony at the point of a bayonet. The precedent of bayonet rule would be as dangerous to American domestic liberty as it would be harmful to the Filipinos. Anti-imperialists insisted that the United States could expand and protect its foreign trade without resort to such imperialism. They recalled Washington's Farewell Address warning against involvement in the quarrels of European powers. But they argued in vain. Imperialists said that modern communications and American power made the Farewell Address obsolete or claimed that acquisition of the Philippines was merely the continuation of America's westward march, which Washington and the other Founding Fathers had initiated. They insisted that American rule would educate and uplift the Filipinos, not degrade or oppress them.

Republicans in the Senate supported McKinley overwhelmingly. Several had their doubts, but in the end only George Frisbie Hoar of Massachusetts and Eugene Hale of Maine could bring themselves to vote against their triumphant president. The Democrats were divided over the treaty. William Jennings Bryan thought it would be difficult to defeat a treaty that promised peace with Spain, so he urged Democrats to accept the treaty and the Philippines, then grant the islands their independence. He probably affected only one or two votes. Nevertheless, with ten out of thirty-two Democratic senators voting aye, the treaty received two-thirds approval by a single vote. Meanwhile, fighting had already broken out between American troops and Aguinaldo's rebels. It was a sign that the United States would find it far more difficult to pacify and govern its empire than to acquire it.

CONTROVERSIAL ISSUES AND FURTHER READING

The United States entered the Spanish-American War with little popular dissent. Contemporaries quarreled over the later decision to take the Philippines far more than they did over the decision to expel the Spanish from Cuba. [John Holladay Latané, *Diplomatic Relations of the United States and Spanish America* (1900); James Morton

Callahan, *Cuba and International Relations* (1899).] When the diplomatic correspondence leading to the war was published in 1901, however, and revealed Woodford's opinion that Spain would have been willing to make more concessions without war, it did generate some criticism.

Most early historical criticism of the war came from conservatives. They feared that overseas colonialism endangered American liberty at home and entangled the United States needlessly abroad, but they did not worry much about the negative impact of American rule on Cubans or Filipinos. They disliked the Cuban rebels as terrorists and thought the Filipinos would be better off under American rule. These authors did not argue that the war was the product of an imperialist plot led by Theodore Roosevelt and Henry Cabot Lodge. Instead, they saw it as the result of the yellow press, ignorant popular enthusiasm, and McKinley's weakness. [Horace Edgar Flack, *Spanish-American Diplomatic Relations* (1906), and Elbert Jay Benton, *International Law and the Diplomacy of the Spanish-American War* (1908). Both books emerged from a Johns Hopkins seminar given by W. W. Willoughby.] Even Admiral French Ensor Chadwick, a member of the naval commission that investigated the sinking of the *Maine* and the author of an encyclopedic defense of the war, moderated his stance in light of this critique. [French Ensor Chadwick, *The Relations of the United States and Spain: Diplomacy* (1909).] But until the post-World War I era, most historians continued to justify America's forcible intervention in Cuba. [See Albert Bushnell Hart, *The Monroe Doctrine* (1916); John Holladay Latané, *America as a World Power* (1907); John Bassett Moore, *The Principles of American Diplomacy* (1918).]

Disillusion after World War I brought with it a reaction against the imperial and interventionist policies initiated in the 1890s. Defenders of the Spanish-American War were few. The conservative critique of the war continued in the works of such prominent historians as James Ford Rhodes and Samuel Flagg Bemis. [James Ford Rhodes, *The McKinley and Roosevelt Administrations* (1922); Samuel Flagg Bemis, *A Diplomatic History of the United States* (1936).] But now liberal and socialist historians added their criticisms and interpretations. Walter Millis, a prominent journalist, wrote a best seller, *The Martial Spirit* (1931), which popularized the view that Roosevelt, Lodge, and other imperialists maneuvered America into a needless war to get the Philippines. Millis was very critical of the annexation of the Philippines, but less so of America's intervention in Cuba. Socialists Scott Nearing and Joseph Freeman were unsparing of this intervention as well. In their popular book, *Dollar Diplomacy: A Study in American Imperialism* (1925), Nearing and Freeman blamed big business and economic interests along with imperial thinkers like Roosevelt, Lodge, and Mahan for America's imperialism. Julius Pratt's still influential study, *The Expansionists of 1898* (1936), tried to absolve business and economic interests of the charge that they had sought war to gain an empire by showing that business had generally opposed the war. It was the imperial-minded intellectuals like Roosevelt, Lodge, and Alfred Thayer Mahan who were responsible for the needless war, he implied. Business became converted to the cause of imperialism during the war, however, and played a major role in the decision to annex the Philippines and other territories in the imperial aftermath to the war.

World War II cast interventionism in a better historical light than had World War I. Many realist historians began to praise the Spanish-American War as initiating America's necessary involvement in world affairs. Nevertheless, historians remained somewhat ambivalent about the way the United States had entered the war and the imperialism that had resulted. Richard Hofstadter and William Leuchtenberg wrote as though the war had been a needless consequence of neurotic belligerence on the part of liberals as well as conservatives, while Foster Rhea Dulles perpetuated the idea that Roosevelt and Lodge had manipulated America into the war to get the Philippines. [Richard Hofstadter, "Manifest Destiny and the Philippines," *America in Crisis*, ed. Daniel Aaron (1952); and *Social Darwinism* (1944); William Leuchtenberg, "The Needless War with Spain," *Times of Trial*, ed. Allan Nevins (1958); and "Progressivism and Imperialism: The Progressive Movement and American Foreign Policy, 1898–1916," *Mississippi Valley Historical Review* (1952); Foster Rhea Dulles, *America's Rise to World Power, 1898–1954* (1955).]

The discovery by J. A. S. Grenville and George Berkeley Young that the Navy Department had devised plans as early as 1896 to attack the Spanish fleet at Manila if war broke out over Cuba undercut the idea that Roosevelt and Lodge had ordered the attack against the wishes of their superiors. [J. A. S. Grenville and George Berkeley Young, *Politics, Strategy, and American Diplomacy* (1966).] Meanwhile H. Wayne Morgan led many historians to revise their estimate of McKinley's weakness and gullibility, arguing that McKinley was purposeful and in complete command of his administration throughout the events leading to war and the acquisition of the Philippines. [H. Wayne Morgan, *William McKinley and His America* (1963); see also Morgan, *America's Road to Empire* (1965); Margaret Leech, *In the Days of McKinley* (1959); Lewis L. Gould, *The Spanish-American War and President McKinley* (1982).] Ernest May was not fully convinced of all this, but his *Imperial Democracy* (1961) argued that Spain had been fully aware of America's demand for Cuban independence and had purposely delayed while trying to get European help against the United States. May was not sure this justified war, but said that McKinley, while he operated primarily out of a cowardly fear for the fate of the Republican party, still "conceived he had some justification for demanding a final end to the violence in Cuba."

Revisionists, of course, were far more critical of the war. Walter LaFeber's highly influential *The New Empire* (1963) argued, contrary to Julius Pratt, that business had not only been favorable to the war, but that its influence had been the primary one in McKinley's final decision to intervene in Cuba as well as take the Philippines. In the wake of Vietnam, Philip Foner argued an even more radical thesis. Using Cuban documents but citing rather thin evidence, Foner claimed that the rebels had actually opposed American intervention and had wanted only arms and munitions. McKinley intervened not to help them, but to expand the American empire. Thus, Foner said, McKinley had purposely omitted a demand for Cuban independence in his ultimatum, refused to recognize the rebel government, and meant from the outset to use the war to take the Philippines. He intended his delays merely to provide time for military preparations. When he was ready, he sent the *Maine* to Havana to create an incident that would justify war. [Philip S. Foner, *The Spanish-Cuban-American War and the Birth of American Imperialism, 1895–1902* (1972).]

Foner's views have not been widely adopted even by radical historians. The best, most judicious summary of the war is now Charles S. Campbell, *The Transformation of American Foreign Relations, 1865–1900* (1976). This book also has an excellent summary of the other events and trends chronicled in this chapter, as does Robert L. Beisner, *From the Old Diplomacy to the New, 1865–1900* (1975).

In addition to these books, the Venezuelan crisis can be studied in Dexter Perkins, *The Monroe Doctrine, 1867–1907* (1937); Gerald Eggert, *Richard Olney* (1973); and Allan Nevins, *Grover Cleveland* (1932). On the subsequent Anglo-American rapprochement, see Bradford Perkins, *The Great Rapprochement* (1968); Charles S. Campbell, *From Revolution to Rapprochement* (1974); Robert G. Neale, *Great Britain and the United States, 1895–1903* (1960). On the rise of imperialism and the anti-imperialist countermovement, see David Healy, *U.S. Expansionism: The Imperialist Urge in the 1890s* (1970); William Appleman Williams, *The Roots of the Modern American Empire* (1969); Ernest May, *American Imperialism* (1968); Robert L. Beisner, *Twelve Against Empire* (1968); and Richard Welch, *Response to Imperialism: The United States and the Philippine-American War, 1899–1902* (1979).

CHAPTER 9

The Surge into Asia: Empire in the Philippines and the Open Door in China

THE SUPPRESSION OF THE PHILIPPINE REVOLUTION

Admiral Dewey's fleet sailed into the Philippines during a recess in a revolution that was already two years old, the first modern colonial revolution in Asia. In August of 1896, the small educated Filipino middle class led an open rebellion against the Spanish. The rebels were especially angry at the Catholic friars' economic control of much of the islands' arable land. Not only did the friars hold huge feudal estates, they maintained political control of many Filipino barrios.

As the Spanish authorities and the rebels drew near to a pitched battle that would have been bloody and costly to both sides, they agreed to compromise. The rebels were not seeking outright independence; they merely wanted to reduce the power of the Church, open the economy to greater participation by the middle class, and introduce more islanders into the higher echelons of government. When Spain offered a series of reforms and a payment of $800,000 for an end to the rebellion, rebel leader Emilio Aguinaldo accepted and went into exile.

Spain never did carry out its promised reforms, and the insurrection broke out again. Aguinaldo had banked Spain's first payment of $400,000 against future contingencies, and he drew on this money to supply arms and materiel to the rebels from his exile in Hong Kong. The Americans helped him because Dewey decided that Aguinaldo and his rebels could furnish the troops Dewey lacked to give ground support to his fleet. Dewey even had Aguinaldo brought to Manila on the fleet's flagship. Aguinaldo maintained ever after that Dewey and his representatives had promised him an independent Philippine nation. Dewey swore he had made no such commitment.

When American troops finally arrived in the Philippines months after Dewey's victory, conflict quickly flared between them and the Filipino rebels. Dewey and the American army commander, General Elwell Otis, refused to permit Aguinaldo's troops to join the attack on the city of Manila, which was still held by the Spanish garrison. The Americans arranged with the Spanish defenders to have a short and harmless fire-fight for the salvation of Spanish honor, whereupon the surrender would be offered and accepted. The battle for Manila became a bit more realistic than intended when some Filipino troops joined the mock attack without authorization. Afterward, the Americans forced the Filipinos to camp outside the city, and resentment smoldered between the two occupying armies.

While American troops took Manila, Aguinaldo and his sympathizers gained control of much of the rest of the Philippines. Aguinaldo declared the Philippines independent, set up a government, and established a capital at Malolos. Nevertheless, William McKinley ignored the Filipinos. He ordered the American peace commission to demand Spanish cession of the islands to the United States. Then, before the Senate even ratified the treaty, he issued an executive order establishing American military government throughout the Philippines. This meant that the American army would have to wrest control of all but Manila from the Aguinaldo government and troops already in place. General Otis tried to disguise the full import of McKinley's order from the Filipinos by judiciously editing McKinley's proclamation before publishing it. This only made matters worse when the deception was exposed by a subordinate's inadvertant publication of the unexpurgated version.

Aguinaldo and his lieutenants were rightly suspicious, tensions heightened, and inevitably an American patrol clashed with the Philippine troops dug in around Manila. The clash came only forty hours before the Senate vote on the treaty and probably contributed to the Senate's narrow consent to it, since few senators wanted to be seen as refusing to back America's soldiers in a foreign land. The convenient timing of this incident outside Manila has led to suspicions on the part of several historians, American as well as Filipino, that McKinley provoked the incident. But there is no evidence of this, and the poor communication between McKinley and his military commanders makes it unlikely he could have contrived it even if he had so desired.

The war for the Philippines lasted more than three years and cost the Americans nearly 5,000 lives. The Filipinos suffered even more. The war cost them the lives of 20,000 soldiers and nearly 200,000 civilians. It was a savage war marked by atrocities and racial hatreds. American soldiers expressed their feelings in a song that was so offensive the American commanders tried to ban it:

> Damn, Damn, Damn the Filipinos
> Cross-eyed kakiak Ladrones,
> Underneath our starry flag,
> Civilize them with a Krag,
> And return us to our own beloved homes.

(A Krag was the army-issue rifle of the United States.)

The Americans expected a quick triumph over people they regarded as inferiors, and the protracted war exasperated them. Exasperation turned to brutality when the Filipinos refused to surrender after a series of American victories and instead dispersed to fight as guerrilla bands. "Water cures" and other forms of torture became commonplace to gain information from villagers or captives about guerrilla locations and identities. Guerrillas also fought savagely. After one especially brutal attack on unarmed American troops in a chow line, the American commander promised to make the entire surrounding area a "howling wilderness."

Ultimately the United States had to station 70,000 men on the islands to control them. The troops converted Philippine villages into garrisons in order to cut off supplies to the guerrillas, tactics reminiscent of Butcher Weyler's reconcentration policy that Americans had found so objectionable. Finally, a daring raiding party captured Aguinaldo, the Filipino middle class lost heart, other Filipino commanders surrendered their forces, and the war ground to a bitter anticlimactic end in 1902.

The war generated much controversy in America. Prominent members of the Anti-Imperialist League publicized the case against American rule in the islands. The Democratic party tried to make an issue of imperialism in the election of 1900, but other issues muddled the election and it never served as the referendum on imperialism that William Jennings Bryan proclaimed it would be. Imperialism was potentially divisive in both parties, so political leaders tended to downplay it. Only after the election did news of American as opposed to Filipino atrocities make headlines in a couple of sensational court martials. By that time the war was nearly over, and no great political movement against the occupation developed.

The relative success of America's colonial government also muted criticism in America and the Philippines. American promises of modernization, better schools, cleaner cities, more roads and factories, and improved agriculture won the grudging cooperation of the most economically progressive upper-class Filipinos, and the United States delivered on many of those promises. Nevertheless, the residual effect of the Philippine war and colonial aftermath left many Americans unsettled. Even Theodore Roosevelt came to believe that acquisition of the Philippines was a mistake. He concluded that the islands were a strategic Achilles heel: They invited attack from other powers in Asia and could not be defended. Consequently, although the United States undertook several more military interventions in the next two decades, popular acceptance of such intervention was reluctant rather than buoyant.

THE OPEN DOOR NOTES

Acquisition of the Philippines naturally prompted greater American interest in Asia. The dream of a great China market, one of the primary reasons the McKinley administration decided to annex the Philippines, now beckoned even more invitingly. American missionaries also began concentrating their efforts on China. Before the 1890s most missionaries were stationed in the

Mediterranean; only 200 were active in China. By 1900 there were over 1,000 American missionaries in China. By 1905, that figure had risen to 3,000, more than 80 percent of all American Protestant missionaries abroad.

Consequently, the McKinley administration regarded the increasing pace of European imperialism in China with a more jaundiced eye after the Spanish-American War. The acceleration of European imperialism had begun after the Japanese victory in the Sino-Japanese War of 1895. First the European powers had forced Japan to limit its spoils to the island of Formosa (Taiwan), the nearby Pescadores, and a sphere of influence in the strategic peninsula of Korea. After checking Japan, the European powers proceeded to carve their own concessions in China. Germany took financial control of the Shantung peninsula and a naval base in the port of Kiaochow. The Russians leased a naval base at Port Arthur on the Liaotung peninsula, which they had forced Japan to disgorge. Russia also secured the right to control railroads through Chinese territory to connect its Trans-Siberian Railroad with Port Arthur and Vladivostok. France extorted a naval base at Kwangchwan.

Great Britain had been no happier with these imperial ventures than the United States. Britain already controlled most of China's trade and one-third of the foreign investments in that beleaguered country. Since Great Britain was becoming increasingly preoccupied with the rising strength of Germany in Europe and wished to concentrate more of its power there, it would have been happier with the earlier status quo in China. Britain did successfully request a new concession at Weihaiwei on the Shantung peninsula, from which it could keep an eye on the Russians. Britain also made China promise not to alienate any part of the Yangtze Valley to other foreigners. But it expended its primary diplomatic effort in trying to get the other imperial powers to maintain an open door for the trade of all nations in their spheres of interest, and it warned against further dismemberment of sovereign Chinese territory.

The British knew the Americans were not in the market for their own sphere of interest in China, and so had a similar interest in restricting the imperial scramble. Prior to the Spanish-American War, the British had approached McKinley about a joint declaration in favor of the open door and the territorial integrity of China, but McKinley had turned them down. Then the victory over Spain and the acquisition of the Philippines changed McKinley's attitude. The continuing European intrusions in China brought him to accept the suggestion of a limited initiative in pursuit of America's East Asian interests.

The suggestion for the initiative came from William Rockhill, acknowledged at the time as one of the few American experts on China. He had gained the ear of John Hay, McKinley's last secretary of state. Rockhill feared that the collapse of China would set off such a scramble among the imperial powers that it might not only close out American trade, but bring world war. He knew that Hay and McKinley would balk at any American engagement to protect China's territorial integrity, but one of his acquaintances, an Englishman named Alfred Hippisley, recommended a more limited course

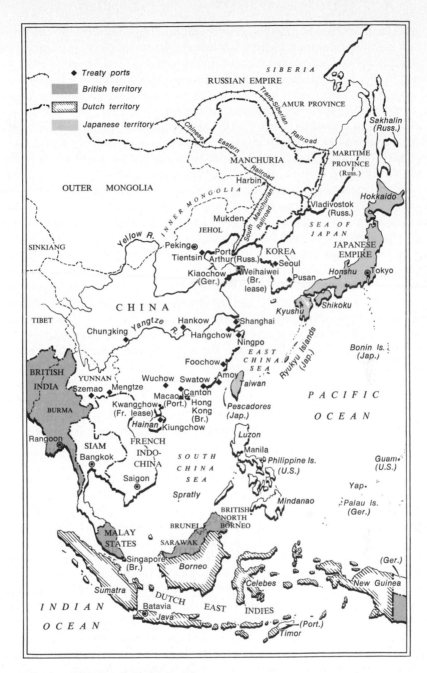

Map 9 China and the Imperialists

that Hay and McKinley might find acceptable. Hippisley was an official of China's semi-autonomous Imperial Maritime Customs Service, which was responsible for collecting the customs duties owed China. These tariffs constituted the major reliable source of income for the moribund Chinese government. If the European powers in China insisted on a monopoly of trade and investment in their new spheres of interest, they might prevent the Imperial Maritime Customs Service from operating there as well. This would destroy the financial underpinnings of China's government.

To forestall this, Hippisley drafted a statement for Rockhill that Hay sent off almost unchanged in September 1899 as the first Open Door note. (The British government by this time had drifted away from its earlier advocacy of the Open Door and had no role in Hippisley's initiative.) In it, the United States requested each imperial power to keep its spheres of interest in China open to trade from foreign nations. This note did not challenge acquisition of those spheres of interest or demand equality of investment along with trading rights in them.

None of the great powers was terribly anxious to accept such an open door to trade, but Russia and Japan were not nearly so concerned with the commerce in their spheres as they were with investments in such strategic enterprises as railroads and mines. Rather than offend the Americans over what they perceived as a minor issue, they and the other powers gave tentative and carefully hedged endorsements of Hay's suggestion. Hay ignored the qualifications and announced that the Open Door was now international policy. None of the nations wanted to contradict him, and his statement passed for an accepted principle among the uninitiated. Many Americans praised Hay's coup as a brilliant stroke that demonstrated America's new prestige and influence in international affairs, along with its shrewdness and idealism in protecting China against predatory powers.

The following year, Hay burnished that image even further with his second Open Door note. Hay sent this one in the midst of a crisis in China known as the Boxer Rebellion. The Society of Righteous and Harmonious Fists, or Boxers as Westerners called them, was a secret organization dedicated to eradicating foreign influence from China. At first the society also opposed the dowager empress and her Manchu court. The empress diverted their efforts exclusively toward the Europeans by quietly throwing her influence behind them and supplying them with arms. She believed the Europeans were trying to restore her son to the throne after she had imprisoned him and exiled or executed many of his advisors for excessive reformist zeal. With the secret encouragement of the empress, the Boxers murdered hundreds of Christian missionaries and their Chinese converts and laid seige to the foreign embassies and compounds in the capital of Peking.

Hay and McKinley sent 2,500 American troops from the Philippine war to join the forces of the other European powers in an expedition that set off from the China coast to rescue the besieged foreigners in Peking. The combined force plundered its way to the capital, with the American troops only somewhat less brutal than their compatriots. Almost every hut and village on the path of the expedition was destroyed. (Kaiser Wilhelm of Germany had encouraged his troops to make themselves as fearsome to the Chinse as Attila the Hun had been to the ancient world. His army obeyed, and his unfortunate turn of phrase earned the Germans an unwanted nickname that would plague them throughout World War I.)

McKinley and Hay quite naturally feared that some of the expedition's participants might be reluctant to remove their troops once their mission had been accomplished. To encourage their withdrawal, Hay sent a second Open Door note urging not just an open door for trade, but also respect for the territorial and administrative integrity of China. He uttered no threats, asked no commitments, and made none on the part of the United States. The note was simply a statement of American interests and wishes. Meanwhile, Hay worked cleverly to bolster Chinese provincial authorities who were suppressing the Boxers in the southern districts of China. He then pointed to the stability being restored there as good reason for the other powers to refrain from carving out further spheres. Once a satisfactory settlement to the Boxer Rebellion had been achieved, the United States withdrew its own troops.

Again Hay and McKinley won plaudits for what seemed a successful intervention on behalf of China. The relief of the besieged legations made a sensational story that entranced many Americans who had never given a thought to foreign policy. After Hay's death in 1905, his friends enshrined the Open Door policy alongside the Monroe Doctrine as a seemingly beneficent if vague foreign policy commandment demonstrating both America's strength and idealism. Naive Americans portrayed the United States as the protector of China, and the Chinese as grateful protégés.

While America's decision-makers did believe they were doing China a good turn in issuing the Open Door notes, their primary concern had been with America's interests in the potential trade offered by China's markets. They also understood the limitations of that interest; only 2 percent of America's exports found their way to China at the time, whatever the potential for the future. Hay and McKinley intended no major commitment to China. America's army was bogged down in the Philippines, its fleet was concentrated in the Caribbean against an imagined German threat to Latin America, and despite the defeat of the anti-imperialist campaign in the United States, the Philippine war had taken its toll on public opinion toward foreign adventures. A single expedition to China in pursuit of the traditional goal of protecting American lives and property might be popular; a significant military commitment on behalf of the Open Door or in pursuit of America's own sphere of influence in China, on the other hand, would be very risky politically as well as strategically. Consequently, Hay and McKinley were willing to support the concept of the Open Door verbally, but they had no intention of risking war.

Recognizing that the second Open Door note's call for the territorial integrity of China had no teeth and could well be brushed aside by the major powers in China, Hay prepared an alternative plan. He sent a discreet feeler to China about the possibility of America acquiring a coaling station at Samsah Bay in Fukien Province. But it was just as tentative and toothless as the Open Door notes themselves. Hay withdrew the request without even waiting for a Chinese reply when the Japanese, who already had a paramount interest in Fukien, pointedly reminded Hay of his own principles. The imperial powers thus were fully aware of the limitations of American interest in and commitment to the Open Door. They were careful of American sensitivities only because the power balance was so delicate in East Asia that for the moment even mild American action might tip the situation in favor of one side or another.

China's leaders also understood the limits of the American commitment and the essentially self-interested character of the Open Door policy. Hay never consulted the Chinese themselves about American decisions affecting their affairs. However much the principles of the Open Door and American hopes for Chinese territorial integrity may have corresponded to China's own interests, it was difficult to maintain that the Chinese should have felt much gratitude. American merchants and diplomats dealing directly with China generally urged forceful policies against supposed Chinese duplicity. Even American missionaries, idealistic as their motives may have been, were subversive of China's own culture.

They were contemptuous of Chinese authority, and their presence was made possible only by the gunboat patrols and diplomatic threats that lay behind the unequal treaty system. Also, at the very time the Americans were issuing the Open Door notes, they discriminated against Chinese residents in California and other western states. When the United States acquired Hawaii and the Philippines, it closed the door almost entirely to Chinese immigration to those islands. China's government was too weak to do anything about this, but educated Chinese who learned of these events made their displeasure known.

THEODORE ROOSEVELT, JAPAN, AND THE LIMITS OF THE OPEN DOOR

Theodore Roosevelt, who succeeded the assassinated McKinley in September of 1901, was under no illusions about the extent and nature of America's commitment to the Open Door policy. Occasionally he would bluster, as he did after the Boxer Rebellion when Russia refused to withdraw its troops from Manchuria and then erected trade barriers against American cotton exports to that area. At that time Roosevelt said he would not mind "going to extremes" with the Russians, but his actual instructions to Hay were far more restrained. Hay put the matter in perspective when he commented privately that both the Chinese and Russians knew the United States position was entirely moral. Hay suspected that neither country would pay much attention, since moral force was "mere flapdoodle."

The British also decided that America's posturing in East Asia was mere flapdoodle. They turned to Japan instead for help in restraining the Russians in China and negotiated the Anglo-Japanese Alliance of 1902. The Japanese were aching to confront the Russians. They resented Russia's role in ousting them from the Liaotung Peninsula and Port Arthur. They regarded Russia as a grave threat to their strategic interests in Korea and to their economic interests in the resources and railroads of Manchuria. Japan feared only that France might come to the aid of its Russian ally. The Anglo-Japanese Alliance protected against that contingency by pledging Great Britain to aid Japan if Japan found itself at war with more than one power. Thus fortified, Japan launched a surprise attack on Russia's Asiatic fleet and sank it while it lay at anchor at Port Arthur. The Russians immediately sent their European fleet into Asian waters, and the Japanese sank it too. Meanwhile, Japanese land forces conquered Port Arthur and Mukden after long and bloody sieges. The world looked on in astonishment as supposedly backward and inferior Asians beat a major European power.

Theodore Roosevelt was gleeful as well as astonished. Japan was doing "our work" in China, he said, and it was "bully" the way the Japanese had started the war with a surprise attack. Yet the extent of the Japanese victory gave him some pause. He did not believe it likely that the United States and Japan would ever go to war, but an increasingly powerful Japan could pose a threat to the nearly indefensible Philippines and Hawaii, perhaps even to the Pacific Coast. Japan might issue its own challenge to the Open Door in China as well. Roosevelt thought America's interest in China was relatively negligible and actually hoped Japan could be induced to spend its energies on the Asian continent rather than in the Pacific, where the United States was more involved. Still, he thought it desirable that Russia remain at least strong enough to keep some semblance of a balance of power in northern Asia.

With these interests in mind, and perhaps even more motivated by his unquenchable thirst for adventure and personal glory (Roosevelt's daughter said he wanted to be the bride at every wedding and the corpse at every funeral), Roosevelt agreed to mediate the Russo-Japanese War. He immediately found himself in difficulties. Russia was willing to make concessions in Korea and Manchuria in exchange for peace, but Japan wanted more. Unknown to most, Japan was at the end of its financial tether and desperately needed money. It demanded a large financial indemnity and the cession of Sakhalin Island. Russia was ready to break off negotiations rather than submit to these additional demands; only Roosevelt's pressure kept the bargaining from breaking down. Russia finally conceded the southern portion of Sakhalin, and Japan gave up its demand for the indemnity. Peace was made. Roosevelt won the Nobel Prize for his success, but he paid a price. The Japanese government was hard pressed to explain to the Japanese people, who had been told that their enormous sacrifices had won a great victory, why there was no indemnity to relieve their financial suffering. Naturally, the government blamed it on Roosevelt.

Nonetheless, the Japanese and the Roosevelt administration were able to compromise their respective positions in Asia. Roosevelt's special envoy to Japan, William Howard Taft, agreed to a memorandum with Japanese Prime

Figure 9 President Theodore Roosevelt stands between the Russian and Japanese delegations at Portsmouth, New Hampshire, where he helped negotiate an end to the Russo-Japanese War. Photo courtesy of the National Archives.

Minister Taro Katsura in 1905 that Japan would not challenge the United States position in the Philippines, while the United States would recognize Japanese predominance in Korea. This Taft-Katsura Memorandum said nothing about Manchuria, but it was no coincidence that a few months later Japan opened Manchuria to American trade.

In 1906 this accommodation faltered when San Francisco demonstrated its resentment of Japanese and Chinese laborers by segregating Asians in the school system. The Japanese were mortally offended. They were not like earlier Chinese governments, which had been apathetic about discriminatory practices in America. Japan encouraged emigration. It was overcrowded, and it saw emigration to the Pacific islands, the United States, and South America as a chance not only to relieve this population pressure, but also to create markets for Japanese goods. Prior to Japan's victory over China in 1895, Japanese leaders had preferred this expansion by Pacific emigration to military and political expansion on the Asian continent. The Sino-Japanese and Russo-Japanese wars had shifted Japan's emphasis toward Asia, but Pacific emigration remained a significant part of Japan's foreign policy goals.

The United States had already spiked some of these ambitions by closing the Philippines and Hawaii to Japanese immigrants and forbidding contract labor. Then riots and the segregation controversy in San Francisco led to a movement in Congress to extend the 1904 law prohibiting Chinese immigration to include Japan. Japan protested vehemently. Some American publicists panicked and warned that Japan, with its fierce military traditions and sense of honor, might declare war.

Roosevelt recognized that despite the depth of Japan's anger, the chance of war was remote, but he still thought it important to resolve the immigration and discrimination issues. When he found sentiment for excluding the Japanese too strong to be countered, he decided his only hope of avoiding a direct insult was to strike a deal. San Francisco would end its educational segregation and Congress would abandon its attempts to prohibit Japanese immigration; Japan itself would take the responsibility for preventing its citizens from emigrating to the United States. Roosevelt brought San Francisco Mayor Eugene Schmitz and the entire city school board to Washington, a major feat since Schmitz was free on bail after being charged with five counts of extortion. Roosevelt got the board to give up segregation, and a skeptical Congress dropped the bill to prohibit Japanese immigration. Japan, as its part of this so-called Gentleman's Agreement, quietly and reluctantly stopped issuing passports to laborers emigrating to the United States.

When anti-Japanese riots continued in California, Roosevelt reversed himself and concluded that war with Japan might indeed be a possibility. He decided to strengthen America's navy not only to deter Japan, but also because Britain's construction of a monster battleship, the HMS *Dreadnought*, set off a new European naval race. To stir public support for his expensive expansion of the American navy, Roosevelt sent the existing fleet on a highly publicized voyage to the Pacific Coast. Then, to impress the Japanese, he ordered the Great White Fleet to continue around the world.

Fortunately for this exposed naval task force, Japan's leaders did not contemplate war as feverishly as some American military leaders and newspaper pundits feared. A new Japanese cabinet made a formal decision to turn away from expansion by Pacific emigration and to concentrate instead on Japan's continental interests in Korea, Manchuria, and China. In this way Japan assumed that it would avoid conflict with America's domestic racism and its possessions in the Pacific. Rather than objecting to the Great White Fleet's voyage of intimidation, the Japanese cabinet invited the American ships to visit Japanese ports. The fleet received a tumultuous welcome.

Roosevelt and the Japanese moved quickly to publicize their détente and dampen war speculation. In November of 1908, Ambassador Takahira Kogoro and Hay's replacement as secretary of state, Elihu Root, exchanged notes reaffirming respect for one another's Pacific possessions, the Open Door, and the territorial integrity of China. In private conversations, the Japanese told Root and Roosevelt that they considered Manchuria, Taiwan, and Korea to be among the Pacific possessions which the United States must respect. Root and Roosevelt made no objection.

The Chinese were not nearly so pleased with Roosevelt's East Asian policies. The Chinese had hoped to make use of America's commitment to the Open Door policy to help them resist Japanese and Russian encroachments in Manchuria. The Chinese had long subscribed to the stratagem of manipulating barbarians to protect China's interests against other barbarians. By the time Roosevelt became president, China's officials were under more than usual pressure to redeem Chinese interests because a national spirit was beginning to rise among some urban and student groups. In 1905, a few Chinese nationalists even organized a boycott against American goods in response to the Chinese Exclusion Act of 1904. No longer would they permit their officials to look with indifference upon the treatment of Chinese in barbarian lands.

Roosevelt sympathized with the boycotters' anger at the indignity of Chinese exclusion. Yet he could do nothing about the law. He could only issue orders for government officials to deal fairly with the Chinese already in America. Then, unwilling to see the Chinese boycott humiliate American businessmen before the merchants of other powers, he insisted that the Chinese government suppress it. He even had America's Asiatic fleet anchor at Shanghai. Chinese officials mildy supported the boycott for a few months, fearful that the boycotters might turn their energies against the regime if it moved against them. When Chinese businessmen began to lose interest, the Chinese government finally responded to American pressure and suppressed the boycott. Roosevelt told Congress afterward that the United States had been much to blame for the conflict because "grave injustices and wrong have been done by this nation to the people of China."

Despite Roosevelt's tentative sympathy for rising Chinese nationalism, he did not make any other dramatic gestures on China's behalf. He protested vigorously when, during the boycott, the Chinese government sought to regain control of a concession it had granted the American China Development Company to build a railroad from Hankow to Canton. The stockholders of the company included such financial powerhouses as E. H. Harriman, Jacob Schiff, and the presidents of National City Bank, Chase National Bank, and Carnegie Steel. Yet by 1903, eight years after receiving its concession, the company had built only ten miles of railroad. Disturbed at the ineptitude and lethargy of the company, China took advantage of the anti-American atmosphere to try to buy back the concession from J. P. Morgan, who had assumed control after the company had passed through the hands of a Belgian consortium. Morgan was perfectly willing to sell, but Roosevelt regarded the Chinese offer as a slap at American prestige. Only after a long meeting with Morgan did Roosevelt abandon his protests and allow the financier to sell the concession back to China.

WILLIAM HOWARD TAFT AND DOLLAR DIPLOMACY IN ASIA

Roosevelt had few compunctions about putting pressure on the hapless Chinese over Morgan's railroad in southern China, but he and Root were very cautious about American activities in northern China, where Japan had its interests. Roosevelt's successor, William Howard Taft, was not so fastidious. He and his secretary of state, Philander Knox, were determined to help China. They devoutly believed that American investment in "backward" countries would aid them at the same time it fulfilled America's own interest in international stability. Taft's emphasis on financial intervention contrasted sharply with Roosevelt's greater concentration on power politics, and the newspapers began to call Taft's foreign policy "dollar diplomacy."

A group of young and vigorous American diplomats urged Taft and Knox toward financial intervention in Manchuria. These diplomats, Willard Straight, Huntington Wilson, and William Phillips, had served in East Asia and were busily and self-consciously replacing William Rockhill as the recognized American experts on the area. When the State Department was reorganized at the end of Roosevelt's administration, they formed the staff of the new Bureau of Far Eastern Affairs. In the course of their earlier duties abroad, all of them had learned to detest the Japanese. They believed it was America's mission to support China against Japan, a policy Rockhill condemned as foolhardy. Their displacement of Rockhill had little impact on such determined leaders as Roosevelt and Root, but they and their attitudes had considerable influence on the administration of Taft and Knox.

The staff of the Bureau of Far Eastern Affairs secured the support of Taft and Knox for a project of railroad baron E. H. Harriman that deeply worried the Japanese. Harriman cherished ambitions to build a round-the-world railway and was eager to acquire a Manchurian route as one link in this grandiose dream. He even induced Willard Straight to resign from the State Department and become his agent. China joined the Taft administration in

Figure 10   William H. Rockhill (left), whose loss of influence under President William Howard Taft (right) signalled a significant shift in U.S. diplomacy toward Japan and China. Portraits courtesy of the National Archives.

supporting Harriman and offered him a concession to build a railroad between Chinchow and Aigun. The Chinese hoped that such a railroad would drain business and influence from Japan's Southern Manchurian Line. When Japan objected angrily, however, the Chinese quickly aborted the project. They knew that the Americans could not protect them from Japan and that the British would not be drawn into a scheme against their Japanese allies. Undeterred, Knox proposed the neutralization of all Manchurian railways and suggested that eventually China be permitted to buy control of them with a loan from the great powers. To Japan's great relief, this scheme also failed.

Taft did succeed in wedging American capitalists into a consortium formed by British, French, and German bankers to float a loan to China. Taft and the Chinese both thought this loan might give China some strength to resist Japan. The Japanese foiled that plan by compelling the consortium to invite them and the Russians to participate as well. This ensured that the consortium would do nothing to imperil the various foreign spheres of influence in China. Yet Taft continued to cooperate; he even accepted the consortium's request to delay recognition of the Chinese Nationalist government that overthrew the Manchu dynasty in 1912. Taft's inconsistency only succeeded in making China as angry as Japan.

Although the president's dollar diplomacy offended Japan, Taft and Knox were not truly anti-Japanese. They did their best to protect Japanese rights in the United States. In 1911 they gave up America's rights under the unequal treaty system to control Japanese tariffs on American products, and they renewed the Gentleman's Agreement. They simply did not understand that Japan would regard their policies as a threat to its vital interests. They did nothing to prepare America's naval or coastal defenses in the Pacific, and they were taken by surprise when Japan drew closer to its old enemy Russia to resist the American drive on Manchuria. Theodore Roosevelt warned Taft and Knox against challenging Japan, but Knox replied that China needed Manchuria as much as Japan did and he accused Roosevelt of abandoning America's historic Open Door policy.

WOODROW WILSON AND MISSIONARY DIPLOMACY IN ASIA

Roosevelt was not the only critic of Taft's dollar diplomacy in East Asia. Many liberals refused to believe that Taft's cooperation with Wall Street bankers and European imperial powers could possibly be intended to help China. His acceptance of Japanese participation in the consortium and nonrecognition of China's new government confirmed their suspicions. In contrast to Theodore Roosevelt, these idealistic liberals thought America should do more to help China. American missionaries in China encouraged these ideas. They greatly influenced the thinking of Woodrow Wilson and his minister to China, a former college professor named Paul Reinsch.

When Wilson became president, he abruptly withdrew government support for the consortium. This caused the participating American bankers to pull out, because the government would no longer guarantee to collect the consortium's loans. Wilson had consulted none of the other nations involved in the consortium when he made his decision; he had not consulted China; he had not even consulted his own State Department. Huntington Wilson resigned in protest. But Wilson, convinced of the righteousness of his position, then announced that the United States would recognize the revolutionary government of China.

Japan argued against recognition by pointing out that the revolutionary government was on the verge of civil war. That government was an unstable coalition between the Nationalists, who had risen to control southern China in 1911, and the commander of the Manchu empire's army, Yuan Shi-kai. Yuan controlled much of northern China; by taking him into the government, the Nationalists had hoped to avoid civil war. After Yuan persuaded the last Manchu emperor to abdicate in 1912, Sun Yat-sen, whom the Nationalists had made their provisional president, stepped aside in favor of Yuan as president of the new Republic of China. Yuan secured recognition and a loan from the European powers in 1913, but many of the Nationalists disliked the terms of the loan and feared that Yuan was using the money to finance the army on which his power depended.

The Nationalists raised a second revolution against Yuan. Yuan put it down easily, and Sun and many of his followers fled to Japan. Yuan then outlawed their Kuomintang party and suspended the national and provincial parliaments. He even contemplated making himself emperor. Open civil war broke out a month after Wilson recognized the new regime. It kept China divided because Yuan could not conquer the Nationalists in the south, and the Nationalists, having no army, could not defeat Yuan in the north. To add to the chaos, Yuan lost control of his own lieutenants, who proceeded to set themselves up as independent warlords in various regions.

Meanwhile a much larger war had broken out in Europe. World War I diverted the attention of Europe and America from the Asian theater, and Japan saw an open field in a weak and divided China. Japan extorted from the European Allies the right to conquer Germany's colonies in China and the Pacific as the price for its entry into the war. Quickly Japan took Shantung and Germany's Pacific islands north of the equator (Australia and New Zealand got those south of the equator). Then, in early 1915, Japan presented China with a list of twenty-one demands. China was to ratify Japanese control of Shantung; extend Japanese concessions in Manchuria and central China; permit no further acquisition of harbors or islands on the China coast by other foreigners; purchase half its armaments from Japan; accept Japanese advisors for all its political, military, and economic affairs; and permit Japanese police to share control of critical points throughout China. In short, China would become a Japanese colony.

The Japanese told China to keep the Twenty-One Demands secret. But the Chinese leaked them to the American missionary community. Paul

Reinsch clamored from China for Wilson to do something. Initially Wilson left the affair to the State Department while he concentrated on the European war, and the State Department reacted rather coolly to China's request for help. State Department counsellor Robert Lansing said it would be "quixotic in the extreme" for the United States to entangle itself in the affair. Secretary of State William Jennings Bryan issued a statement recognizing the legitimacy of Japanese concerns in Shantung and Manchuria and expressed only mild concern for the Open Door and the territorial integrity of China. Nevertheless, other voices in the State Department, led by Paul Reinsch, warned Wilson that China's very existence was in danger.

Wilson told Bryan he wanted the United States to be the champion of China. He wrote a stern note warning that the United States would not recognize any agreement between Japan and China that impaired American rights, Chinese political and territorial integrity, or the Open Door. Great Britain joined the protest because the Twenty-One Demands infringed on its sphere in the Yangtze and Hupeh areas. This opposition, along with some internal dissent within Japan, caused the Japanese to abandon the most far-reaching of the demands. But Japan forced the Chinese to accept the rest of its ultimatum, and the Japanese now resentfully regarded the United States as their primary obstacle in Asia.

With Japan operating almost unchecked in China, Wilson swallowed hard and agreed to a new consortium to loan money to the Chinese. Japan would be a member of the consortium, but at least Wilson thought Japanese influence might be diluted if America furnished some of the loan money. In this way Wilson established a measure of superficial cooperation with Japan. As the United States entered the war in Europe in 1917, Wilson thought it important to cool the Japanese-American rivalry still further. Neither Wilson nor Japan was willing to make substantial concessions, so Robert Lansing and Japanese special minister Ishii Kikujiro agreed to a set of notes papering over the disagreements. Japan would respect the Open Door and the territorial integrity of China, while the United States would accept Japan's "special interests" there. Just what constituted Japan's special interests was left to the imagination, although a secret protocol pledged both sides to respect the status quo in China for the duration of the war.

Japanese-American relations remained strained despite the Lansing-Ishii Agreement of 1917. When Japan insisted on sending an expeditionary force into Siberia following Russia's withdrawal from World War I, a reluctant Wilson dispatched an American force to Siberia as well, in large part to keep an eye on the Japanese. Then, at the Paris Peace Conference, Wilson tried unsuccessfully to get the Allies to withdraw their cession of the Shantung Peninsula to Japan. He was also instrumental in defeating a clause Japan sought to insert into the peace treaty recognizing racial equality, a clause Wilson opposed personally and feared would prevent Senate consent. Japanese-American relations remained distrustful and contentious for the next twenty-five years.

CONTROVERSIAL ISSUES AND FURTHER READING

The Open Door policy in Asia was an immensely popular one in the United States after John Hay enunciated it at the turn of the century. Newspapers, popular magazines, and politicians praised Hay for devising a clever diplomacy that supposedly saved China from predatory imperialists while protecting American interests, all without entangling the United States in foreign alliances or war. [See, for example, A. L. P. Dennis, *Adventures in American Diplomacy, 1896–1906* (1928).] Hay knew how little influence his declaration of policy had had in the absence of any disposition on the part of the United States to enforce it. Nevertheless, he and his successors did nothing to stop the popular portrayal of the Open Door as the savior of China. Consequently, the Open Door notes rapidly acquired an aura of sanctity approaching that of the Monroe Doctrine. This popular image proved tenacious through the years, especially in those sectors of the public influenced by the reports of American missionaries in China. Even today, many Americans continue to see the United States as having been the friendly protector of China, fighting Japan in the 1940s to save China's independence, only to be betrayed by the triumph of Mao Tse-tung and the Communists in 1949.

Academic historians have never been so enamored of the Open Door or America's actions in East Asia, and they have differed strongly about their effect. The first group of historical critics in the 1920s and 1930s was isolationist. They saw the Open Door as having entangled the United States in European imperial rivalries. Then, when the Europeans pulled back, the United States was left standing alone as the primary obstacle to Japan's ambitions. Isolationists thought the United States should have avoided foreign entanglements in both Asia and Europe, and confined its military power to the defense of North America or perhaps at most the Western Hemisphere. They particularly condemned the United States for supposedly defending the interests of the British Empire by declaring the Open Door in China. [See, for example, A. Whitney Griswold, *The Far Eastern Policy of the United States* (1938), and Samuel Flagg Bemis, *A Diplomatic History of the United States* (1936).] The other great pre-World War II historian of American policy in East Asia, Tyler Dennett, wrote his major works to demonstrate that the United States should have allied itself with Great Britain and been willing to use force rather than mere words and diplomacy to ensure the Open Door and the survival of China. But by the 1930s he had come around to the isolationist view. [See Tyler Dennett, *Americans in Eastern Asia* (1922), *Roosevelt and the Russo-Japanese War* (1925), and *John Hay* (1933); and Dorothy Borg, "Two Historians of the Far Eastern Policy of the United States: Tyler Dennett and A. Whitney Griswold," in Dorothy Borg and Shumpei Okamoto, eds., *Pearl Harbor as History* (1973).]

After World War II, realist historians joined the chorus condemning America's interventionist policy in Asia, but they did not denounce American intervention in World War II in Europe, as the isolationists did. Instead, they thought the United States should have tried to stay out of the war with Japan so it could concentrate its efforts against the greater threat of Hitler's Germany. These historians pointed out that the China market never amounted to anything, that American interests in Asia were too few and unimportant to justify taking any risks for them, and that the United States would have been better off if it had allowed Japan to exert some control

over China. Perhaps if the Japanese had not been threatened by American obstruc-
tion, they would have been more moderate in China and never attacked Pearl Harbor. The realists argued that the war with Japan endangered the effort against Hitler
without doing China any good and without winning any real loyalty from the Chinese. China soon went Communist anyway, and the United States began its equally
ineffective attempts to control communism in Asia, leading to the wars in Korea and
Vietnam.

The primary quarrel among realist historians has been over which actions and
leaders were most to blame for the tragic policy in Asia. Some have seen it as stem-
ming inevitably from the decision to keep the Philippines and then issue the Open
Door notes. [See, for example, Louis J. Halle, *Dream and Reality: Aspects of American
Foreign Policy* (1959), and George F. Kennan, *American Diplomacy, 1900–1950* (1951).]
But most realists now argue that John Hay and Theodore Roosevelt were well aware
of the limitations of American interest in Asia, were quite willing to accommodate
Japan, and confined their activities to diplomacy and verbal expressions of American
desires. Their only fault was their failure to explain their policies adequately to their
successors and the general public. These realist historians blame William Howard
Taft, Woodrow Wilson, and pro-Chinese State Department officials rather than
Roosevelt and Hay for America's supposedly blind and excessive attachment to
China, the Open Door, and confrontation with Japan. [See Raymond A. Esthus, *Theo-
dore Roosevelt and Japan* (1966); Charles E. Neu, *An Uncertain Friendship: Theodore Roose-
velt and Japan, 1906–1909* (1967); Charles E. Neu, *The Troubled Encounter: The United
States and Japan* (1975); Akira Iriye, *Pacific Estrangement: Japanese and American Expan-
sionism, 1897–1911* (1972); Akira Iriye, *Across the Pacific: An Inner History of America–East
Asian Relations* (1967); Burton Beers, *Vain Endeavor: Robert Lansing's Attempts to End the
American-Japanese Rivalry* (1962).]

As realist historians dated America's overcommitment in Asia from the accession
of Taft to the presidency in 1909, naturally John Hay's Open Door notes lost much of
their previous significance. The significance of the notes was further undermined by
historians of Chinese-American relations who pointed out that Hay did little more
than confirm policies America had been supporting since its first contacts with China
in the eighteenth century. Certainly Americans did not need the British to dupe them
into adoption of the Open Door, especially since Great Britain was in the midst of
changing its policy when Hippisley was approaching the Americans without British
government authorization. [R. G. Neale, *Great Britain and United States Expansion,
1898–1900* (1966); Paul A. Varg, *Open Door Diplomat: The Life of W. W. Rockhill* (1952).]

Historians who concentrated on China have generally been less sympathetic to
Japan than those realists or other historians who have concentrated on Japanese relations with the United States. They have argued that the United States never supported China to the point that it risked war with Japan or seriously threatened
Japanese interests until 1940, when Japan allied itself with Germany and truly menaced American security. These historians agree that the United States could have followed a more enlightened Japanese policy before 1940, but, unlike some realists, they
have little hope that a better policy would have avoided Pearl Harbor. Meanwhile,
they point out that American policy was actually harmful rather than helpful to the
Chinese. American diplomats and businessmen condescended to China and exploited it, while the missionaries, however good their intentions, undermined China's
culture and national self-confidence. The regrets of most historians of China are not
for the war against Japan, but for America's self-delusion about the supposed benevolence of its policy toward China, its sense of outrage and betrayal at the Communist

revolution, and the consequent refusal of recognition and ultimate war with Mao's China over Korea. [See John King Fairbank, *The United States and China* (1958); Paul A. Varg, *Missionaries, Chinese, and Diplomats: The American Protestant Missionary Movement in China, 1890–1952* (1958); Paul A. Varg, *The Making of a Myth: The United States and China, 1897–1912* (1968); Marilyn Blatt Young, *The Rhetoric of Empire: American China Policy, 1895–1901* (1968); Warren I. Cohen, *America's Response to China* (2nd ed., 1981); Charles S. Campbell, Jr., *Special Business Interests and the Open Door Policy* (1951); Roy Curry, *Woodrow Wilson and Far Eastern Policy, 1913–1921* (1957); Russell H. Fifield, *Woodrow Wilson and the Far East: The Diplomacy of the Shantung Question* (1952); Shih-shan Henry Tsai, *China and the Overseas Chinese* (1984); Michael H. Hunt, *The Making of a Special Relationship: The United States and China to 1914* (1983); James Reed, *The Missionary Mind and American East Asian Policy* (1982).]

Revisionists dissent even more strongly from the realists who wish America had appeased Japan. They think the United States should have been far more supportive of China. They regard the Open Door as simply a policy of informal empire and economic exploitation. They argue that Americans were so confident of their industrial dominance as to believe the United States could control the Chinese economy and through the economy China itself if simply given a chance to compete openly in the China market. Americans had no real interest in China's territorial integrity or general well-being, only in the opportunity for profits. If the United States had been truly anxious to help China, it would have joined the Soviets in supporting the Chinese nationalists. This would have created a strong China capable of withstanding Japan and therefore deterring it prior to Pearl Harbor. [See William Appleman Williams, "China and Japan: A Challenge and a Choice of the Nineteen Twenties," *Pacific Historical Review*, 26 (1957), pp. 259–279; Charles Vevier, *The United States and China, 1906–1913* (1955); Thomas J. McCormick, *China Market: America's Quest for Informal Empire, 1893–1901* (1967); Jerry Israel, *Progressivism and the Open Door: America and China, 1905–1921* (1971).]

For information on the Philippine war and occupation, see Richard Welch, *Response to Imperialism: The United States and the Philippine-American War, 1899–1902* (1979); Stuart Creighton Miller, *"Benevolent Assimilation": The American Conquest of the Philippines, 1899–1903* (1982); Peter W. Stanley, *A Nation in the Making: The Philippines and the United States, 1899–1921* (1974); and for a strong revisionist denunciation, William J. Pomeroy, *American Neo-Colonialism: Its Emergence in the Philippines and Asia* (1970).

CHAPTER 10

The Surge into Latin America: Varieties of American Empire

THE NATURE OF THE AMERICAN EMPIRE IN LATIN AMERICA

Throughout its history, the United States has been wary of the idea of imperialism. Americans have prided themselves on the fact that their revolution was the first successful rebellion against European colonialism. Their political ideology has been based on the principle of government by consent of the governed. Although they have subscribed to other competing values—desire for national security, economic prosperity, and the prestige associated with great power status—they have suffered considerable discomfort when they sacrificed the principle of democracy too easily and blatantly to those other desires. Prior to the Spanish-American War, Americans found it relatively easy to rationalize the contradictions between their actions and their commitment to democratic self-determination. They ignored the Indians and visualized the westward movement as expansion into "empty lands" which they would ultimately incorporate into the Union as equal states. But it was difficult for them to conceive of making states out of the Philippines, the South Sea Islands, Hawaii, or Puerto Rico. The Supreme Court even decided in the famous Insular Cases that the inhabitants of America's new colonies were not entitled to all the basic liberties granted American citizens by the Constitution. To add to the dilemmas the United States faced in its new colonies, many Americans thought it essential to ensure stability in still other nations that were economically or strategically important.

The United States could no longer escape the fact that it was an imperial and interventionist power. In the first flush of victory, the thrill of arrival as a great world power overrode the sense of guilt and the anti-imperialist movement that had exploited that guilt. Then, as the thrill waned in the blood and atrocities of the Philippine revolution, Americans began to regard their colonial experiment and intervention in general with an increasingly jaundiced eye.

Still, intervene they did. They may not have done so enthusiastically;

they may have considered intervention only the lesser of evils; yet most came to feel that the United States had no other choice, especially in Latin America. Even many politicians and historians who opposed the annexation of the Philippines or an activist policy in defense of the Open Door in Asia were ready to defend the acquisition of colonies and protectorates in Central America and the Caribbean. They reasoned that Latin America was closer to home than Asia and believed that it was strategically vital for the United States to control the isthmian canal routes.

By the end of the Spanish-American War, the United States was well on its way to achieving the goal of an isthmian canal. America displaced Spanish rule in two critical islands guarding the Caribbean approaches to the canal routes, Cuba and Puerto Rico. Great Britain was slowly but surely reducing its power and presence in the Western Hemisphere to concentrate on the European theater. The United States wanted nothing to tempt Spain or Great Britain to return to the Caribbean or Central America, and it hoped to deter the recently united and aggressive Germany from intruding there as well.

As the strategic interest of the United States in Latin America increased, so did its direct economic stake. Cuba was especially valuable. It supplied sugar and tobacco; it served as an important market for American manufactured goods; and Americans invested heavily there in tobacco and sugar plantations, banks, railroads, and public utilities. Mexico, where Americans were developing similar markets and investments, was equally valuable. The rest of Latin America was not, although several American corporations had substantial interests in various areas and sought protection from the U.S. government. The United States had always assumed that protection of American lives and property abroad was a proper goal of diplomacy, so the government became more inclined to intervene as its Latin American economic interests increased and the obstacles posed by major rivals decreased.

Americans naturally managed to find ideological rationales for their multiplying interventions. They convinced themselves that American rule could never be like European colonial oppression because the United States would educate the native peoples for liberty. As time wore on, this took the concrete form of a decision to free the Philippines and to consider granting statehood to the largest and most compatible of the colonies. Where the United States felt compelled to intervene militarily or to exert a rather heavy-handed economic and diplomatic influence, Americans were at least half convinced that this too could work for the good of all. American trade and investments would increase the economic wealth of those nations. U.S. military power would protect Latin America against European colonial exploitation and preserve peace among the weaker nations. Political supervision could help bring stability and democracy. American influence would work against dictatorship, corruption, and the chaos that indigenous romantic nationalists or radicals might bring in their wake.

Events quickly exposed the problems and contradictions involved in colonizing or intervening in foreign areas. The clash of cultures between the native inhabitants and Americans was often bitter and ugly. Most Americans shared a condescending attitude toward non-Europeans. When Americans served abroad in positions of authority as factory owners, colonial officials, teachers, and missionaries, they often aroused nationalistic hostilities. American troops stationed in foreign countries caused special difficulties: Most soldiers were uneducated and unsophisticated. They regarded foreigners as strange and inferior and treated them as such. Consequently, American military intervention often created more problems than it solved.

The United States usually intervened in hope of establishing reasonably stable and democratic regimes. Nevertheless, those who were the targets of the intervention generally regarded any government established or supported by the United States as collaborationist. Such a government could not survive by democratic means. It would resort to oppression, invite rebellion and chaos, and tempt American intervention once again. The events of Theodore Roosevelt's administration exposed many of these problems. Roosevelt's successor, William Howard Taft, tried to circumvent the need for military intervention by substituting dollar diplomacy. By encouraging American investment to enrich and buttress weaker economies, Taft hoped he would stabilize the politics of those nations as well. But dollar diplomacy failed; American investment and trade usually enriched a few Americans and a small group of Latin Americans without raising the general standard of living.

Most Latin American countries began to concentrate on one or two cash crops or natural resources that might be exchanged in the United States for manufactured items and luxury goods. The upper classes might benefit from this trade and from the American investments and loans that made possible the railroads, port facilities, and public utilities necessary to commerce; few peasants did. The economies of these nations became almost totally dependent on the United States, whose superior economic strength permitted its citizens in large measure to control the price of both Latin American exports and imports. Latin Americans paid more for the manufactured goods they imported than they received for the agricultural products or raw materials they exported.

Woodrow Wilson recognized some of the problems with dollar diplomacy and thought they were caused by the greed of Wall Street investors. He believed that a greater dedication to democracy abroad and less concern for selfish profits in American trade and investment would resolve the difficulties. But to his chagrin, his attempt to establish just and democratic governments led to more conflict and intervention than the policies of either of his predecessors.

The dilemma Wilson, Taft, and Roosevelt faced is still with us and still generates controversy. Revisionists condemn America's historic policies toward Latin America in toto. Like the Latin American Left itself, they believe that the United States intervened in Latin America primarily for economic gain, to protect and increase American trade and investments. American interventions were not motivated by fears for national security, because no outside power posed a credible threat to Latin America after the British retreated at the turn of the century. The United States intervened instead to perpetuate the dictatorship of the Latin American upper classes, which have been allied with the economic interests of the United States. It has sought to protect its collaborators against indigenous revolutionaries who had no choice but to seek nationalization of land and resources because wealth was concentrated in so few hands. Obviously the United States had no interest in democracy, or it would have supported such revolutionary movements.

Restrained realists also have been highly critical of U.S. policy toward Latin America, but for different reasons. They do not believe economic interests provided the primary motivation for U.S. interventions. Instead, they think the United States intervened out of naive notions of national security and hopes for Latin American democracy. They agree with the revisionists that the United States has exaggerated the security threats to Latin America. Therefore they believe that most of the interventions have been foolish ones which generated hostility toward the United States and did little good. Most realists do not regard Latin America as terribly vital to U.S. economic or strategic interests and therefore agree that the United States should follow a much more restrained policy there. The implication of their view, however, is that the United States should not hesitate to intervene when its national security truly is at stake, even though such intervention might be harmful. They see it as inevitable that a powerful nation should influence and to some extent dominate its weaker neighbors and believe the best the United States can hope to do is to mitigate the effects of that situation.

Nationalists do not regard the Latin American policy of the United States to have been such an unmitigated failure. Like the realists but unlike the revisionists, they do not place as great an emphasis on economic motivations. Nationalists also do not believe that U.S. trade and investment have done that much harm. They argue that Latin America needed capital and would have been far worse off if the United States and its corporations had not furnished it. They are not so willing to discount the threats of outside nations to the Western Hemisphere, past or present. Nationalists also believe that the encouragement of democracy in Latin America was a sincere and worthy goal, even if U.S. intervention and influence failed to secure it in very many places. They blame the failure of democracy more on the Latin Americans themselves than on the United States and refuse to equate U.S. policy there with European imperialism.

But even nationalists find it hard to argue against the idea that the United States created at least an informal empire in Central America and the Caribbean area after the turn of the twentieth century. Along with annexing the formal colony of Puerto Rico, the United States made a protectorate of Cuba, acquired all but absolute sovereignty over the Panama Canal Zone, intervened militarily in several Central American and Caribbean nations, and exerted a profound economic influence over the rest of Latin America. Meanwhile, the United States successfully excluded all of the military and much of the economic influence of the European powers.

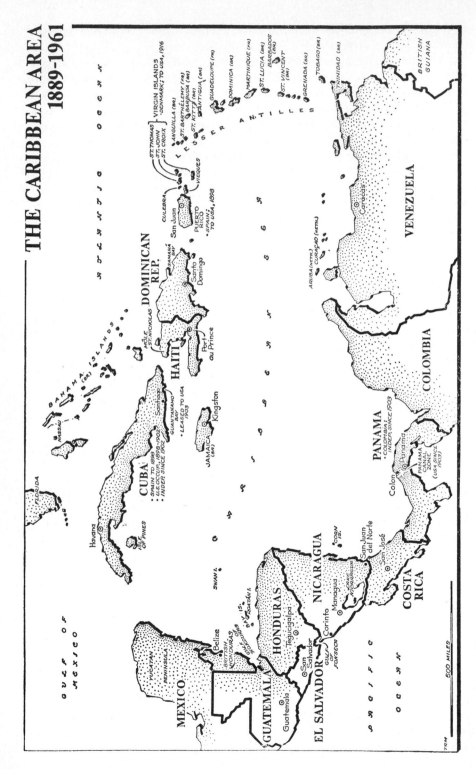

Map 10 The Caribbean Area, 1889–1961

PUERTO RICO: GOVERNING A COLONY

The United States had met little opposition in seizing Puerto Rico during the Spanish-American War. Americans conducted no land campaign at all. Puerto Rican revolutionaries in New York, cooperating to some extent with the Cuban junta, invited American intervention. Thus, Americans found their presence welcomed for the first two years of their occupation of the island. The Puerto Ricans had little reason to mourn the demise of the Spanish empire. Puerto Rico had shared the tragic experience of the rest of the Caribbean, including European conquest, extermination of most of the Indian population, and establishment of a brutal slave system by absentee owners of large sugar plantations. The African slaves ultimately had been emancipated, but the society remained fixed in a rigid class system with a small upper class dominating a large mass of landless, racially mixed peasants. In 1898, only 21 percent of Puerto Rico's land was under cultivation. There were no banks and only two or three roads.

Nevertheless, this was no "empty land" available for mass American immigration. The island was already overpopulated as well as poverty-stricken. Americans would come to Puerto Rico as colonial officials, entrepreneurs, missionaries, or tourists, not as farmers and settlers. Some American capital did flow into the island, and Americans replaced Spaniards as absentee landlords. They shifted Puerto Rican agricultural enterprise even more toward sugar, away from the cultivation of coffee produced by the smaller and relatively independent farmers of Puerto Rico's interior. The United States had abundant supplies of coffee from elsewhere and saw sugar as more profitable.

By 1930, American absentee owners controlled more than half of Puerto Rico's sugar, 80 percent of its tobacco, 60 percent of its banks and public utilities, and under special government protection, 100 percent of its shipping. Some 70 percent of the profits from Puerto Rico's large enterprises went to foreigners, including Americans. Much of the other 30 percent went to rich Puerto Ricans, who in turn spent it on manufactured and luxury goods from the United States. Lower-class Puerto Ricans had to buy food from the United States at tariff-protected prices or produce their own on small, inadequate farms. Existence was possible only at a low subsistence level. Many fled to the cities or to the United States itself to escape their dilemma, so no middle-class farming population developed. The Puerto Rican middle class was essentially a set of bureaucrats or lower-level managers in the larger enterprises and almost totally dissociated from the peasants.

Meanwhile, the Anglo-Calvinist civilization of the United States conflicted with the Catholic Spanish-Creole culture of the island. Puerto Ricans, themselves ambivalent and uncertain in their attitudes toward race, were shocked to find themselves considered black by their American masters. The middle and upper classes considered themselves white and looked with disdain and some alarm at what they considered to be the shallow imported materialistic culture of their supposed racial superiors. This economic and cultural scenario was repeated to a lesser or greater extent throughout Central America and the Caribbean.

The impact of the United States was somewhat different on Puerto Rico than on the rest of Latin America because Puerto Rico was a formal rather than an informal colony. The Insular Cases dictated that the United States did not have to govern Puerto Rico and the Philippines with the expectation that they would become states, as had been the rule with previous American territories. The Organic Act of 1900 gave Puerto Rico a territorial government that allowed election of Puerto Rican representatives, but guaranteed an American governor and an American majority on the governing council. Various American administrations usually reserved these offices for loyal party workers, without regard to their knowledge of Puerto Rico or the Spanish language. Often these officials did little to disguise their patronizing attitudes.

The United States did extend citizenship to the Puerto Ricans in 1917. Americans improved sanitation, utilities, and roads, although the primary benefits of these went to the cities and larger agricultural enterprises rather than to the ordinary peasant. Americans also did much for education on the island. Puerto Rico's literacy rate rose to better that 80 percent, compared to Haiti's 15 percent or the Dominican Republic's 26 percent. Still, this did not offset the growing resentment of the Puerto Ricans toward their American overlords.

It was not until the early 1940s that Puerto Rico tenuously accepted its position within the American empire. During those years, a remarkable Puerto Rican leader, Luís Muñoz Marín, organized a political party that finally convinced the United States to allow Puerto Rico to elect its own governor. Muñoz Marín then gained commonwealth status for Puerto Rico, corrected some of the most glaring of the island's economic inequalities, lobbied successfully for large economic benefits from Congress, and attracted considerable private capital. Yet Puerto Rico's consent to its United States connection remained unstable and laced with considerable hostility. This boded ill for U.S. relations with the rest of Latin America, where the problems raised by the overwhelming North American presence were not balanced as they were in Puerto Rico by the investment of some $500 million between 1898 and 1945 and by the right of free passage to the United States.

CUBA: SHAPING A FORMAL PROTECTORATE

William McKinley committed the United States to abstain from annexing Cuba when he accepted the Teller Amendment, but he also avoided recognizing the Cuban rebel government. This left him free to set the ground rules under which Cuba could remain independent. He forced the Spanish to surrender Cuba to the U.S. military, not to the Cuban rebels. The United States then established a temporary military government and managed to disband the Cuban army by making liberal payments to its commanders and soldiers.

After complaints from Cubans and Americans alike that the first U.S. governor was too liberal toward the defeated Spanish, McKinley appointed General Leonard Wood to succeed him. Wood was a medical doctor who was able, confident, energetic, and sympathetic to the "large policy" of his friends Theodore Roosevelt and Henry Cabot Lodge. Wood did much to improve sanitation, eradicate yellow fever, establish public schools, and bring a measure of efficiency to Cuba's government and public services. Yet he distrusted Cuban abilities and always put North Americans in charge of these projects. He even established a paternalistic code of discipline that prescribed public whippings for violaters of his new civic codes.

Wood and Secretary of War Elihu Root formulated the terms on which the United States would turn Cuba over to an indigenous government. Wood and Root wanted a stable Cuba that would protect U.S. trade and investment and that would welcome a U.S. military presence to defend the island, the approaches to the Caribbean, and the peninsular canal routes. To achieve this, Root circumvented a congressional prohibition against permanent economic concessions in Cuba by granting supposedly temporary ones instead. He and Wood also worked through Senator Orville Platt of Connecticut to attach the so-called Platt Amendment to the Army Appropriations Bill of 1901. This prohibited Cuba from granting foreign economic concessions without U.S. permission or doing anything to impair independence. The Platt Amendment required Cuba to keep its debt at a low level, grant the United States sites for military and coaling stations, and permit the United States to intervene if necessary to protect Cuban independence and maintain stability.

To persuade a Cuban constitutional convention to accept these stipulations, Root promised that the United States would intervene only in the most extreme circumstances. Wood proclaimed that the U.S. occupation force would not leave until Cuba accepted the terms of the Platt Amendment. The Cubans reluctantly acquiesced, and in 1902 Wood turned over the government to a newly elected Cuban president. U.S. troops left, but in conformance with a treaty negotiated on the basis of the Platt Amendment, the U.S. navy moved into the strategic port of Guantánamo to establish its major Caribbean base. A reciprocal trade treaty was also part of the bargain. Cuba received tariff concessions on exports of sugar to the United States and gave U.S. products special privileges in Cuban markets. U.S. investments also increased rapidly. In 1898 U.S. citizens had some $50 million invested in Cuban sugar; by 1920 that figure was $1.25 billion.

Cuban stability did not last very long. President Tómas Estrada Palma refused to accept the verdict of the polls when he was defeated for reelection. His opponents announced a revolution, and Estrada Palma begged for U.S. support. Theodore Roosevelt sent an American warship to Havana, but decided Estrada Palma himself was the major problem. Roosevelt appealed to the Cubans to resolve the issue fairly to avoid American intervention. No one wanted a repetition of the Philippine war. On the other hand, Roosevelt and his special envoy to the island, William Howard Taft, did not want to turn the government over to rebels and thus reward armed insurrection. They preferred that Estrada Palma stay on temporarily while new and fair elections were held.

Estrada Palma and the rebels, however, refused to negotiate. They both angled for U.S. intervention in hopes that Roosevelt would support their position. Estrada Palma resigned rather than accept a new election, and Roosevelt sent Taft, supported by the landing of 5,000 American troops, to establish himself as head of a provisional government. The U.S. provisional government itself held new elections while Roosevelt warned the Cubans that "if the elections become a farce, and if the insurrectionary habit becomes confirmed in the Island, it is absolutely out of the question that the Island should continue independent." Taft's successor as governor, Charles Magoon, tried to encourage reform and strong political parties, but the parties had few roots among the people. Party leaders were mostly intent on the spoils of office. They felt little responsibility because they knew they could induce U.S. intervention in a crisis by threatening revolution and chaos.

After Taft's elections established a new government, the United States withdrew its troops in 1908, some two years after it had intervened. Nevertheless, the Cuban political system remained unstable, corruption increased, and the army set up by the new government became an expensive source of political favoritism and boodle.

In 1912, the United States intervened once again in Cuba. President Taft sent 500 marines to support the Cuban regime against a rebellion of army officers and blacks who were protesting political discrimination. Woodrow Wilson denounced such interventions, but he too felt compelled to threaten intervention to deter a revolt against the incumbent Cuban regime on the eve of U.S. entry into World War I. His action won the consent of a grateful Cuban government to station U.S. troops on the island to guard against any potential German threat. The crisis of World War I temporarily silenced opposition in the United States to Wilson's action, but it was increasingly clear that military intervention in Cuba was self-defeating.

THE PANAMA CANAL: ACQUIRING A FORMAL ENCLAVE IN AN INFORMAL COLONY

By establishing a colony in Puerto Rico and a protectorate over Cuba, the United States took two major steps toward securing control of the Caribbean access to any canal built through Central America. The strengthened U.S. position affected Great Britain as well as Latin America. The United States had been trying for years to rid itself of its obligations under the Clayton-Bulwer Treaty of 1850 to share control of any Central American canal with Great Britain, and in December of 1898, the British decided to open new negotiations on the issue.

After a year of hard bargaining, Secretary of State John Hay and British Ambassador Lord Julian Pauncefote concluded a pact that gave the United States sole control of the potential canal, but ensured its neutrality by forbidding the canal's fortification. Theodore Roosevelt and his "large policy" cohorts campaigned against this first Hay-Pauncefote Treaty because it prohibited fortification, and the Senate responded by mangling the treaty so thoroughly that it had to be renegotiated. By the time the second Hay-Pauncefote Treaty was signed in January 1902 Roosevelt himself was president, and the British were ready to retreat still further from Latin America. This second treaty was silent on fortification, implicitly according to the United States the right to full military control of the canal.

All that remained was for the United States to choose between Nicaragua and Panama as the canal route. A commission appointed by McKinley, the so-called Walker Commission, had reported in favor of Nicaragua in 1901. The commission's engineers admitted that Nicaragua's river system might be too shallow for easy construction, but the Panama route had an even more serious drawback. The successor to De Lesseps' bankrupt New Panama Canal Company demanded the exhorbitant sum of $109 million for the purchase of its works and concessions. The House of Representatives accepted the Walker Commission report and authorized construction through Nicaragua.

William Nelson Cromwell, a remarkable U.S. lobbyist for the New Panama Canal Company, refused to accept this House action as final. He convinced the Panama Company to reduce its demand from $109 million to $40 million. Then he persuaded the U.S. Senate to authorize the money and to urge the negotiation of a treaty with Colombia for canal rights through Panama with the proviso that if negotiations failed, Roosevelt would return to the Nicaragua option. Cromwell got his way in Congress through liberal application of money. His allies distributed Nicaraguan stamps showing an erupting volcano to counter Nicaraguan claims that its route would be perfectly safe.

The Roosevelt administration quickly negotiated the Hay-Herrán Treaty with Colombia, which gave the United States a ninety-nine-year lease on a canal zone six miles wide in exchange for an initial payment of $10 million plus $250,000 annually. But the Colombian Senate balked. It wanted an increase in payments and greater acknowledgment of Colombian sovereignty over the canal zone. Colombia had reason to stall. The New Panama Company's concessions ran out in 1904, and Colombia would then receive the money for De Lesseps' works as well.

The stall enraged Roosevelt. He might have turned to Nicaragua, but instead he resolved to get the better of the "contemptible little creatures in Bogotá." You could no more make a binding agreement with them than you could "nail currant jelly to the wall," he later complained. When an influential Panamanian suggested that Panama might rebel against its Colombian overlords and sign its own treaty with the United States, Roosevelt was ready to listen. Roosevelt knew rebellion was endemic in Panama. The United States, in its role as guarantor of transit rights across the isthmus of Panama, had intervened four separate times in recent years to protect the railroad against rebel attacks. The man who suggested that a convenient rebellion might break out again was Philippe Bunau-Varilla, an official of the New Panama Canal Company who was desperate to strike a deal before the company's concession ran out.

Bunau-Varilla wanted the United States to protect the revolution against Colombian reconquest by using its rights as guarantor of transit to block Colombian landings or use of the Panamanian railway. Panama needed the help because its revolutionary forces consisted of a fire brigade, a few local police, and a small contingent of Colombian soldiers whose commander had been bribed. Roosevelt told Bunau-Varilla that he could not encourage revolution, but he let John Hay inform Bunau-Varilla that the American ship *Nashville* was steaming toward the isthmus. Roosevelt later commented that Bunau-Varilla would have been a very dull man not to have known what America would do in case of a revolution.

Bunau-Varilla was not dull. He delayed the revolution until the *Nashville* was lying off Colon. When the revolution began, however, the commander of the *Nashville* failed to prevent the Colombians from landing an invasion force because orders to do so had been too late in arriving. A quick-thinking railroad supervisor saved the day. He had already sent all the rolling stock to the Pacific side of the isthmus, stranding the Colombian force. He then invited the Colombian commanders aboard one of the last available trains and sent them off also, leaving the troops leaderless. The *Nashville* landed some U.S. sailors to "keep the peace," and the revolution was secure.

Panama's new leaders gratefully authorized Bunau-Varilla to negotiate a canal treaty with the United States. They told him at the same time to protect Panama's sovereign rights over the canal, but Bunau-Varilla was so anxious to guarantee the American Senate's approval of the treaty that he gave away even more than Hay requested. Hay wanted American control of a canal zone six miles wide for ninety-nine years. Bunau-Varilla insisted the United States govern "as if it were sovereign" a ten-mile zone in perpetuity. In return, the United States would protect the sovereignty of Panama, especially against Colombia. The Panamanian leaders protested Bunau-Varilla's giveaway, but accepted it rather than face Colombia alone.

The treaty with Bunau-Varilla ran into considerable opposition in the United States from the press and Congress. The Democrats particularly denounced Roosevelt's unscrupulous tactics. They argued that America should have turned to the Nicaraguan route rather than encouraging the Panamanian revolution. The Senate could not resist the handsome concessions the president had won, however, and it accepted the treaty by a vote of 66 to 14. Roosevelt defended his actions as perfectly legal. When he asked his cabinet if he had successfully vindicated himself, Elihu Root replied that he certainly had: "You have shown that you were accused of seduction and you have conclusively proved that you were guilty of rape." Later, in 1911, Roosevelt was quoted as telling an audience at the University of California: "I took the Isthmus." His alleged comment triggered a congressional investigation, and Woodrow Wilson subsequently apologized to Colombia while trying to get Congress to appropriate $25 million as an indemnity. Roosevelt succeeded in getting his Republican friends in Congress to defeat Wilson's move, but two years after his death in 1919, Congress did grant Colombia the indemnity.

Ironically, as Colombia became mollified, Panama became less so. The United States completed the canal in 1914 and eliminated yellow fever in the process, but it established the canal zone as a protected enclave against the Panamanians themselves. The American flag gradually replaced the Panamanian flag. The Americans set up separate schools and commissaries. They made English the language of the zone and imported English-speaking West Indians to replace Panamanians in jobs on the canal. The United States officially segregated the canal zone by race and grouped the Panamanians with the West Indians as blacks. American labor bosses, often white southerners, treated the Panamanians and West Indians as they had treated blacks at home. Discrimination even extended to the currency in which laborers were paid. American citizens received gold, while the Panamanians and West Indians were paid in less valuable silver. The United States also exerted tremendous authority in Panama outside the zone. It controlled all lakes and streams necessary to the operation of the canal; it had a monopoly of all communications and utilities; and it tied Panama's economy to the American dollar.

Although the United States maintained the right of direct intervention in Panamanian politics and foreign policy, it tried to leave this sphere to the Panamanians as much as possible. Panamanian politics degenerated into a struggle for power within an economic elite of older families that considered themselves "white" and whose main goal was protection of their private interests. If this political system did little for the mass of Panamanians, it permitted efficient and uninterrupted operation of the Panama Canal by the United States.

THE ROOSEVELT COROLLARY: STAKING OUT AMERICA'S SPHERE OF INFLUENCE

As the United States strengthened its hand in the Caribbean through acquisition of formal colonies and protectorates in Cuba, Puerto Rico, and the Panama Canal, Theodore Roosevelt reconsidered America's policies toward the other independent nations of the area. At first he did not seem to think that anything more than the traditional adherence to the Monroe Doctrine was necessary. In 1902, when Great Britain and Germany approached him with a plan to use naval power to force Venezuela to pay its long-overdue debt, Roosevelt made no objection beyond warning that the venture must lead to no territorial acquisitions by the two European powers. He even wrote the German ambassador that if any South American country misbehaved toward a European country, the European nation should "spank it." He had a change of heart, however, after Britain and Germany sank several Venezuelan gunboats, blockaded the Venezuelan coast, and proceeded to bombard several coastal forts.

When the Venezuelans offered to submit the debts to international arbitration, Roosevelt urged a reluctant Germany and a somewhat less reluctant Great Britain to accept. In 1915, at the height of Roosevelt's fight to bring the United States into the world war against Germany, the former president even declared that he had sent an ultimatum to the kaiser that had finally forced the Germans to accept arbitration. There is no record of such an ultimatum in German or American archives, but Roosevelt had deployed the fleet in Latin American waters and used leaks to the press to threaten Germany.

This second Venezuela crisis stirred some soul-searching in many nations. Financial chaos, indebtedness, and political instability were endemic throughout Latin America. Other crises like the one in Venezuela were bound to arise. Sooner or later, a major European power would acquire control of a Latin American country, either by conquest or by gaining command over its economy and finances. This would pose a direct challenge to the Monroe Doctrine, which Roosevelt and the United States took far more seriously after the Spanish-American War.

Roosevelt considered two alternatives beyond the enforcement of the traditional injunctions of the Monroe Doctrine. The first of these was suggested by the Argentine foreign minister, Dr. Luís Drago. He proposed a new international principle: Public debts should not justify the use of force or territorial occupation. This Drago Doctrine, however, contradicted the European and American diplomatic tradition that a nation had the right to protect the lives and property of its citizens abroad. Roosevelt was willing to accept the Drago Doctrine, but he insisted that if a debtor nation refused to submit the issue to arbitration, then force was justified. He supported this modified Drago Doctrine at the Hague Conference of 1907 and the conference accepted it.

Many Latin American nations refused to sign the Hague modification of the Drago Doctrine because they rejected forcible collection of debts under any circumstances. The United States also had an incentive to ignore the Hague agreement. In the arbitration of the Venezuelan debt following the second Venezuelan crisis, the arbitrators favored the debts of the British and Germans over those of the United States. Since the British and Germans had used force to secure their debts while the United States had not, Roosevelt feared this precedent would undermine whatever authority was left to the Drago Doctrine after so many Latin American countries had refused to sign it.

Roosevelt turned to a very different alternative. He declared that if worse came to worst, the United States itself would intervene in Latin America to see that Latin American nations behaved justly toward their European creditors. U.S. intervention would eliminate any pretext for European intervention. This policy of "preventive intervention" became known as the Roosevelt Corollary to the Monroe Doctrine.

The occasion for Roosevelt's announcement was a crisis in the Dominican Republic. The Dominican Republic was the scene of continuous political and economic chaos. In seventy years, it had had nineteen revolutions and fifty-three presidents. The latest civil war had broken out in 1903, while European creditors were clamoring for payment of their debts and their war vessels sailed Dominican waters. In 1904, the harassed Dominican president asked the United States to intervene by sending arms, guaranteeing Dominican sovereignty, and paying its debts. Roosevelt had no desire for a new territory. He said he would as soon annex the island as swallow a porcupine wrong-end to.

He suggested instead that the United States take over Dominican customs collections, pay off creditors, and turn the remainder of the revenue over to the Dominican government. The suspicious Dominicans accepted out of fear of the Europeans, but the U.S. Senate recoiled after hearing Roosevelt claim that in cases of "chronic wrongdoing, or impotence" among Western Hemisphere nations, the United States "however reluctantly" would have to exercise "an international police power." Roosevelt seemed ready to extend the Platt Amendment to the whole of the Caribbean and Central America.

Roosevelt established the Dominican customs house receivership on his own authority until the balky Senate finally accepted the treaty with the Dominican Republic in 1907. Yet he hoped to keep the intervention limited and to avoid any further ones. He managed to do so until the end of his term; his successors were not so fortunate.

WILLIAM HOWARD TAFT AND DOLLAR DIPLOMACY

Taft tried to avoid interventions under the Platt Amendment or the Roosevelt Corollary by stabilizing Latin regimes through the infusion of private American capital. The new bureaucracy in the State Department advocated this dollar diplomacy in Latin America just as it did in China. And just as in China, it brought little but trouble.

Roosevelt had tried to promote stability in Central America by sponsoring a tenuous treaty arrangement among the fractious republics of the area. Taft tried to secure the area further by negotiating a customs receivership in Honduras to stave off potential British intervention. The arrangement was frustrated by the objections of the U.S. Senate and by various Honduran governments and agencies embroiled in their own civil wars.

In Nicaragua, Taft used greater force to accompany his dollar diplomacy. Nicaragua was meddling in other Central American states, including Honduras, and had contracted major loans with British institutions. Taft and Knox threw their support to a rebellion that promised a more pliant regime. They landed U.S. marines in rebel-held territory to protect North American property and lives, which just incidentally deterred the government from reconquest. After many twists and turns, the U.S.-sponsored government took power, and it accepted an American loan and a customs receivership to guarantee repayment. The U.S. Senate delayed its consent to the arrangement, but under Knox's urging, U.S. banks funded the loan anyway. These North American financiers also established the Bank of Nicaragua and chartered a corporation for operating Nicaragua's rail and steamship lines, all in defiance of the Nicaraguan constitution, which forbade special concessions to foreigners. U.S. marines then helped to put down another rebellion that charged the incumbent Nicaraguan regime with selling out to Wall Street. As the marines withdrew, leaving behind a one-hundred-man legation force to help keep order, Taft and Knox proclaimed their policy of stabilizing Central American economies a success.

WOODROW WILSON AND MISSIONARY DIPLOMACY

Woodrow Wilson disagreed with Taft's proclamation that dollar diplomacy had been successful. As he had criticized such diplomacy in Asia for its self-ish economic motivations and its favors to Wall Street, so he denounced the loans and customs receiverships in Nicaragua and Honduras. Wilson apologized to Colombia for Roosevelt's "taking" of Panama and tried to get Congress to appropriate $25 million as compensation. He also announced that the United States would never seek another foot of territory in Latin America.[1] Although neither Roosevelt nor Taft had sought more territory, Wilson's pledge, along with his denunciation of dollar diplomacy as unwarranted interference in the affairs of sovereign nations, implied that he would seek a less interventionist policy than his predecessors.

Yet for all of Wilson's denunciations of dollar diplomacy, he still assumed that an orderly free economy open to "legitimate" U.S. trade was a vital part of the proper democratic system every nation should enjoy. This devout belief in democratic political procedures and a free economy actually gave Wilson more incentive to intervene in the affairs of the Caribbean and Central American nations than had the more overt strategic doctrines of Roosevelt or the dollar diplomacy of Taft. That Wilson's missionary diplomacy would override his initial commitment to nonintervention was demonstrated most graphically on the island of Hispaniola. The two nations that shared the island, Haiti and the Dominican Republic, both endured long military occupations initiated by Woodrow Wilson.

The most systematic and extensive intervention took place in Haiti. That country had had a long history of suffering and turmoil since the legendary slave revolt led by Toussaint L'Ouverture at the turn of the nineteenth century. American ships and marines had intervened there eight times between 1867 and 1900 to protect American lives and property. A thin upper class of French-speaking Creoles arbitrarily and rather contemptuously ruled a great mass of peasants. The elite was tied to France by culture, religion, and the exchange of Haitian coffee for French tobacco. An influential coterie of German merchants also resided in Haiti. U.S. economic interests were less important than those of France or Germany until 1900. Then a rapid rise of activity brought the United States control of 60 percent of Haiti's import

---

[1] Apparently he did not regard purchasing the Virgin Islands from Denmark under threat of seizure, as he did in 1916, to be in violation of this pledge.

market by 1910. With State Department support, U.S. bankers pried their way into a French and German consortium that controlled Haiti's national bank. The 50 percent share they acquired allowed America to dominate Haiti's customs office, since the bank was empowered to collect customs duties.

Before the Spanish-American War, Haiti's fine port at Môle St. Nicholas had given the country strategic importance, and the United States had tried to secure the harbor several times. After the United States had acquired Puerto Rico and Guantánamo in Cuba it seemed less important. But the United States still did not want to see Môle St. Nicholas fall into the hands of a rival European power like Germany. The continuing turmoil in Haiti thus led to considerable sentiment for intervention in the state and war departments of the United States. American bankers also encouraged such interventionist sentiments in hopes of gaining government protection for their financial concessions.

Racial prejudices inclined American officials to think the worst of Haiti's potential for stable and humane government. These prejudices were reinforced by the fact that between 1911 and 1915, seven of Haiti's presidents were assassinated or forcibly removed from office, one of them by being blown up in his palace. The final straw came in 1915 when the president tortured and executed 167 political prisoners and in turn was dismembered by angry revolutionaries.

The United States had already made the decision to intervene if fighting broke out in the capital because a staunch opponent of U.S. influence seemed prepared to overturn the government. Wilson sent in marines, established martial law, and installed a hand-picked government. The marines forced this government to accept a treaty empowering the United States to supervise Haiti's customs collection and finances, establish schools, build roads, and train a national guard. The marines and their national guard protégés then carried on a running battle with bands of Haitians who were menacing the roads the Americans were building with conscripted labor. Americans also began buying land in Haiti after forcing repeal of Haiti's constitutional provision prohibiting foreigners from owning property.

U.S. military courts constituted the Haitian judicial system until 1929. The Americans improved government efficiency and established roads and schools, but at great cost. A rebellion in 1919 cost 3,000 Haitian lives. American racism was rampant and bred much resentment. The second U.S. commander in Haiti, U.S. Marine Colonel Littleton W. T. Waller, expressed his disgust with "bowing and scraping to these coons." The Haitian national guard, organized by the United States to maintain order, became a force of its own. The guard continued the conscription of labor after the U.S. occupiers had formally abandoned it and waited in the wings to take control when the United States left.

A year after U.S. marines landed in Haiti, they occupied the neighboring Dominican Republic. The United States had operated the Dominican Republic's customs since 1905, and this helped maintain financial and political stability there while satisfying the country's European creditors. Such stability demonstrated the virtue of the customs receivership to many Americans. The United States failed to recognize how much Dominican stability owed to that nation's powerful president, Ramón Cáceres. When Cáceres was shot in 1911, the country became a revolving door for presidents, each of whom gutted the treasury before he abandoned office. The Dominican Republic was left with no public sanitation, a 90 percent illiteracy rate, only sixty-five kilometers of roads, and not a single public school. Bandits roamed the interior, and even the capital city became a wasteland.

The Taft administration intervened briefly in 1912 to end one civil war by helping to install a provisional president. The civil war resumed immediately after the U.S. ship left, however, and the provisional president resigned. Wilson's administration pressed the Dominican factions to end the turmoil and insisted that the United States be given supervisory control to ensure free elections and clean government. When even the factions most sympathetic to the United States resisted, the marines landed. After a brief effort to find a compliant government, the American military took full control. It tried to confiscate all private weapons, and it replaced the politicized national guard with a new independent one officered primarily by Americans. Again the United States built roads, established schools, provided public sanitation, and reformed government finances, but the occupation also raised almost universal resentment against the U.S. overlords. In addition to the racism that plagued the U.S. reputation everywhere it intervened, the occupation authorities established a particularly noxious press censorship. And, as in Haiti, Cuba, Panama, and Nicaragua, the local guard established under U.S. auspices overran its bounds.

MISSIONARY DIPLOMACY IN MEXICO

Wilson's intervention in Mexico was more sensational than his interventions elsewhere, but Mexico's size and the power of its nationalist resistance also made the intervention much shorter and more embarrassing. In the thirty-five years before the Mexican Revolution of 1910, General Porfirio Díaz's dictatorship had given the United States little reason to consider intervention. Díaz's ruthlessness had provided order and rapid economic growth, and he had invited U.S. businessmen to share the profits. The United States was the market for 75 percent of Mexico's exports. Europeans shared more equally in Mexico's import markets, investments, and loan portfolios, but Americans dominated the railroads and communications. Americans owned many of Mexico's mines and much of its agricultural land; after 1901, they invested heavily along with the British in the extraction of oil.

Foreign economic domination naturally roused nationalist antagonism in Mexico. Resentment was especially strong toward the United States, the most prominent foreign presence and the well-remembered despoiler of Texas, California, and the Southwest. Even Díaz, who generally welcomed foreign investment, disliked the dominance of foreign technicians and the use of English as the official language on the railroads. He began to buy out foreign investors. When his grip on the country faltered, there was a reservoir of anti-American nationalism ready to be tapped by the revolutionary contenders for his power.

A loose alliance of local leaders headed by Francisco Madero finally overthrew Díaz in 1911. Fighting then broke out between Madero and his erstwhile allies, who included Francisco "Pancho" Villa, Bernardo Reyes, and Emiliano Zapata. Madero had to rely on the regular army, led by Victoriano Huerta, to suppress these local rebellions. Huerta ultimately joined Madero's enemies, overthrew and murdered him, and then made himself provisional president.

President William Howard Taft and Secretary of State Philander Knox followed a cautious policy toward the revolution. Madero had considerable sympathy in the United States, and Taft and Knox had no desire to get entangled in Mexican politics. On the other hand, their ambassador to Mexico, Henry Lane Wilson, had no such compunctions. He regarded Madero as a visionary and wrote urgent and distorted analyses of Madero's supposed radicalism and anti-Americanism. Before Huerta overthrew Madero, Huerta worked out an agreement with the other rebel leaders at the American embassy under the auspices of Henry Lane Wilson. The ambassador also did nothing to prevent Madero's murder.

Henry Lane Wilson's policies and actions came under strong criticism from American liberals and certain sectors of the press, who pointed out the ambassador's connections to American investment interests that had long opposed the Madero family. Taft consequently resisted the ambassador's urging to recognize Huerta's government immediately and left the touchy issue to the new American president, Woodrow Wilson. Woodrow Wilson came to office with little knowledge of Mexico but with strong liberal commitments to legitimate democratic practices at home and abroad. He decided to make Mexico an example of the virtues of democracy. He told Huerta that the United States would withhold recognition of his government until Huerta established a cease-fire and held proper elections in which he would refrain from running. When Huerta balked, Wilson dismissed Ambassador Wilson and cut off arms to Huerta's government. Huerta persuaded President Wilson to cut off arms to his opponents as well by hinting that he would not run in the coming elections. As Huerta saw his power slipping, however, he arrested most of his congressional opponents, declared the subsequent election void, and stayed on as provisional president.

Woodrow Wilson responded by trying to induce the European powers to withhold recognition and arms. Then he settled down to a policy he called "watchful waiting" as various Mexican rebel groups under the umbrella title of Constitutionalists carried on the fight against Huerta. The Republican party ridiculed Wilson's policy and demanded vigorous military intervention in Mexico to ensure stability and protect American economic interests. As the turmoil in Mexico continued and Republican political pressure mounted, Wilson removed the embargo on arms to the Constitutionalists.

Then he found the opportunity for an even more sensational gesture. In

April 1914, an American naval vessel patrolling Mexico's Gulf coast sent a whaleboat ashore to purchase gasoline, only to have the crew arrested by Mexican soldiers for trespassing. The Mexican commanding officer released the eight crewmen with an apology in a couple of hours, but the American fleet commander demanded far more—a written apology, a court martial for the arresting officer, and a twenty-one gun salute to the American flag. President Wilson supported him and ordered the Atlantic fleet to Mexico. He did not want a confrontation; but he insisted on the twenty-one gun salute, and he let it be known to Huerta that the United States would return the salute. When Huerta continued to hesitate, Wilson ordered the occupation of Vera Cruz, Mexico's second city.

After a bloody invasion costing 100 American and 500 Mexican casualties, Americans took the city. But Wilson did not know what to do with it. American intervention had strengthened Huerta's position with his countrymen rather than weakened it. Wilson wanted to withdraw as quickly as possible, yet saw no way to do it gracefully. His chance came when the ABC powers—Argentina, Brazil, and Chile—offered mediation. Wilson accepted but insisted that the settlement include replacement of Huerta's government by the Constitutionalists until new elections could be held. Even the leader of the Constitutionalists, Venustiano Carranza, refused such direct interference in Mexico's internal affairs. Carranza took power on his own two weeks after the ABC mediation had offered a meaningless declaration to paper over the Mexican-American dispute. He refused to hold elections or cater to America in any way—and he left the embarrassed Wilson still with no graceful way out of Vera Cruz.

Finally, Carranza found himself in desperate need of the port at Vera Cruz to defeat the rebellions of Pancho Villa and Emiliano Zapata. He pledged to avoid reprisals against collaborators and political opponents in Vera Cruz, and with this face-saving concession in hand, Wilson withdrew the American forces. Carranza immediately arrested or fired everyone who had cooperated with the Americans in Vera Cruz.

When Carranza's forces gained the upper hand over those of Villa and Zapata in the following year, 1915, Wilson decided to recognize the Carranza government. He also cut off arms to Carranza's opponents. Pancho Villa retaliated angrily: His troops massacred seventeen Americans while robbing a Mexican train, and Villa himself led a raid across the U.S. border on the New Mexican town of Columbus in March 1916. Against the protests of Carranza, Wilson sent a military force under General John Pershing into Mexico in pursuit. Pershing found himself fighting not just Villa's forces, but Carranza's troops and the populace of several towns as well. After one particularly fierce fight with Carranza's troops at Carrizal, open war between Mexico and the United States seemed probable. Perhaps it was prevented only by the growing conflict with Germany that ultimately led the United States into World War I. In February 1917, the distracted Wilson withdrew Pershing's troops unilaterally.

Relations between Mexico and the United States remained strained in the

Figure 11 Pancho Villa (top) and his pursuers—General John (Black Jack) Pershing is fourth from left. Immediately to his right is George Patton, who would make his reputation in World War II. Photos courtesy of the National Archives.

succeeding years. Germany even proposed an alliance to Mexico if the United States entered World War I on the Allied side. Germany offered the reconquest of Texas and the Southwest as a reward. Mexico did not consider the offer seriously, but when the famous Zimmermann telegram proposing the alliance came to light, it reemphasized the tenuous state of Mexican-American relations. The constitution adopted by Carranza's revolutionary government damaged relations even further. It established a liberal labor code to be enforced against foreign as well as Mexican employers. The constitution also gave the Mexican government the right to expropriate any property necessary for the good of the Mexican society. Carranza could take over foreign investments in Mexico's mines, agricultural land, and oil fields. He began by imposing a royalty tax on oil drillers. Thus he directly challenged America's commitment to protect the property of its citizens abroad.

Wilson protested but kept a low profile to avoid war, since the United States was deeply involved in the European conflict and needed Mexican oil. Wilson's dilemma in Mexico illustrated the basic issues that would bedevil American relationships with the Third World in the twentieth century. America's interest in foreign trade and investment would often conflict with indigenous economic interests, beget dislike of economic dependence on the United States, and lead to conflict if the United States adhered to its historic belief in the right of a nation to protect the property of its citizens abroad. American insistence on stability and to a lesser extent on democratic procedures in nations of strategic or economic importance would lead to military interventions. American racial and cultural prejudices, borne by its military forces, merchants, missionaries, or travelers, further aroused nationalist resentments.

Some of these difficulties were no doubt inevitable. Relationships of weaker to stronger nations cannot help but be tinged with a degree of dependency and consequent resentment. Even the most enlightened nations and peoples have radiated a degree of cultural smugness and disdain for foreign ways. Regardless, many people will agree that a serious threat to vital national strategic and economic interests may justify forcible intervention. Yet it seems clear in retrospect that Germany, Great Britain, and Japan did not really jeopardize vital American interests in East Asia and Latin America. With the possible exception of the isthmian canal, it is difficult to find interests in East Asia and Latin America that the United States could rightly consider vital. Neither the strategic threats nor the economic trade and investments in those areas were significant enough to justify the extent and forcefulness of America's interventions in this pre-World War I era. A more restrained diplomacy could have protected most American interests without breeding the resentment that America's imperial surge did.

CONTROVERSIAL ISSUES AND FURTHER READING

American historians writing in the post-Spanish-American War era almost unanimously supported American intervention in Central America and the Caribbean as necessary to national security. None were very enthusiastic about it, but almost none could bring themselves to oppose it outright. They often demonstrated their reluctance by accompanying their defense of the Roosevelt Corollary or dollar diplomacy with ironic asides about the self-righteousness of Americans in denying their imperialistic tendencies. [See, for example, Archibald Cary Coolidge, *The United States as a World Power* (1918).] Their reluctance also could show up in partisanship. Democrat historians often limited their criticisms of intervention to those undertaken by Republicans, especially Roosevelt's "taking" of Panama. Republicans, on the other hand, praised Roosevelt's interventions while ridiculing Woodrow Wilson for trying to remove the problems of Latin American republics by "removing their independence." [For criticism of Roosevelt's intervention, see John Holladay Latané, *America as a World Power* (1907); for defenses of Roosevelt accompanied by criticisms of Wilson, see Albert Bushnell Hart, *The Monroe Doctrine: An Interpretation* (1916).] Still, historians were clearly in the interventionist camp. [Chester Lloyd Jones, *Caribbean Interests of the United States* (1916).] Some even condemned Wilson for being too restrained in his policy toward Mexico. [See, for example, Frederick A. Ogg, *National Progress, 1907-1917* (1918).] The author of the only full condemnation of American intervention written in this period, Hiram Bingham, recanted only a few years later by saying that the United States owed it "to the progress of the world . . . to see to it that the republics of Tropical America behave." [Hiram Bingham, *The Monroe Doctrine: An Obsolete Shibboleth* (1913). For his recanting, see Thomas L. Karnes, "Hiram Bingham and his Obsolete Shibboleth," *Diplomatic History* (Winter 1979).]

Following World War I, there was a general acknowledgment in the United States that military interventions in Latin America were undesirable and in many cases had been mistaken. This trend would culminate in the Good Neighbor Policy of the 1930s. Among historians, it would lead to a widespread belief that restraint toward Latin America was necessary, but significant divisions remained over the reasons for such restraint and over evaluations of America's past and present policies.

Nationalist historians generally defended America's past interventions as necessary under existing conditions to prevent the chaos that could have invited intervention by Germany or other European powers. Nationalists were ready to show more restraint following World War I because they said that the Latin American nations themselves were becoming more stable and capable of self-defense. This made American intervention less necessary. They implied, however, that if instability were again to invite intervention by outside powers hostile to the United States, strategic interests would require the United States to resume its interventionist policy. [The classic work of this genre is Samuel Flagg Bemis, *The Latin American Policy of the United States: An Historical Interpretation* (1943). Another broad text with a similar outlook is J. Lloyd Mechem, *A Survey of United States-Latin American Relations* (1965). Works in this vein restricted to the Caribbean are Chester Lloyd Jones, *The Caribbean since 1900* (1916), and Howard C. Hill, *Roosevelt and the Caribbean* (1927). On Cuba, see Russell Fitzgibbon, *Cuba and the United States, 1900-1935* (1935), and two modern works which argue that the United States abandoned its occupation too soon, Allan R. Millet, *The Politics of Intervention: The Military Occupation of Cuba, 1906-1909* (1968), and

James Hitchman, *Leonard Wood and Cuban Independence, 1898–1902* (1971). Not many other recent historians are willing to defend America's post-Spanish-American War interventions, but Julius W. Pratt's survey *America's Colonial Experiment: How the United States Gained, Governed, and in Part Gave Away a Colonial Empire* (1950), is considerably more sympathetic to the occupations than one might have expected from his earlier books.]

Most historians since World War I have been more critical of America's military interventions. They have argued that neither Germany nor any other power posed a serious threat to American security in the Western Hemisphere in the early twentieth century. Therefore American interventions were generally mistaken overreactions to imaginary threats that did great harm to the image of the United States in the minds of Latin Americans. But most also have implied that if ever there had been or was to be a true threat to American security, however remote the possibility, the United States would have to intervene. Liberal internationalists hoped the unpleasant necessity might be mitigated by making intervention a cooperative enterprise through international or regional organizations like the Organization of American States or the United Nations. [See, for example, Dexter Perkins, *A History of the Monroe Doctrine* (1963), and J. Fred Rippy, *The Caribbean Danger Zone* (1940).] Realists urged that the United States simply face up to the fact that although it needed to use far more restraint in Latin America, "A nation which has tremendous economic strength and world-wide strategic concerns must develop a political philosophy which will take account of unavoidable dependency, whether it be economic or strategic, or as it sometimes must, political as well." [Whitney T. Perkins, *Denial of Empire: The United States and Its Dependencies* (1962), pp. 351–352.]

As in the case of historians of U.S. Asian policy, these realist historians are generally less critical of Theodore Roosevelt's frankly power-oriented interventions than of Taft's idealistic dollar diplomacy or Wilson's even more idealistic missionary diplomacy. Also they do not believe American interventions were much motivated by narrow economic interests, but harshly condemn the few instances they find. [Broad surveys that criticize the United States from a realist outlook are Edwin Lieuwen, *United States Policy in Latin America: A Short History* (1965), and Donald Dozer, *Are We Good Neighbors?* (1959). A better and more recent survey, although slightly more restricted in its coverage, is Lester Langley, *The United States and the Caribbean, 1900–1970* (1980). The classic survey of American policy toward the Caribbean is Dana G. Munro, *Intervention and Dollar Diplomacy in the Caribbean, 1900–1921* (1960). Another excellent work emphasizing the political aspects of American intervention is Whitney Perkins, *Constraints of Empire: The United States and Caribbean Interventions* (1981). For Theodore Roosevelt's policies, see Howard K. Beale, *Theodore Roosevelt and the Rise of America to World Power* (1956). For Taft's dollar diplomacy, see Walter V. Scholes and Marie V. Scholes, *The Foreign Policies of the Taft Administration* (1970). For Wilson's missionary diplomacy, see Arthur Link's multivolume biography, *Woodrow Wilson* (1947–   ). For Mexico, see Karl M. Schmitt, *Mexico and the United States* (1974); P. Edward Haley, *Revolution and Intervention: The Diplomacy of Taft and Wilson with Mexico, 1910–1917* (1970); Kenneth J. Grieb, *The United States and Huerta* (1969); and Robert E. Quirk, *An Affair of Honor: Woodrow Wilson and the Occupation of Vera Cruz* (1962), an excellent book. For Cuba, see Lester D. Langley, *The Cuban Policy of the United States* (1968).]

Although some of these realist analyses of U.S.–Latin American relations can be quite critical of American intervention, revisionist analyses are generally more so. Revisionists do not regard American policy as having been motivated by benevolent if mistaken liberalism or concerns for imaginary security threats. They see it as intentional rapine motivated mostly by economic greed. [One of the oldest of these analyses is that of Scott Nearing and Joseph Freeman, *Dollar Diplomacy: A Study in American Imperialism* (1925). A somewhat milder book, and an excellent one, is Leland H. Jenks, *Our Cuban Colony: A Study in Sugar* (1928). The most recent critical surveys of U.S.–Latin American relations are Cole Blasier, *Hovering Giant: United States Responses to Revolutionary Change in Latin America* (1978), and Gordon Connell-Smith, *The United States and Latin America: An Historical Analysis of Inter-American Relations* (1974). For a look at Cuba from this point of view, see Jules Robert Benjamin, *The United States and Cuba: Hegemony and Dependent Development, 1880–1934* (1977). A milder revisionist account is David F. Healy, *The United States in Cuba, 1898-1902: Generals, Politicians, and the Search for Policy* (1963). The best recent work on Panama is Walter LaFeber, *The Panama Canal: The Crisis in Historical Perspective* (1979). For Haiti, see Hans Schmidt, *The United States Occupation of Haiti, 1915–1934* (1971). A mild revisionist account of U.S. relations with Mexico is Robert F. Smith, *The United States and Revolutionary Nationalism in Mexico, 1916–1932* (1972). Gordon Lewis's excellent work, *Puerto Rico* (1963), is written in a similar spirit.]

CHAPTER 11

Europe, America, and World War I

GERMANY DISRUPTS THE EUROPEAN BALANCE OF POWER

The rise of the United States and Japan at the end of the nineteenth century challenged the stability of the international system and resulted in three potentially disruptive conflicts: the Sino-Japanese, Russo-Japanese, and Spanish-American wars. But at least the United States and Japan intruded into areas relatively remote from the existing major powers of Europe. No similar power vacuums cushioned the rise of Germany in the late nineteenth and early twentieth centuries. When Germany joined the roster of world powers, it threatened the heart of Europe and disturbed the precarious balance that had been the basis of peace since the defeat of Napoleon.

In 1860, Germany had been little more than a geographical expression, thirty-nine principalities sharing a heritage of German language and culture but little sense of political or economic unity. The central plain of Europe offered few natural boundaries, and Germans were mixed liberally into surrounding areas such as Schleswig-Holstein (Denmark), Alsace-Lorraine (France), Luxembourg (Holland), Switzerland, Austria, Poland, and the Baltic fringes of Russia.

The architect of modern Germany was the chancellor of Prussia, Otto von Bismarck. Using the small but efficient Prussian army, he combined with Austria to seize Schleswig-Holstein from Denmark. Then he turned on his Austrian ally in a contest for influence over the numerous principalities that lay between the two Germanic rivals. Bismarck won this war at the Battle of Sadowa in 1866, but he refrained from occupying Vienna and managed to avoid alienating Austria permanently.

Five years later, Bismarck's rising Germany shocked Europe by attacking and defeating France. Bismarck was not as successful in reconciling France to its defeat as he had been in pacifying Austria. His military commander, the great Prussian general Helmuth von Moltke, refused to accept the easily defended Rhine River as Germany's western border. Instead, he insisted on annexing Alsace-Lorraine, with its large French population, in order to secure the province's resources of iron ore and a defensive perimeter in the Vosges

Mountains. The annexation all but guaranteed permanent Franco-German enmity. To sustain the memory of its lost territory, France draped black veils over the statues in Paris's Place de la Concorde that represented the capital cities of Alsace and Lorraine.

Following the Franco-Prussian War, Bismarck set out to protect his new Germany by juggling the balance of power among the major European states. After winning an alliance with Austria in 1879, he lured Russia into the arrangement by emphasizing the common interest of the emperors of Germany, Austria, and Russia in resisting France. Although France had lost most of its revolutionary fervor domestically, it continued to advocate liberalism and nationalism in the rest of Europe. French-encouraged nationalism in Poland worried the three empires especially, since they had divided Poland among them in the previous century.

Bismarck had to work mightily to hold the Three Emperor Alliance together. Russia and Austria could agree on Poland and France, but they were bitter antagonists in the Balkans. There Russia encouraged the rebellions of its kindred Orthodox Slavs against the rule of Ottoman Turkey, "the sick man of Europe," in order to extend the czar's sway through the Balkan Slavs to the Dardenelles. These straits would give the Russian navy access from the Black Sea into the Mediterranean. Austria feared that the independence movements Russia was encouraging would spread to Slavic groups within the Austro-Hungarian Empire and rip that multi-ethnic state to shreds. Bismarck dampened some of this Balkan rivalry between his allies by acting as an "honest broker" in the area and by encouraging Russia to direct its expansion toward China and India, where it would not conflict with the interests of Austria or Germany.

Bismarck's convoluted policy began to unravel when Kaiser Wilhelm II came to the German throne in 1888. Wilhelm found Bismarck's policy too conservative and constraining. He dismissed the Iron Chancellor and permitted the treaty of alliance with Russia to lapse. France leapt at the chance to end its isolation in Europe, loaned money to the czar, and in 1898 began a series of contracts and agreements that led to a military entente. Europe looked on aghast as the autocratic czar of Russia bared his head at the playing of the *Marseillaise,* the anthem of revolutionary France. Kaiser Wilhelm naturally drew closer to Austria. Then both Germany and France began casting half-apprehensive, half-inviting glances at Great Britain.

Great Britain stood aloof from most of this maneuvering. So long as no European nation threatened the British Isles directly, Great Britain preferred to concentrate on its overseas imperial interests, especially the Suez Canal, India, China, and southern Africa. These interests brought the British more frequently into conflict with France and Russia than with Germany or Austria. France, whose citizens had built the Suez Canal, challenged Britain for control of Egypt and the Mediterranean, Britain's lifeline to India. France and Great Britain came within a hair's breadth of war in 1898 when rival military expeditions confronted one another at the small Egyptian-Sudanese outpost of Fashoda. France, finding itself at a military disadvantage, withdrew, but the Fashoda Incident was almost enough to make France forget Alsace-Lorraine and turn to Germany for help against Britain. France's ally Russia also posed a major threat to Britain. Its push toward the Dardenelles made Britain fear for its control of the Mediterranean and Suez. Russian pressure on Persia and Afghanistan threatened the British colony of India. Russian movement into Manchuria, Korea, and northern China challenged the British position in southern China as well.

Compared to Britain's problems with France and Russia, Bismarck's cautious probes for colonies in Africa and the Pacific (such as Samoa) seemed minor and temporary irritants. Neither Bismarck nor Kaiser Wilhelm looked on Great Britain with any special enmity, although both German statesmen found it necessary to protect the imperial throne and the aristocratic class structure against rising German liberalism by appealing to German nationalism with bold foreign policy adventures that challenged the position of Britain and its empire.

Bismarck had managed to keep his expansionist initiatives limited enough to avoid provoking a permanent alliance of offended powers against him. The kaiser did not. He angered London by demanding that it leave railroad concessions in Turkey to Germany, and he began to build a railroad to Baghdad. He sent his flamboyant Jameson telegram of support to the Boers of South Africa and in it denied British claims to the Transvaal. To support his push for overseas colonies, he began a huge naval building program in 1897 and extended it in 1900. The fleet he built in his North Sea ports seemed aimed particularly at Great Britain's traditional naval supremacy. At the instigation of the kaiser's chief naval advisor, Grand Admiral Alfred von Tirpitz, Germany constructed battleships capable of taking on the British fleet, rather than fast cruisers that might raid colonial commerce. The kaiser and Tirpitz drummed up domestic support for their heavy naval expenditures with shrill anti-British rhetoric.

A surge of German industrial and military growth accompanied all these developments. For two centuries France had been the major continental power, but by 1910 Germany towered over its rival. Germany led France in population by 65 to 39 million, in coal production by 222 to 38 million tons, in steel by 14 to 3 million tons. The German army also replaced that of France as the most powerful in Europe. Germany pioneered the efficient general staff system, the development of elaborate contingency war plans, and the use of masses of trained civilian reserves to supplement professional troops. After 1910, Germany sought to improve on its advantages by doubling its military appropriation. None of its neighbors could afford to match this expenditure.

Even before 1910, the British began to fear that Germany could overrun France and the Low Countries, which would make possible a successful invasion of England. Since Germany's industrial output surpassed that of Great Britain as well as France, and since Germany's navy seemed intent on challenging British supremacy, Britain grew nervous about its policy of "splendid isolation" and the emphasis on imperial affairs. To counter Germany's threat to the European balance of power, the British sought to resolve their conflicts with the United States. Great Britain accepted a secondary status in the American sphere and returned its Western Hemisphere fleet to home waters to guard against the German threat from the Continent. It concluded an alliance with Japan in 1902 to protect British interests in East Asia, thus enabling it to bring home major elements of its Asian fleet as well. It began a bitter internal debate over whether it was necessary to abandon its open market policy in the British Empire to protect British commerce from the rising economic power of Germany. Finally, in 1904, Great Britain and France determined to put aside the bitterness of the Fashoda Incident and move toward a closer understanding. France traded its claims in Egypt for British support of the French colonial position in the rest of North Africa.

THE UNITED STATES AND THE EUROPEAN BALANCE OF POWER: THE ALGECIRAS CONFERENCE

The reconciliation between Great Britain and France shocked Germany. Leading German diplomats wanted to disrupt the Anglo-French entente before it could be extended from a minor colonial agreement to a continental alliance aimed against Germany. They believed that if they challenged French control of Morocco, where Germany also had some treaty claims, Great Britain would back away and expose the hollowness of its support for France. The German army approved the timing of this challenge because France's ally, Russia, had been at least temporarily shattered by its humiliating defeat in the Russo-Japanese War of 1904 and the subsequent abortive revolution of 1905. The German navy, however, opposed the Moroccan maneuver because its fleet was not ready to confront Great Britain. Even the kaiser was reluctant to trigger a crisis at that moment. Nevertheless, his foreign policy advisors bullied him into a visit to Morocco, where he delivered a speech encouraging the sultan to resist French supervision and make an independent agreement with Germany. Caught between the great powers, the sultan appealed for an international conference to resolve the issue.

Although the United States had stood apart from these European struggles, Kaiser Wilhelm sought the support of Theodore Roosevelt for the German position on Morocco. Wilhelm appealed to America's time-honored dislike of European colonialism and desire for open doors for trade by insisting that Germany sought nothing more than equality of treatment for all nations in Morocco. He warned that war might result if France disregarded German rights and interests in North Africa, and that the victors might then partition China to America's disadvantage. The German ambassador to the United States, Roosevelt's personal friend Speck von Sternburg, tried to give further emphasis to the kaiser's goodwill toward the United States by writing Roosevelt that the kaiser would accept any advice Roosevelt chose to give him for a settlement. (Sternburg had been authorized only to say that the foreign ministry would urge the kaiser to abide by Roosevelt's suggestions.)

Roosevelt responded to this extraordinary expression of Germany's respect with much flattery and words of sympathy. But after the Venezuela crisis, Roosevelt harbored some concern for the growth of German power and intentions in the Western Hemisphere. He was more favorably disposed toward Great Britain because the British had removed the last barrier to Anglo-American friendship in 1903 by accepting the decision of an American-stacked commission on the disputed border between Canada and Alaska. So Roosevelt determined to use the influence Sternburg's indiscreet letter had given him to back France and preserve the Anglo-French entente in the face of German threats. He persuaded France to accept the call for a conference by promising that the United States would participate and support France against any German demands that Roosevelt considered unreasonable. Roosevelt hoped the conference would avoid war and at the same time maintain the balance of power against Germany's growing strength.

America's official delegates to the Algeciras Conference of 1906 operated strictly as observers. Behind the scenes, however, Roosevelt persuaded a reluctant Kaiser Wilhelm to accept French dominance in Morocco by threatening to publish Sternburg's letter, which supposedly committed the kaiser to abide by Roosevelt's advice. Afterward, Roosevelt ingenuously congratulated the kaiser on a diplomatic triumph. Thus Roosevelt had helped avert war and maintain the Anglo-French entente. But, to his great frustration, he had to keep the full extent of his role in the outcome secret because he knew he had no support from the American people for meddling in European politics.

ISSUE OF NEUTRAL RIGHTS ON THE EVE OF WAR

Roosevelt did not have to be so secretive about his role in the Second Hague Peace Conference of 1907. Like the First Hague Conference of 1899, the second conference was called by the Russian czar to discuss means of preventing or limiting war, and the American public approved of such efforts. But the results were disappointing. The conferees could not agree on military budget limitations, restrictions on the size of ships, reduction of army enlistment terms, or the composition and powers of a world court. They did agree on a modified version of the Drago Doctrine prohibiting forcible debt collection unless the debtor state refused arbitration, but most Latin American nations refused to sign.

In the Second Hague Conference's one concrete accomplishment, the conferees managed to set up an International Prize Court of Appeals to judge cases involving neutral rights on the high seas. Unfortunately, they could not agree on the neutral rights it was supposed to enforce. They scheduled a conference for the following year to devise such a code, and surprisingly the British reversed their naval policy of centuries to agree to a broad range of neutral rights. The resultant formulation of international law, embodied in the Declaration of London of 1909, seemed to eliminate the issue that had driven Great Britain and the United States to war in 1812 and had hung over Anglo-American relations ever since.

But the Declaration of London masked internal disagreements over maritime issues in both nations, disagreements that would play a vital role in America's entry into World War I. Just as American diplomats were winning the long struggle for neutral rights at the Hague and London conferences, Alfred Thayer Mahan and some other important naval officers had changed their views of America's interest in that struggle. Since the United States had become a major naval power, they wanted to avoid restrictions on the navy's operations and adopt the old British view of belligerent rights. (Some of these officers had the inflated notion that the Union navy had won the Civil War for the North by invoking the doctrine of continuous voyage to prevent neutrals from trading with the Confederacy through Mexico and thus circumventing the Union blockade.) For once Theodore Roosevelt ignored such strategic balance of power arguments and nonchalantly instructed his delegates to the London conference, including Mahan, to continue their traditional advocacy of neutral rights. The other delegates overcame Mahan's obstructionism and negotiated the London agreement.

The British delegation endorsed the Declaration of London amid almost equal confusion. The British navy supported the declaration's provisions on neutral rights because the admirals no longer thought it necessary to stop all neutral trade with Europe in wartime. If war broke out with Germany, the British navy planned only a limited blockade sufficient to draw the German battle fleet out of port so it could be destroyed. Thus Great Britain would not need to invoke the doctrine of continuous voyage to stop neutral trade from reaching Germany through nonbelligerent neighbors like the Netherlands. The British navy also was willing to restrict the contraband list, for the British Isles were far more dependent on imported food than they had been in Napoleonic times, and the declaration would prohibit the confiscation of food shipments as contraband.

A number of British leaders, however, challenged this strategy. These leaders, who came to be known as Continentalists, worried that the French might abandon the entente if the navy strategy were followed. It would leave France the entire burden of fighting the Germans on land. Besides, most Continentalists assumed that the war would be over quickly, like the Austro-Prussian, Franco-Prussian and Russo-Japanese wars. (They assumed that the only exception to the rule of short wars in the previous half-century, the American Civil War, had degenerated into a lengthy war of attrition only because American military men were inept amateurs.) In such a short land war, a naval blockade, which took a long time to be effective, would be irrelevant.

The naval strategists and the Continentalists fought continuously among themselves and never fully rationalized British strategy. The Continentalists, with their assumption that the next war would be too brief for a blockade to be effective, had little more objection to the neutral rights protected by the Declaration of London than their naval rivals. But the bickering between the two groups made it possible for those outside either clique to make their voices heard. Many of these outsiders in Parliament and the press denounced the declaration for giving up too many belligerent rights, while others condemned it for placing too few restrictions on the capture of food as contraband. Even politicians who considered such objections silly had difficulty resisting the political gains to be made by attacking the declaration. Consequently, Parliament deferred ratification time and again. When war finally came in 1914, the British still had not formally ratified the declaration, and as the war dragged on they once again turned to a rigid blockade that violated the neutral rights the Americans and the Germans had both assumed would be universally accepted.

THE OUTBREAK OF WORLD WAR I

While the Second Hague Conference and London Conference were seeking international agreement, Great Britain came to its own private arrangement with its long-time antagonist, Russia. Great Britain had believed it necessary to find some common ground with the ally of its entente partner. Russia, after its defeat at the hands of the Japanese, was ready to forego the Asian ambitions that clashed with British interests and return its attention to European questions, particularly the Balkans. In this atmosphere, the British successfully urged the reconciliation of the interests of their Japanese ally with Russia, reached an accommodation with Russia on the Persian approaches to India, and tabled their historic opposition to Russian ambitions for the Dardenelles. This Anglo-Russian Entente of 1907 quickly brought cries of "encirclement" fron Kaiser Wilhelm and his allies.

But the two great European alliances were not yet facing one another with unalloyed enmity. Russia and Austria even worked out a secret Balkan deal. Russia would stand by while Austria annexed Bosnia; Austria would not object when Russia took the Dardanelles. Suddenly, Austria double-crossed its rival in the Balkans by annexing Bosnia before Russia was ready to move. This added to the legacy of bitterness between the two nations. Tensions increased during the Second Balkan War of 1912–1913 in which Serbia, a Russian client and the chief Balkan instigator of the Slavic nationalism that threatened to destroy the Austro-Hungarian Empire, acquired another great bite of Turkey's territory. When the heir to the Austro-Hungarian throne, the Archduke Franz Ferdinand, and his wife were assassinated in Bosnia's capital city of Sarajevo by Bosnian dissidents who had entered Sarajevo with help from the Serbian secret police, the stage was set for calamity.

Austria used the occasion to send an ultimatum to Serbia with demands for control over its internal affairs. Austria purposely made the demands harsh enough to force a Serbian rejection and provide a reason for war. Foolishly, Kaiser Wilhelm gave Austria a "blank check" and promised support for whatever action Austria thought necessary in the wake of the assassination of the Hapsburg heir. Russia, having already been humiliated once by Austria in the Bosnian annexation affair, believed it could not afford to stand by again while Austria swallowed Russia's Serbian protectorate. Russia mobilized its troops along the Austrian border, then extended the mobilization along its German border as well.

Mobilization in that era constituted a threat almost guaranteeing war, for a mobilized nation using modern transportation could conquer an unmobilized nation before any resistance could be mounted. So Germany mobilized against Russia. But Germany's plan for war with the entente, the so-called Schlieffen Plan, called for a holding action on the eastern front, where Germany thought the backward Russians would be very slow in bringing their potential force to bear, while an all-out invasion quickly conquered a more formidable France. Consequently, Germany mobilized against the French as

Map 11 Alignment of the European Powers in World War I

well as the Russians, and the French responded with their own mobilization.

As the Continent plunged toward war, Great Britain wavered. The British cabinet appealed desperately for a mediated peace. It had forsworn British interests in the Balkans and might have stayed out of the war entirely if the conflict had remained limited to that area. But when the German armies slashed through neutral Belgium, threatening the conquest of France and the destruction of the continental balance of power, Great Britain honored its treaty obligations, declared war, and sent its expeditionary force to France.

The French and British finally managed to stop Germany's westward drive in the great Battle of the Marne. In turn, Germany thwarted a Russian invasion of Prussia. The war settled into a long and bloody stalemate. At the outset, the British had launched their long-planned attempt to draw the German fleet into battle by instituting a limited blockade of Germany. Then, as World War I degenerated into a prolonged war of attrition, Britain's allies pressed for a total blockage of trade to their enemies. The British never declared an official blockade. That would have required them to station ships directly at the mouth of German harbors, a suicidal action after the invention of long-range artillery and submarines. But the British found other ways to stop almost all trade to the Central Powers.

They turned away the United States request that all belligerents abide by the unratified Declaration of London. They extended the contraband list to include such American exports as copper, oil, lead, rubber, aluminum, and ultimately cotton. They declared food contraband on the pretext that the German government had nationalized all food distribution, even though the rumor of nationalization proved false. They used the doctrine of continuous voyage to extend their blockade to neutral Holland, arguing that food sent to the Netherlands was destined for Germany. The British navy even sowed mines northward from Scotland into the open ocean to block the approaches to the North Sea. These actions did more than contravene the unratified Declaration of London; they violated doctrines of international law that even Britain had accepted over the past two centuries.

WILSONIAN NEUTRALITY

Woodrow Wilson watched in horror and surprise as the world around him exploded into war. The first inkling that the Sarajevo crisis might bring general war did not reach him from his ministers abroad until the very day the shooting started. He had remarked on his accession to the presidency how ironic it would be if he, with all his preparation for presiding over domestic reforms, were called upon to lead the United States in a foreign war. Like all Americans, he was determined to stay out of the conflict. He told his countrymen to remain neutral in deed as well as name, impartial in thought as well as action.

Wilson's call for neutrality and his sincere desire to stay out of the war did not mean that he was personally impartial, however. He was a profound admirer of Great Britain's parliamentary tradition, and he regarded Germany as militaristic, brutal, and a threat to civilization. If Germany won the war, he feared it would "change the course of our civilization and make the United States a military nation." He told the British ambassador to the United States, "Everything that I love most in the world is at stake." These sentiments might not have been strong enough to push Wilson into immediate war with Germany, but they certainly determined him to avoid a clash with Great Britain over neutral rights. He did not want conflict between American exporters and the British fleet to bring the United States into the war on the wrong side, as Wilson believed had happened in 1812. Wilson did not suspect that the United States could be drawn into the war in any other way. Germany had neither the fleet nor the geographical proximity to clash with American interests or retaliate for America's tolerance of the British blockade. Wilson saw a conciliatory policy toward the British as the best way to gratify his desire to check the ambition of militaristic Germany and keep America out of the conflagration.

Despite Wilson's strong feelings about Great Britain and Germany, he did not immediately take full charge of American policy toward the war. His wife died a day after Great Britain declared war on Germany, and he spent much of the energy that remained to him shepherding his domestic reform program through Congress. He did not think it necessary to worry about the intricacies of neutral rights under international law in any case. He assumed, along with the Europeans, that the war would be over before the posture of the United States could have serious consequences.

With Wilson preoccupied, the task of shaping American policy fell largely to William Jennings Bryan, the ill-prepared secretary of state, and Robert Lansing, a narrow and somewhat devious international lawyer who served as the chief legal advisor to the State Department. Bryan left the technicalities of international law to Lansing and set out to restore peace in Europe. He offered immediate American mediation between the belligerents. Bryan either did not understand or did not think it important that immediate mediation would enable Germany to demand large concessions from the Allies, since the German invasion force had occupied much of Belgium and northern France in its march toward Paris. The shocked Allies rejected Bryan's mediation proposal and held their breath. If the Central Powers accepted, Germany might appear to the United States as the advocate of peace and win American public opinion.

Fortunately for the Allies, the German chancellor, Theobold von Bethmann Hollweg, rejected Bryan's offer. Bethmann would have been happy to have accepted and escaped from the war with minimal annexations, but his country was split. The right wing was buoyed by the early German victories and demanded that the war be pursued until the Allies conceded Belgium, Poland, the Baltic states, parts of France, and the dismemberment of much of the British Empire. The German left wing, having debated furiously within itself whether its duty to the international laboring class and peace out-

Figure 12   Secretary of State William Jennings Bryan (center) and his State Department staff on the eve of World War I. Photo courtesy of the National Archives.

weighed its duty to support the fatherland, had assuaged its conscience after deciding for war by insisting that the conflict was purely defensive and should end with no annexations. Bethmann tried to pacify the two sides with a "diagonal policy," contriving to agree with both and remaining silent on war aims until the progress of the war brought some hope of agreement between the factions. His rejection of Bryan's mediation proposal bought him some time, but at the cost of sacrificing his best chance to ensure that the most powerful of all noncombatant nations did not come into the war against Germany.

If Bryan did not understand the significance of his actions, another of Wilson's entourage did. "Colonel" Edward M. House held no official position in Wilson's administration, but he was the president's closest confidant and advisor. He was a wily, soft-spoken, somewhat effeminate man who managed to remain close to the strong-willed president by listening well, avoiding any contradiction of Wilson, and accompanying all suggestions with abundant flattery while insinuating that his ideas were mere rephrasings of Wilson's own. He played on Wilson's idealism and vanity with great virtuosity. This honorary Texas colonel felt even more strongly than Wilson that the Allies were fighting a war for civilization. He was not anxious to see Germany totally defeated and the balance of power in Europe destroyed, but he certainly did not want to see a German victory of any sort. He warned Wilson against Bryan's mediation approach, and Wilson privately agreed to entrust Colonel House with any further attempts at mediation. House henceforth would be sure to clear all diplomatic initiatives with the Allies before presenting them to the Central Powers. This would ensure that the United States would never be lined up with Germany, pressing the Allies to accept unwanted peace terms.

Meanwhile, Robert Lansing was trying to devise a response to Great Britain's announcement that it intended to ignore or revise parts of the Declaration of London in order to stop German commerce. Lansing composed a rather stiff note of protest. Colonel House told Wilson that the note was exceedingly undiplomatic, and Wilson decided to pursue private negotiations with the British to remove any bones of contention that might bring conflict. During a month of quiet contacts, Wilson and his advisors tried to induce the British to make at least sufficient gestures to America's neutral rights to avoid raising a popular outcry among the American people that might force the government into a hostile posture. The British refused to do anything that might restrict their naval warfare, so Wilson and Lansing finally issued a blunt official protest to Britain's policies. But they made clear in subsequent contacts that they would not push a general protest to the breaking point. Instead, they would protest each individual case of interference with American ships or goods as it came up and would be willing to accept a settlement after the war.

The relieved British continued to tighten their blockade and to funnel all American goods to themselves and their allies. Wilson's protests were muted, and so were those of American shippers and exporters. Accelerated trade with Great Britain more than offset the loss of potential trade with Germany. Vast exports of food, raw materials, and arms to the British revived an American economy that had been in a recession since 1911.

Meanwhile, Wilson made several other decisions that encouraged the growth of this one-sided trade with the Allies. At the outset of the war, Wilson and Bryan had decided to forbid private citizens from making loans to the belligerents. Soon it became clear that Great Britain would not have the ready cash to continue its volume of purchases. Without credits from American suppliers and banks, the booming trade that was lifting the United States out of recession would dry up. Wilson, with Bryan's reluctant consent, quietly removed the ban on private loans. There was nothing legally unneutral about the decision; international law did not forbid loans to belligerents from neutrals. Germany itself agitated for removal of the ban, unaware as yet that the Allied blockade would be effective enough to prevent supplies Germany might buy on credit from reaching the Central Powers.

In another significant decision concerning his nation's neutral stance, Wilson refused to prohibit exports of arms to the nations at war. Again, this was no violation of neutrality: All belligerents would have the right to purchase American arms, and Germany did not argue with the decision at first. Only after it became clear that the British blockade would ensure that the

Allies alone benefited from neutral armaments did Germany object. Wilson refused to change his mind. He believed that a ban on arms shipments would encourage militarism, since the neutral arms trade would benefit primarily nations that had not made prewar preparedness a fetish. Wilson also argued that to revise America's neutral stance in midwar after the course of combat had made it disadvantageous to one or the other of the belligerents would itself be unneutral.

Finally, Wilson refused to order a strong protest against the British mining of the North Sea approaches. Since American ships preferred the English Channel route, the mines did little or no harm to American trade, and Wilson did not think the issue warranted the risk of conflict with Britain.

THE GERMAN RESPONSE: SUBMARINE WARFARE

Throughout the last months of 1914, the Germans protested long and loud against Great Britain's illegal interference with neutral trade to the Central Powers and against Washington's refusal to enforce those rights at the risk of conflict with the Allies. The German navy was particularly frustrated. Its battle fleet was too weak to meet the British navy head-on; it had to remain in port and watch helplessly as the British fleet swept up German merchant ships and then proceeded to stop neutral vessels headed for Germany or any other nation that might trade with the Central Powers. The only ships in the German navy that did anything at all in the early days of the war were a few submarines which, through a combination of luck and British carelessness, managed to sink four aged British warships. The German navy formerly had regarded U-boats as experimental and auxillary craft, but these early successes seemed to promise a chance for the navy to help win the war. The submarines might turn the tables on Great Britain and blockade the British Isles. Great Britain was far more dependent on overseas commerce than Germany, and an effective blockade would be devastating to the Allied cause.

Unfortunately for Germany, an attempt to blockade England with submarine warfare inevitably would run afoul of international law. International law permitted enemy warships to be sunk on sight, but required that merchant or passenger ships be warned and that safety be provided for their crew and passengers before they could be sunk. Submarines were unable to fight under such rules. Even small weapons could penetrate their thin hulls, and a merchant or passenger ship was perfectly capable of ramming a U-boat if the submarine surfaced to give warning.

Germany could afford to ignore such niceties in its dealings with the British, since the British already were doing as much harm to Germany as they could. But Germany could not afford to offend the United States to the point that it joined the Allies. Submarine warfare had the potential to do just that. Under international law, citizens of neutral nations had the right to work or travel aboard belligerent merchant or passenger vessels. If Germany violated international law by failing to warn civilian belligerent ships and provide for the safety of passengers and crew, it might kill American citizens as well as British subjects. Germany also had to fear that submarines, operating under conditions that made visibility very difficult, might sink American ships by mistake. British ships often used the ruse of sailing under an American flag, which increased the chances of mistaken sinkings even further.

Chancellor Bethmann Hollweg thought these were reasons enough to avoid the use of submarines against British commerce. He believed that American entry into the war would be fatal to Germany's hope for victory. And he did not think the submarine could effectively blockade the British Isles in any case. In early 1915, Germany possessed a grand total of twenty-one submarines, of which only about half could be on station at any one time. This was far too few to sink the hundreds of ships carrying goods to the Allies. Germany had estimated before the war that it would take 221 submarines to mount an effective blockade. But German naval officers maintained that a U-boat campaign could frighten ships from even attempting to reach Great Britain. These officers ignored the disparity between the force they previously had insisted would be necessary and the U-boat fleet they actually had. They wanted to get the German navy into the war. Admiral von Tirpitz warned his fellow officers: "If we come to the end . . . without the fleet having bled and worked, we shall get nothing more for the fleet, and all the scanty money that there may be will be spent on the army."

Tirpitz orchestrated a colorful newspaper campaign on behalf of submarine warfare and raised considerable sentiment for it among the right and center parties in the German Reichstag. The admiral also made use of his privilege as a military leader to carry his argument directly to Kaiser Wilhelm without having to go through the civilian chancellor. Tirpitz finally won over the emperor to a declaration of U-boat warfare in February 1915. That declaration established a war zone around Great Britain in which enemy merchant ships would be sunk without warning. Germany suggested that neutrals keep their citizens and goods off belligerent vessels, and also warned that neutral ships might be sunk in cases of mistaken identity. Germany acknowledged that its actions went beyond the customary rules of warfare, but argued that this was justified as reprisal against Great Britain's flagrant violations of international law and neutral rights.

WILSON'S TEMPORARY VICTORY: "HE KEPT US OUT OF WAR"

Woodrow Wilson had several options when he realized that Germany's declaration of submarine warfare would endanger American citizens and ships. William Jennings Bryan urged him to do nothing that would endanger America. He advised Wilson to treat Germany as he treated Great Britain— protest, but reserve settlement until after the war. He further asked Wilson to warn American passengers and seamen away from belligerent vessels and to couple his protest to Germany with one to Great Britain against its violations of neutral rights. Thus Wilson would be able to retreat from his protests by claiming that both belligerents violated American rights and that neither was worthy of American sacrifice.

Although none of Wilson's advisors suggested it, later critics of Wilson and American entry into World War I have argued that there was a better way to avoid the war. Wilson could have forced Great Britain to respect American neutral rights and to abandon much of the blockade by embargoing supplies and credits to the Allies or convoying neutral ships and goods to Germany. Internal British cabinet reports and memos indicate that the British probably would have backed down rather than face a confrontation with American convoy escorts or loss of American materiel. But wartime emotions made the British response unpredictable, and an embargo or convoys could have led to war with Great Britain. It also is doubtful that enforcing neutral rights would have deterred Germany's decision for submarine warfare. Germany did not embark on submarine warfare in retaliation for the British blockade or American lack of neutrality; it did so because German leaders gambled that the submarine could win the war. Only the threat of war with the United States kept the German navy from sinking any ships sailing toward Great Britain. To avoid confrontation with Germany, Wilson would have had to keep all American vessels and citizens away from the waters around Great Britain or to overlook it when submarines attacked them.

Wilson was not willing to do that. He regarded submarine warfare on civilian vessels as a drastic and barbaric challenge to international law and humanity. He sent a stiff note to Germany warning that the United States would take "any steps necessary to safeguard American lives and property" and would hold Germany to a "strict accountability" for the actions of its U-boats.

Wilson's "strict accountability" note bristled like an ultimatum but it fell short of one. It did not say whether Germany would be held accountable before or after the war, and Bryan signed the note thinking it meant afterward. Wilson encouraged Bryan's hopes that "strict accountability" did not presage war when he sent a parallel protest to Great Britain, albeit a far weaker one, warning against the use of the American flag as a ruse by British ships. His policy in the weeks following issuance of the note cast further doubt that Wilson was prepared to enforce his protest at the risk of war. The United States sent a note to Germany suggesting that the Germans trade their submarine warfare on merchant ships for a British promise to permit foodstuffs to reach Germany. As Wilson and the State Department wrestled with the new and complex issues surrounding the use of undersea weapons, protests against German sinkings that affected American ships or property were delayed and muted. During a brief period of German fright at the "strict accountability" note, Bethmann urged revocation of the submarine order to chairman of the Senate Foreign Relations Committee refusing to accept a [sin]gle abatement of American rights. Then, on March 24, a submarine at[tac]ked the French channel steamer *Sussex*. The *Sussex* did not sink, but eighty [pe]ople died and four of the twenty-five Americans aboard suffered serious [in]jury.

Wilson sent the Germans a public ultimatum. The United States would [b]reak relations if Germany did not halt all submarine attacks on passenger [a]nd freight-carrying ships, armed or unarmed. Bethmann had anticipated [s]uch a crisis. He had convinced the kaiser that since the German navy did not possess enough U-boats to blockade Great Britain effectively, continuation of submarine warfare was not worth the risk of war with the United States. Bethmann also had maneuvered the resignation of Admiral von Tirpitz. This enabled him to answer Wilson's protest with amazing concessions. The German note conceded that the attack on the *Sussex* had been wrong and promised no further sinkings without warning. This *Sussex* pledge was a remarkable victory for Wilson's diplomacy. Wilson campaigned for and won the presidency in 1916 with the slogan, "He kept us out of war."

AMERICA ENTERS THE WAR

In the euphoria that followed the *Sussex* pledge, few noticed that Germany's *Sussex* note claimed the right to resume submarine warfare if the United States did not compel Great Britain to respect international law. No one in America could know that the German navy was continuing to build U-boats with the intention of reopening the issue when it had enough to enforce an effective blockade of Great Britain. Nor could Americans know that Bethmann was losing his power to resist the naval campaign. General Paul von Hindenburg had replaced Falkenhayn in command of the German armies, and he and his chief subordinate, General Erich Ludendorff, had enough influence with the kaiser to override Bethmann on the U-boat if they chose. The Centre party also gave up its opposition to the submarine campaign, depriving Bethmann of his parliamentary majority in the Reichstag. Bethmann decided his only chance to prevent all-out submarine warfare in the near future was to make peace.

Bethmann had at least a slim chance to succeed in getting American support for a peace conference. Once the *Sussex* pledge seemingly ended the crisis with Germany, Wilson had turned harshly on Great Britain. He was disillusioned by Britain's refusal to ask him for mediation in line with the House-Grey Memorandum, and he was increasingly angered by British contempt for American neutral rights. He was prepared to offer neutral mediation and call for peace terms from both sides without preconditions, a dangerous course for the Allies so long as Germany had the military advantage and occupied Allied territory.

Wilson recognized this danger and it caused him to hesitate, especially after Germany began to deport Belgian civilians to work in German factories.

prevent American entry into the war. But the Germans soon concluded that Wilson was not prepared to fight. The kaiser then instructed submarine commanders to stop risking their own ships in the attempt to identify the nationality or nature of potential target vessels.

Sinkings increased. The British steamer *Falaba* went down, taking an American citizen with it. Another German submarine mistakenly torpedoed the American ship *Gullflight*. Wilson waited three weeks before protesting the *Falaba* incident and was still wrestling with the *Gullflight* issue when the destruction of the *Lusitania* abruptly ended his hesitation.

The *Lusitania* was a giant British passenger liner carrying over 1,900 people from New York to England. On May 7, 1915, a German submarine torpedoed it off the coast of Ireland, and it sank within twenty minutes. Nearly 1,200 passengers drowned, including 124 Americans. The Germans had posted signs in New York warning people not to sail on the ship, and they correctly claimed that the vessel carried some arms and ammunition. Germany thus felt the sinking was justified, and some Germans even celebrated it by declaring a school holiday.

Wilson and America were horrified at the deaths of over a thousand civilians; they were not yet accustomed to the routine killing of civilians in war. The British enhanced the shock of the *Lusitania* by releasing a report signed by the famous and respected British commentator on American life, Lord Bryce, which detailed and exaggerated German atrocities during the "rape" of Belgium.

At first Wilson reacted somewhat tentatively. He announced that America was a nation "too proud to fight." But then he sent a protest note to Germany harshly condemning the sinking of the *Lusitania* and calling for an end to submarine warfare against civilian ships. To strengthen the note even more, he deleted an indication that the United States might defer compensation until after the war. When Germany delayed its response, he sent a second and still harsher note. He rejected Bryan's advice to couple his notes with parallel protests against the British, even though the British had exploited the period of outrage against the sinking of the *Lusitania* to tighten their blockade drastically. Wilson also refused the suggestion of his secretary of state that he order Americans off belligerent ships and out of the war zone. Bryan refused to sign the second *Lusitania* note and resigned on June 8, complaining, "Colonel House has been Secretary of State, not I. I have never had your full confidence."

Wilson's reaction to the *Lusitania* convinced Bethmann that Germany had to stop torpedoing passenger ships or it would face a new and powerful enemy on the battlefield. The Army Chief of Staff, General Erich von Falkenhayn, agreed that the danger of American intervention outweighed the benefits of U-boat warfare, and he refused to support the adamant naval officers in a ferocious debate before the kaiser. The kaiser finally permitted Bethmann to prohibit submarine attacks on large passenger liners and to order greater caution against sinking neutral vessels, but Wilhelm insisted that the order be kept secret so Germany would not be seen as retreating. Since Wilson could not know that his protests had had some effect, he continued to press the case and relations remained tense. Then a German U-boat mistakenly sank the British passenger liner *Arabic,* and two Americans died in the attack. Wilson could only see this as an obdurate refusal to heed his warnings. Failure to take strong action would expose his protests as hollow and destroy both his own prestige and that of his nation.

Still, as in the *Lusitania* crisis, Wilson was willing to exert some patience. Rather than issue an immediate public ultimatum, he had his new secretary of state, Robert Lansing, privately inform the German ambassador that the United States would sever relations with Germany if it did not stop submarine attacks against innocent ships and passengers. The German ambassador, Count Johann von Bernstorff, violated his orders and informed Lansing of the earlier secret instructions against attacks on large passenger liners. He said the *Arabic* sinking was a mistake and promised compensation. Confusion and hesitation on the part of Berlin in confirming Bernstorff's promises caused new concern and consternation, but after another struggle between the navy and Bethmann for the mind of Kaiser Wilhelm, the German government gave a further public pledge that no passenger liners of any kind would be sunk. Bethmann also issued secret orders to withdraw all submarines from the west coast of England, where passenger liners most commonly traveled. Temporarily, Bethmann had managed to stifle the threat of American intervention. But the German navy and its political allies were merely biding their time. Winter and the shortage of U-boats would have rendered submarine warfare relatively ineffective for the following months anyway. The return of operational weather and the growth of the U-boat fleet would inevitably bring new pressures on the German chancellor.

Wilson could not know of the debates within the German hierarchy, but he was aware of how fragile America's peace was. He had staked the prestige of the nation on his warnings against illegal submarine warfare. If Germany embarked again on all-out U-boat warfare, he would face a choice between humiliating retreat and measures almost sure to bring war. Britain added its own reminders of possible future conflict with America: It placed cotton on the contraband list. As usual, the British waited until a German-American crisis could divert attention from the blow and issued the order immediately after the sinking of the *Arabic*. Britain also signed a contract to purchase large amounts of U.S. cotton to support the market price and pacify American farmers. Still, Wilson and Lansing felt they had to respond with a long and detailed protest against British policies toward neutral trade.

Such tensions convinced Wilson that the only sure way the United States could stay out of the hostilities and maintain its honor was to end the war. He approved a plan offered to him by Colonel House that involved an enormous gamble to bring the war to an end through American mediation. Wilson would call for a peace conference and threaten war against whichever side refused. But first House would consult with the Allies and, by promising that American mediators at the conference would be sympathetic to Allied war

aims, ensure that they would not be the ones to refuse. F[...] don and induced the British cabinet to accept this plan, a[...] so-called House-Grey Memorandum.

Wilson would wait until the Allies informed him that th[...] tion was propitious. Then he would issue a call for a peac[...] Germany refused, the United States *probably* would join the A[...] If Germany agreed to the conference but then rejected reason[...] peace, the United States *probably* would leave the conference a [...] the side of Great Britain. (Wilson personally added the "probab[...] memorandum of understanding, the first before House negotiate[...] British, the second afterward.) Meanwhile, House tried to tempt th[...] to accept the call for a peace conference by telling them that Gre[...] was unlikely to accept. At the same time, he assured the Allies that t[...] conference was nothing but a gimmick to pave the way for America[...] vention on the side of Britain and France.

Wilson's wait for the British signal to call the conference and me[...] peace was interminable. The British never did decide the time was p[...] tious. David Lloyd George, the new British prime minister, later claimed[...] Wilson's "probablies" undermined the whole plan. No doubt he wor[...] even more that Wilson's ideas of reasonable terms could never satisfy [...] war aims the Allies had developed during a year of bloody warfare. Fran[...] would not be satisfied without moving Germany out of Alsace-Lorraine an[...] all other lands west of the Rhine. Great Britain would insist on the reduction[...] of the German fleet. Both would want Germany weakened so it could not attack through Belgium again. Russia insisted on concessions in the Balkans. Only a complete Allied victory, not a Wilson-mediated peace, could achieve those goals.

Wilson became desperate for Britain to give him the signal to call the conference, because by the time House returned to America in February of 1916, the danger of American intervention had increased drastically. On February 10, Germany had announced resumption of submarine warfare against armed merchant ships. Bethmann thought he could get away with this because while House had been bouncing around Europe, Secretary of State Lansing had been trying to work out a *modus vivendi* between Germany and Great Britain. Lansing wanted the British to cease arming merchant ships in return for Germany abandoning submarine sinkings of unarmed ships without warning. The British rejected this trade of a practice long sanctioned by international law for a submarine warfare they regarded as totally illegal. Bethmann thought this British rejection would dispose Wilson and Lansing to accept resumption of U-boat attacks on armed merchants.

But German U-boats "mistakenly" sank many neutral merchants and one Dutch passenger liner. It was only a matter of time before a ship went down with American passengers or a submarine sank an American merchant vessel. Many members of Congress tried to forestall the crisis by promoting the Gore-McLemore Resolutions, warning Americans off armed merchant ships or ships carrying contraband. Wilson defused this movement with a letter to

In the interim Bethmann asked the neutral powers, including the United States, to communicate to Great Britain an offer of a peace conference. Wilson proposed his own mediation as a substitute. He claimed that the objects for which each side said it was fighting were "virtually the same" and invited the belligerents to send him their peace terms. Bethmann refused to take this last chance to split America and the Allies. He distrusted Wilson and the Americans, so he refused Wilson's mediation offer and insisted on talking directly to the Allies.

The British did not make the same mistake. They were greatly offended that Wilson could equate their objectives with those of the German militarists and they feared that Wilson's mediation offer was part of a German plot, but they were coaxed to give an answer by Secretary of State Lansing. Lansing had no desire to see the British refuse to answer and cast themselves as the enemy of Wilson's ambition to be a peacemaker. Lansing believed the true policy of the United States should be to "join the Allies as soon as possible and crush the German Autocrats." He assured the British and French that Wilson's mediation offer was not part of the German proposal and that the president preferred the democracies enough to support any demands they might devise. Lansing even encouraged the Allies to make their peace terms as extreme as they wished. Lansing's unauthorized maneuvers helped convince Great Britain to spell out its war aims, and it was even more encouraged to do so when Germany refused to state its own terms.[1]

The Allies insisted on restoration of all territories conquered by the Central Powers, by which it turned out they meant Alsace-Lorraine as well as Belgium, Serbia, Montenegro, and parts of France, Russia, and Rumania. They also demanded liberation of the nationalities dominated by the Austro-Hungarian Empire and Turkey, along with reparations for war damages. Wilson considered these demands a bluff and continued private negotiations with the belligerents. He added pressure to his peace initiative by making a dramatic speech to the Senate in which he appealed brilliantly for "peace without victory," a peace that would replace the balance of power with a community of power. The peace settlement would be based on the concepts of national self-determination, government by consent of the governed, arms limitations, and freedom of the seas. He promised that the United States would contribute its power to a league of nations designed to maintain this peace.

Wilson did not know that his great appeal for mediation and peace was doomed before he set foot in the Senate. The British believed that there could be no return to the *status quo ante bellum* and that only an Allied victory could produce the world Wilson desired. They also feared they might lose the war unless the United States intervened soon on their side. They essen-

---

[1] Historians still debate why Lansing wrote such strong protest notes against the British blockade early in the war if he was so pro-Allied. Opponents of American entry like Charles Tansill have speculated that he changed his policy to conform to the opinion of Colonel House in hopes of furthering his own career. Others, like Daniel Smith, argue that his initial response was simply that of a narrow legal mind confronted with violations of international law.

tially ignored Wilson's initiative and hoped it would go away. The Germans too believed that the war must end in a victorious rather than a compromise peace, and they too feared they would lose the war if it continued much longer. But they knew the United States would not enter on their side to save them. They put their faith instead in their submarines.

By January 1917 Germany had nearly a hundred U-boats, and the navy claimed that if given free rein, these submarines could reduce Great Britain to starvation in six months. Germany's leaders realized that renunciation of the *Sussex* pledge would mean American intervention, but they gambled that they could win the war before the United States could do much to help the Allies. The choice seemed to be between winning the war quickly with the submarine or losing without it. The kaiser secretly decided on January 9, nearly two weeks before Wilson's "Peace without Victory" speech, to launch unrestricted submarine warfare. On February 1, the German government announced that its U-boats would sink without warning all ships sailing in the war zone around Great Britain, including neutral vessels. This was the first time Germany had declared it would sink American ships purposely. The United States would have to fight or back down ignominiously from the stand it had taken since the sinking of the *Lusitania*.

Wilson immediately broke relations with Germany and pressed the Germans to go back to the *Sussex* pledge. But he did not ask Congress for a declaration of war; he told the Senate he would wait for "overt acts" before taking extreme measures. Three weeks later, the British turned over to the United States a telegram to Mexico from the German foreign secretary, Arthur Zimmermann. Zimmermann proposed an alliance between Germany, Mexico, and Japan against the United States if America joined the war, and he offered to help Mexico regain the territory it had lost in the Mexican War. This Zimmermann telegram convinced Wilson that Germany preferred war to abandonment of its submarine campaign. Two days later, Wilson asked Congress for permission to arm American merchant ships to resist German attacks. A Senate filibuster by what Wilson condemned as "a little group of willful men" blocked the measure. So Wilson ordered this interim step toward war on his own authority. He hoped arming American merchant vessels might be enough to protect American ships and avoid full-scale war. But within two weeks he received news that German submarines had sunk three American ships with the loss of fifteen lives. After two more days of mental agony and soul-searching, he accepted the advice of his cabinet and asked Congress for a formal declaration of war.

Wilson accepted that tragic alternative with immense sorrow, but with one great consolation. If the United States was an active and powerful participant in the war, Wilson would have great influence over the peace settlement. He would have the opportunity to create a just peace that would promote democratic government and eliminate the causes of war that had plagued the Old World for so long. Since the February Revolution in Russia had just overthrown the czar and installed a democratic socialist government, Wilson could portray the war against Germany to himself and the American people as one of free nations against militaristic tyrannies. In ringing tones he asked Congress to enlist the United States in a crusade to "make the world safe for democracy."

CONTROVERSIAL ISSUES AND FURTHER READING

The vast majority of historians of Wilson's day, like the vast majority of Congress and Americans at large, approved Wilson's decision for war and had no doubts about the reasons behind it. They agreed that Wilson had tried to be neutral. They approved Wilson's refusal to do more than protest British illegalities, for to have done more might have made Americans participants in the war on the side of Germany. This was unthinkable; Germany's violation of Belgian neutrality, its subsequent atrocities in that unhappy country, and its brutal submarine campaign confirmed that Germany was "a horrible menace to civilization" which, if it won the war, would form a great empire that would "dominate Europe and imperil the safety of the Americas." [John Bach McMaster, *The United States in the World War* (2 vols., 1918–1920). See also John Spencer Bassett, *Our War with Germany* (1919); Christian B. Gauss, *Why We Went to War* (1920); Carleton J. H. Hayes, *A Brief History of the Great War* (1920).] Historians who criticized Wilson argued only that he had not entered the war soon enough. Frederick A. Ogg censured the president for leading Americans to believe that they were unconcerned with the causes and objects of the Great War "until he and the country were rudely awakened by what had become clear to many much earlier—that this was a contest between democracy and autocracy," that the United States would have to fight imperialistic Germany alone if "the Teutonic powers" were victorious. John Holladay Latané shuddered to think that if Germany had not violated international law so flagrantly with its submarines, Wilson would have permitted a German victory and its grave consequences for the security of the Americas. [Frederick A. Ogg, *National Progress, 1907–1917* (1918); John Holladay Latané, *From Isolation to Leadership: A Review of American Foreign Policy* (1918). There was only one significant book criticizing Wilson for entering the war at all, socialist Scott Nearing's *The Great Madness* (1917).]

Within five years after the end of the war, historical opinion began to change. The refusal of the European powers at the Paris Peace Conference to abandon the more self-interested of their war aims in the interest of America's ideas of a just peace undermined the conviction that America had joined a crusade for democracy. Revelations from the historical archives of the defeated powers destroyed the Allies' accusation that Germany and Austria had purposely plotted world war. This raised further questions about why the United States should have intervened. Early critics of American intervention took a rather conspiratorial view of Wilson's decision for war. They accused munitions makers of pushing the Wilson administration into the conflict as a means of increasing their war profits. They charged that Wall Street bankers had maneuvered America into war to prevent the Allies from losing and then defaulting on the vast loans granted them by American financial institutions. Critics claimed that a vicious British propaganda campaign had twisted facts, created German atrocities out of whole cloth, and made use of Britain's control of the single communications cable to the United States to delude American opinion into supporting intervention on the side of the Allies. [John Kenneth Turner, *Shall It Be Again* (1922); C. Hartley Grattan, *Why We Fought* (1929); Harry Elmer Barnes, *The Genesis of the World War* (1927); Frederick Bausman, *Let France Explain* (1922) and *Facing Europe* (1926).]

Later, World War I revisionist critics returned a broader indictment. Charles Beard pointed out that America's high volume of trade with the Allies and the loans that encouraged it tied the prosperity of all Americans, not just big business, to the survival of the Allies. The original mistake of encouraging this trade gave the United States no choice but to intervene to save the British and French from defeat. Charles Tansill was not so ready to let big business off the hook in the most extensive of these revisionist studies. He argued that big business had influenced Wilson to encourage trade with the Allies in the first place and to violate America's neutral duties by refusing to make an effective challenge to Britain's illegal blockade. An embargo or convoy system would have broken the blockade easily and without danger of war with the dependent Allies. Germany would not have had to use the submarine, and America could have continued neutral. [Charles A. Beard, *The Devil Theory of War* (1936); Charles C. Tansill, *America Goes to War* (1936). See also Walter Millis, *The Road to War: America 1914–1917* (1936), and C. Hartley Grattan, *Preface to Chaos* (1936). These World War I revisionists, as opposed to the modern revisionists writing in the Cold War era, were very diverse politically. Turner and Grattan were socialists; Barnes, Beard, and Millis were disillusioned liberals; Tansill and Bausman were right-wing conservatives who detested the British Empire, partly because of their nineteenth-century American nationalism and, in Tansill's case at least, ethnic sympathies with the Irish and Germans. But their books did not reflect these political divisions.The socialists and liberals denounced British propaganda and America's pro-British bias as ardently as the conservatives, and the conservative Tansill denounced the influence of big business on intervention as thoroughly as those historians on the left.]

These World War I revisionist histories had a great impact on American opinion in the years before World War II. They helped lead Congress to pass a series of neutrality acts to prevent the United States from being drawn into World War II in the ways the revisionist historians claimed it had been drawn into World War I.

But Wilson had many defenders among historians as well as the population at large. These defenders argued that Wilson was the last person to have been influenced by big bankers or munitions makers. Wilson had defended neutral rights with no initial expectation that this would bring war, and then felt the United States could not abandon its stand in midwar without itself being unneutral. They agreed with Wilson that Germany's offenses were more heinous that Britain's, since submarine warfare destroyed people as well as property. If Wilson had instituted an embargo or convoy system, destroying American prosperity while risking war with Britain on the side of Germany, he would have provoked a revolt against his administration. Nothing Wilson could have done would have kept Germany from resorting to submarine warfare anyway. Germany had to stop all British trade to win the war, and this required either sinking or terrorizing neutral ships as well as Allied ones.

Yet even Wilson's defenders in this pre-World War II era no longer asserted, as the wartime historians had, that the United States had had to intervene to protect itself from invasion by a ruthless Germany bent on world conquest. They agreed that Wilson had intervened not to protect American security, but to defend America's neutral rights and prestige against submarine warfare. All agreed that Wilson had tried to maintain American neutrality and had joined the war only reluctantly. But one of his most prominent defenders, his official biographer and former press secretary Ray Stannard Baker, accused Wilson's advisors House and Lansing of disloyally trying to maneuver the president into the war. [Ray Stannard Baker, *Woodrow Wilson: Life and Letters* (6 vols., 1927–1937). Charles Seymour, *Woodrow Wilson and the World War* (1921), *American Diplomacy during the World War* (1934), and *American Neutrality, 1914–1917* (1935); Newton D. Baker, *Why We Went to War* (1936).]

World War II revived American fears of Germany as a menace to civilization and made the next generation of historians more willing to believe that American intervention in World War I had been essential. Walter Lippmann wrote a highly influential book during World War II in which he bewailed the naïveté he had shared with the American people and urged a return to a realistic foreign policy based on national interest and power politics. In the course of his argument, he claimed that Wilson had intervened in World War I on these realistic grounds, had recognized that unlimited submarine warfare would cut Atlantic communications, starve Great Britain, and leave the United States to face a "new and aggressively expanding German empire which had made Britain, France, and Russia its vassals, and Japan its ally." [Walter Lippmann, *U.S. Foreign Policy; Shield of the Republic* (1943).]

Other realist historians like George Kennan and Robert Osgood accepted the contention that Wilson should have intervened in the war to protect Britain and the balance of power. But they did not believe that Wilson or the American people had done so for that reason. Osgood conceded that House and Lansing might have thought intervention necessary to American security, but pointed out that Wilson paid his advisors little heed. In any case, most American interventionists, including the leaders of the preparedness campaign, had not thought of security in terms of the subtle interest the United States had in the European balance of power. They spoke instead of the chimerical threat of a direct German invasion of the United States or the Western Hemisphere.

Neither Wilson nor most Americans took the threat of a direct invasion seriously. Osgood pointed out that at the time Wilson and Congress made their decision for war, no one in the United States believed the U-boat campaign would break the great stalemate and defeat the Allies. It was only months later, when Great Britain was weeks from running out of food, that the prospect of German victory became imminent. Thus Wilson had chosen war because he was offended by German conduct, not because he thought it posed a threat to American survival. Wilson's failure to understand and explain America's self-interest in joining the war to preserve the European balance of power left the American people open to the suggestion that the United States had fought for no good reason at all, that it had been duped into rescuing the Allies by British propaganda and international bankers. Psychohistorians bolstered these contentions as they attempted to explain the strange quirk of character that had led Wilson to deal in rigid moralistic and legalistic terms with matters he should have handled pragmatically in terms of power and self-interest. [Robert E. Osgood, *Ideals and Self-Interest in American Foreign Policy: The Great Transformation* (1953); George Kennan, *American Diplomacy, 1900–1950* (1951). The best of the psychohistorical biographies is Alexander L. and Juliette L. George, *Woodrow Wilson and Colonel House: A Personality Study* (1956). The worst is by Sigmund Freud himself, with William C. Bullitt, *Thomas Woodrow Wilson: A Psychological Study* (1966). See also John M. Blum, *Woodrow Wilson and the Politics of Morality* (1956).]

A plausible defense of Wilson against this realist onslaught was slow to emerge. Even Arthur Link, most prominent of all Wilsonian scholars and defenders, at first accepted the realist contention that Wilson had ignored the hard-headed advice of

Lansing and House and gone to war because submarine warfare violated American neutral rights. He differed only in that he believed this reason was good and sufficient. [Arthur S. Link, *Woodrow Wilson and the Progressive Era, 1910–1917* (1954).] But Edward Buehrig noted Wilson's subtle recognition of the European balance of power in the president's hopes for a negotiated peace that would avoid total defeat of either the Allies or the Central Powers. Buehrig thought this showed Wilson was realistic, even though Wilson often said the peace should transcend balance of power considerations. [Edward H. Buehrig, *Woodrow Wilson and the Balance of Power* (1955).] Link seized on Buehrig's point. He admitted that Wilson might have contented himself with armed neutrality after Germany's declaration of unlimited submarine warfare if Germany had avoided sinking American ships. Thus he might have permitted a German victory. Yet his decision for war when German submarines did sink American ships represented more than just a defense of neutral rights; Wilson knew that failure to react strongly to the German provocation would have sacrificed all America's prestige and leverage abroad, giving him no chance to influence the peace. With what Link called a "higher realism," Wilson intervened at least in part to ensure that the peace would be a just one that did not sow the seeds of future war by inciting revenge or disrupting the balance of power. [Arthur S. Link, *Wilson: The Struggle for Neutrality, 1914–1915* (1960); *Wilson: Confusions and Crises, 1915–1916* (1964); *Wilson: Campaigns for Progressivism and Peace, 1916–1917* (1965); *Wilson the Diplomatist: A Look at His Major Foreign Policies* (1957), revised as *Woodrow Wilson: Revolution, War, and Peace* (1970).]

Most recent historians have accepted Link's formulation of Wilson's motivation. Their differences are subtle ones, except in their evaluations of Wilson's advisors. Some modern historians praise House and Lansing for their realism. Most follow Link (and Ray Stannard Baker of the earlier era) in arguing that House and Lansing were disloyal and devious. [Favorable to House and Lansing are Ernest May, *The World War and American Isolation, 1914–1917* (1959), still the best one-volume history of American intervention; Daniel S. Smith, *Robert Lansing and American Neutrality, 1914–1917* (1958), and *The Great Departure: The United States and World War I, 1914–1920* (1965). Closer to Link's view of House, Lansing, and Ambassador Walter Hines Page are Patrick Devlin, *Too Proud to Fight: Woodrow Wilson's Neutrality* (1975), which agrees that Wilson fought primarily to protect America's prestige but regards this motive with a more jaundiced eye than Link; Ross Gregory, *The Origins of American Intervention in the First World War* (1970), which diminishes Wilson's desire to shape the peace as a motive for his intervention; John Milton Cooper, Jr., *Walter Hines Page: The Southerner as American* (1977); and Julius W. Pratt, *Challenge and Rejection* (1967).]

Curiously, modern revisionists have not made much attempt to revive the earlier revisionist critiques of Wilson. [One exception, Sidney Bell's *Righteous Conquest: Woodrow Wilson and the Evolution of the New Diplomacy* (1972), is rather ham-handed and has generally been disregarded by recent historians.] John W. Coogan, however, has argued strongly that Wilson never was truly neutral by proper standards of international law, that he undermined the entire system of international relations by his favoritism toward Great Britain, and that even though it may have been to America's interest to prevent Germany from defeating the Allies, it was even more to America's interest to defend American neutrality, prevent a crushing victory by either side, and maintain both the balance of power and the prewar structure of international law. [John W. Coogan, *The End of Neutrality: The United States, Britain, and Maritime Rights, 1899–1915* (1981).]

Coogan also presented interesting new information on negotiations and strategic planning in Europe prior to World War I. [For further information on the plunge of Europe into the war, see Paul Kennedy, *The Rise of Anglo-German Antagonism* (1980); A. J. P. Taylor, *The Struggle for Mastery in Europe* (1954); Laurence Lafore, *The Long Fuse* (1965); Dwight E. Lee, *Europe's Crucial Years: The Diplomatic Background of World War I, 1902–1914* (1974); Samuel R. Williamson, *The Politics of Grand Strategy: Britain and France Prepare for War, 1904–1914* (1969); and Gerhard Ritter, *The Schlieffen Plan* (1979). On American-European relations prior to the Wilson administration, see Howard K. Beale, *Theodore Roosevelt and the Rise of America to World Power* (1956); Raymond Esthus, *Theodore Roosevelt and International Rivalries* (1970); Frederick Marks, *Velvet on Iron: The Diplomacy of Theodore Roosevelt* (1979); Calvin Davis, *The United States and the First Hague Peace Conference* (1962), and *The United States and the Second Hague Peace Conference* (1975). Richard Challener investigated American military planning and influence in *Admirals, Generals, and American Foreign Policy, 1898–1914* (1973), while Holger Herwig wrote of German planning for war with the United States in *The Politics of Frustration: The United States in German Naval Planning, 1889–1914* (1976).]

INDEX

ABOUT THE AUTHOR

Jerald A. Combs did his undergraduate work at the University of California, Santa Barbara, and received his Ph.D. from UCLA in 1964. Since that time he has been on the faculty of San Francisco State University. He is the author of three books: *The Jay Treaty: Political Battleground of the Founding Fathers; Nationalist, Realist, and Radical: Three Views of American Diplomacy;* and most recently, *American Diplomatic History: Two Centuries of Changing Interpretations.*